VEGETARIANA

Also by Nava Atlas

American Harvest

The Wholefood Catalog

Vegetarian Celebrations

Soups for All Seasons

VEGETARIANA

A Rich Harvest of Wit, Lore, and Recipes

REVISED AND UPDATED

Written and Illustrated by

Nava Atlas

Little, Brown and Company
Boston Toronto London

Revised Edition

Library of Congress Cataloging-in-Publication Data
Atlas, Nava.
Vegetariana : a rich harvest of wit, lore, and recipes / written and illustrated by Nava Atlas.—Rev. and expanded.
p. cm.
Includes bibliographical references and index.
ISBN 0-316-05743-6 (pb)
1. Vegetarian cookery. 2. Vegetarianism. I. Title.
TX837.A85 1993
641.5'636 — dc20 92-13452

10 9 8 7 6 5 4 3 2 1

RRD-VA

Published simultaneously in Canada by Little, Brown & Company (Canada) Limited

Printed in the United States of America

Reproduction of "Beans as Ballots" by Nava Atlas courtesy of the collection of the Wichita Art Museum, Wichita, Kansas. Photo of original artwork by Henry Nelson.

The author also wishes to thank the following for lending original artworks from the first edition for the production of this new edition: Maxine and Steven Rabinowe, Diana Price and Jeff Hill, Peter Elek, Carl Scarbnick, Jack and Shirlee Iden, Blanche Rose, Arnold and Carol Saltzman, Janet Stein and Joe Cancelmo, Arlene and Larry Siegel.

In memory of my father

CONTENTS

FOREWORD TO THE NEW EDITION

In the introduction to the original edition of this book, written in the early 1980s, I stated that vegetarianism was not so much of an oddity as it had been ten years earlier, when I myself had given up meat. If that was the case, then being a vegetarian is still less unusual today, a decade later, when an estimated eight to ten million Americans have gone meatless and millions of others have drastically reduced their meat intake. Can vegetarian diets be—dare I say it—becoming almost mainstream?

As growing numbers of people are turning to meatless diets, there is an increasing variety of reasons for doing so. Health factors may once have been the primary reason for giving up meat, but now environmental and humane concerns rank just as high. I've always believed that vegetarianism is not just a way of eating but a way of life, so it's exciting to me to see it become more and more accepted.

I've now written five book on vegetarian cooking and natural foods, of which *Vegetariana* was my first, and of all, the greatest labor of love. My main intent when first producing the book was to put vegetarian cooking in a lighthearted context, so that the broad range of delicious foods and flavors would be showcased in an inviting, nonintimidating way. Why a new edition? Since the book was first written, many fascinating and healthful foods have become better known or more widely available. I wanted to include new recipes for foods such as tempeh, quinoa, seitan, and others. More tofu recipes are here, too, since this versatile food is practically a supermarket staple and I'm constantly asked for ideas for its use.

Some of the original recipes have been slightly defatted in accordance with the current trend of keeping fat content low. While there are still some rich, special-occasion dishes here, most of the recipes will serve as basic, everyday fare for anyone who wants tasty and uncomplicated meals that are healthful as well as fun to make and eat.

Margarine has replaced butter in the recipes, since the former is better suited to low-cholesterol or dairy-free diets. And in addition, nondairy soy alternatives have been suggested in many of the recipes. Those who use no dairy, as well as vegans, will find a wider range of recipes that they can use in this edition.

Above all, this new edition of *Vegetariana* is the continuation of the celebration of vegetarianism and the vegetarian cookery that so many are embracing as a healthful and satisfying way of life.

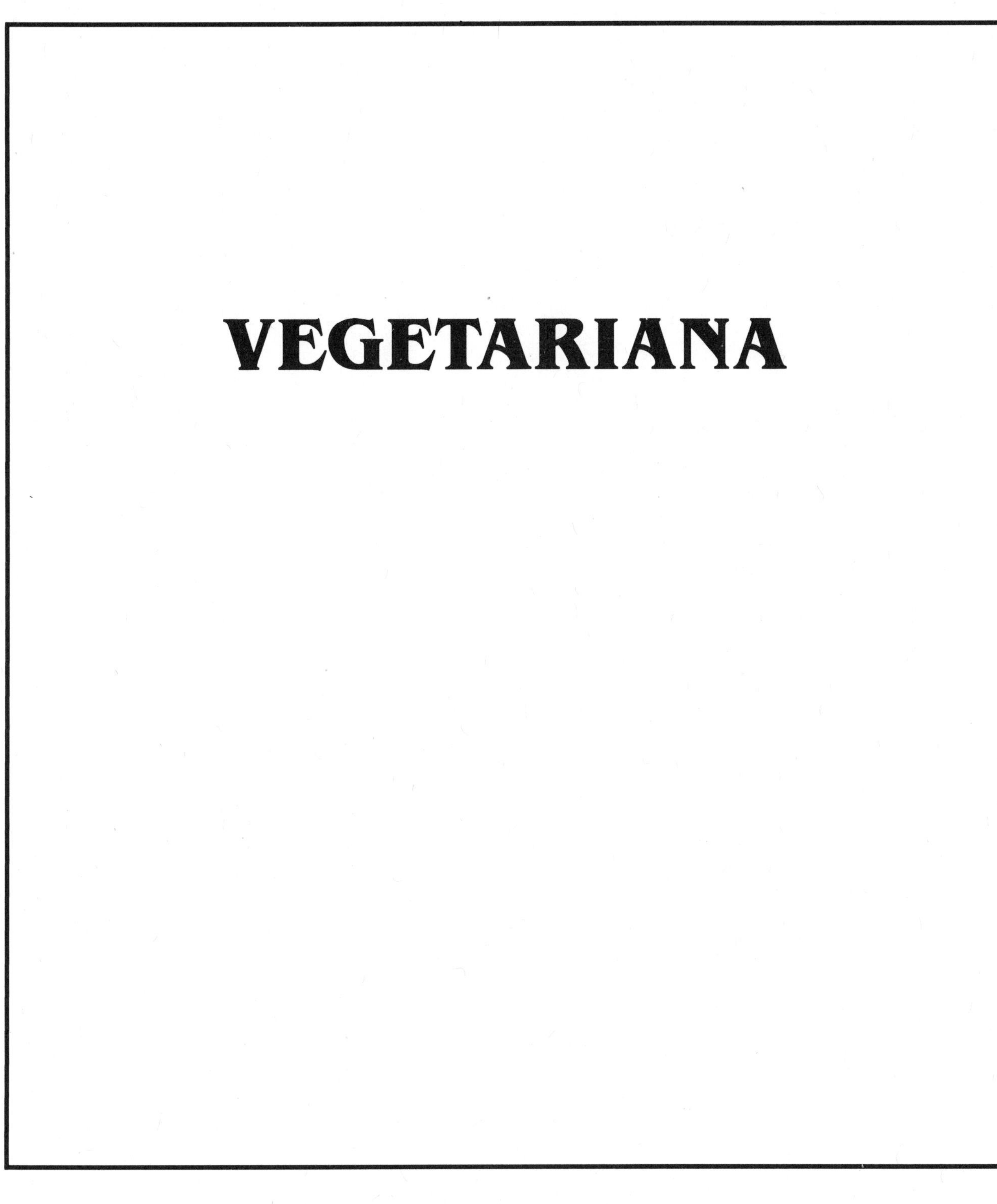

VEGETARIANA

INTRODUCTION

"What on earth do you eat?" was a question I was often asked when I first became a vegetarian, in the early 1970s. Back then, meatless diets were not as widespread and accepted as they are today. I rarely hear this question anymore because so many people have cut down on meat or eliminated it from their diets altogether; they have learned that the answer is, of course, a wealth of fresh vegetables and fruits, grains, legumes, tofu, nuts, seeds, dairy products, pastas, soups, salads, good breads, and, yes, the occasional dessert.

Growing up with a drawing pencil in my hand, I learned early to scrutinize the things around me, and that included what was on my dinner plate. As a child I had to be urged not to "finish your vegetables" but to "eat your meat." Somehow that meat or fish on my plate never appealed to any of my senses.

It was not until I was sixteen years old that I was "adult" enough to assert myself in the kitchen and declare myself a vegetarian. At first this decision was not met with cheers from my family, but interestingly, within a few years, my parents and both of my brothers, in their separate situations and life-styles, all became enthusiastic vegetarians. Having given up meat simply because I didn't like it, I became interested only after the fact in exploring the health benefits and philosophies of vegetarianism, which I found fascinating. It was equally fulfilling to discover that the variety of foods I could eat broadened considerably, and I loved to experiment with these exciting new options in cookery.

My career as an illustrator and graphic designer began almost simultaneously with my move to New York City and my marriage to a fellow artist. A veteran of artist-bachelorhood, in which eating meat and fish was a matter more of supposed convenience than of desire, my husband promptly became a vegetarian after we met. Although dinners were often quick, improvised concoctions after our long days in the studio, I took pleasure in making them fun and memorable, with interesting flavors, textures, colors, and aromas and fresh, whole ingredients. My husband's enthusiasm for these unusual meals convinced me to write down some of those recipes so that I could repeat them.

Later, as I began making dinners that pleased even nonvegetarian guests, I found myself with dozens, if not hundreds, of recipes and a desire to combine them, somehow, with my illustrations. It was *Pudd'nhead Wilson,* by Mark Twain, with its witty homilies opening each chapter, often referring to a food item to make a point (see pages 73 and 147), that inspired me to use literature and lore as the basis for those illustrations. The result is *Vegetariana,* a collection not merely of recipes but also of the surprisingly literary, legendary, folkloric, poetic, and even erotic contexts in which the marvelous variety of foods in the realm of vegetarian cookery is celebrated.

In researching this book, I had at first expected to find a few quotations here and there with which to embellish the recipes. I was unprepared for the avalanche of material that kept me captivated in the library for months. It was an unexpected pleasure to find American humorists such as Mark Twain and Josh Billings writing on cauliflower, corn, and even cherries, and to discover that Beethoven gave serious thought to soup. It was a delight to find in Shakespeare's plays a virtual garden of herbs, and to browse through another garden—*The Perfumed Garden,* a fourteenth-century erotic manual—to unearth recipes that promised to provoke great lust. In other realms, certain foods were honored as aids to magic, fertility, and divination, affirming the important role the edible plant kingdom has played on a multitude of levels throughout history.

Equally fascinating and full of surprises was my exploration of the world of vegetarianism itself. Many of my generation believe that vegetarianism sprang up in the 1960s and blossomed in the new age of health-consciousness of the 1970s. However, the roots of vegetarianism run as deep as ancient India, classical Greece and Rome, and the Old and New testaments of the Bible. More recent but perhaps ever more obscure is the story of the almost concurrent, widespread vegetarian movements in nineteenth-century America and England, which attracted scores of prominent writers and reformers.

A GATHERING OF SOME EMINENT VEGETARIANS

These estimable figures represent but a small sampling of well-known vegetarians of the past. Although all were staunch advocates of vegetarianism for one reason or another, some practiced this diet with greater consistency than others.

LEONARDO DA VINCI (1452–1519)

Leonardo, despite his fascination with military machinery, was a compassionate humanitarian and a vegetarian for much of his life. His love of animals is cited as the basis for his dietary beliefs; legend has it that he bought caged birds just to set them free.

GEORGE BERNARD SHAW (1856–1950)

"It is nearly fifty years since I was assured by a conclave of doctors that if I did not eat meat I should die of starvation."

Shaw confounded this conclave and most likely outlived them, surviving well into his nineties as a staunch vegetarian.

LEO TOLSTOY (1828–1910)

"And there are ideas of the future, of which some are approaching realization and are obliging people to change their way of life . . . such ideas in our world are those of freeing the labourers, of giving equality to women, of ceasing to use flesh food, and so on."

MOHANDAS GANDHI (1869–1948)

This great Indian leader was a vegetarian almost all his life and gave credence to both the health benefits and ethical issues in his books and lectures. Vegetarianism, he believed, was not only a way of eating but a way of life, and contributed to one's spiritual progress.

PERCY BYSSHE SHELLEY (1792–1822)

"There is no disease, bodily or mental, which adoption of vegetable diet and pure water has not infallibly mitigated whereever the experiment has been fairly tried."

FRANZ KAFKA (1883–1924)

"I was sad in the evening because I had eaten anchovies. In the morning, the doctor comforted me; why be said? After all, I ate the anchovies, not the anchovies me."

EASTERN AND WESTERN ROOTS

Vegetarianism's Far Eastern roots are well known and stem almost exclusively from the doctrine of *ahimsa,* which is common to Buddhism, Hinduism, and Jainism. *Ahimsa* is the doctrine of the sanctity of all life, of kindness, and of noninjury. It originated in Indian Vedic literature, although it was Gautama Buddha, who lived around the sixth century B.C., and the Jains who popularized the doctrine. Although kindness toward all creatures was a principle of the Buddhists, avoiding meat was not an absolute, as it was with the Jains and, for a time, among certain Hindus.

Legend has it that the Buddha's conviction of noninjury toward all creatures arose from his sorrow at seeing a family of insects destroyed by a plow.

A contemporary of the Buddha was the Greek philosopher and mathematician Pythagoras, who is perhaps better known as the originator of the Pythagorean theorem than as the "father of Western vegetarianism." Pythagoras, like many other important Greek philosophers after him, favored a natural, meatless diet, stressing that "the earth affords a lavish supply of riches."

Plato, who lived around the fourth century B.C., also advocated this diet, although there is no evidence that he himself was a vegetarian. In *The Republic,* after describing the meatless bounty of which the citizens partake, he states that with such a diet they "may be expected to live in peace and health to a good old age."

THE BRITISH VEGETARIANS

The "Pythagorean diet" is referred to by many writers, among them Ovid, Voltaire, Emerson, and Shelley.

Percy Bysshe Shelley, the English poet, staunchly advocated vegetarianism for both health and ethical reasons but was unable to stick to it consistently. Shelley apparently did not know how to eat well and was generally rather sickly, and so had to be constantly on the defensive about his diet:

> ***The advocate of a new diet is held bound to be invulnerable [to] disease, in the same manner as the secretaries of a new religion are held to be more moral than other people.*** (from a letter dated 1817)

Shelley wrote of the ideals of vegetarianism in both prose and poetry, and it was his rather graphic verse that influenced George Bernard Shaw, the caustic English playwright, to become a vegetarian. Shaw adhered strictly to a meatless diet for nearly seventy years, until his death, at age ninety-four. Luckily for him, his wife and later his housekeeper were excellent cooks and prepared a wide assortment of imaginative dishes for him. Although he could be self-righteous on the subject of vegetarianism (he even sent his friends "vegetarian postcards" that he had printed himself), he could also be wittier than most in the same regard. An example of his humor may be found on page 34.

Right between Shelley and Shaw, in the mid–nineteenth century, the British Vegetarian Society was established. This movement, like its almost concurrent American counterpart, was instigated by clergymen and stressed the health benefits of such a way of life, which also included temperance. Like the American movement, it was joined and promoted by prominent reformers, among them the radical feminist Annie Besant, who embraced a form of Eastern spiritualism. For all their similarities, the two movements seem to have had little contact until Mrs. Besant and some Indian teachers traveled to the United States in 1893 and introduced a certain mystical element into American vegetarianism.

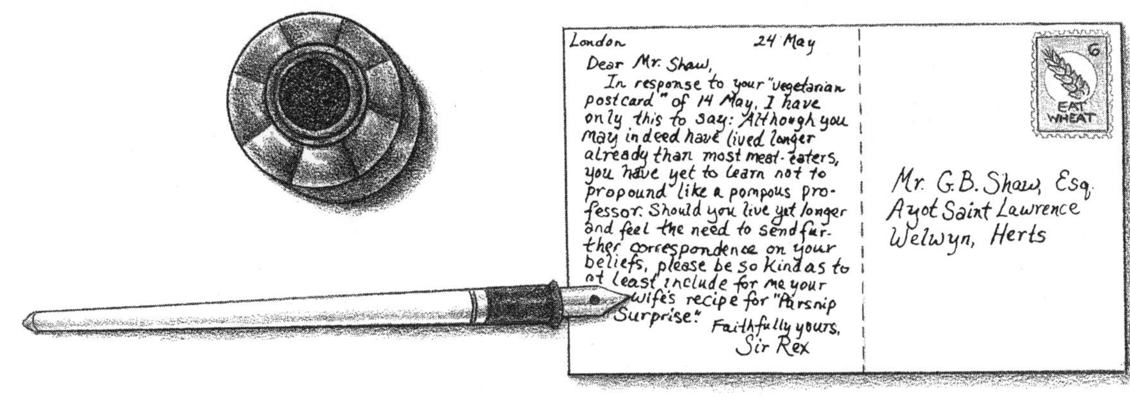

London 24 May
Dear Mr. Shaw,
In response to your "vegetarian postcard" of 14 May, I have only this to say: Although you may indeed have lived longer already than most meat-eaters, you have yet to learn not to propound like a pompous professor. Should you live yet longer and feel the need to send further correspondence on your beliefs, please be so kind as to at least include for me your wife's recipe for "Parsnip Surprise."
Faithfully yours,
Sir Rex
6
EAT WHEAT
Mr. G.B. Shaw, Esq.
Ayot Saint Lawrence
Welwyn, Herts

VEGETARIANA AMERICANA

Possibly the strongest vegetarian movement in the United States prior to the one that blossomed in the 1960s occurred around the mid–nineteenth century. Its members included many renowned reformers and literary figures. As in the British movement, the leaders were mainly clergy; perhaps the best known of these was Sylvester Graham (1794–1851), the father of graham crackers. Originally the name was associated with Graham Bread, a coarse, whole wheat bread that Graham developed and promoted in his widely heard lectures, along with a natural vegetarian diet, good hygiene, and temperance.

In 1850, the American Vegetarian Society was born in New York City, instigated primarily by two clergymen who had separately established "vegetarian churches." Graham was still alive to participate in the first year's meetings of the society, which was also joined by two prominent members of the Alcott family, Dr. William Alcott and Bronson Alcott (father of Louisa May Alcott, the author of *Little Women*).

These meetings, which stressed the health and longevity benefits of vegetarianism, went on well into the 1850s, with many notable guests attending the vegetarian feasts. Among these were the feminists Amelia Bloomer, Susan B. Anthony, and Lucy Stone. The society was very much in favor of women's rights and other reforms.

Noted guests at Vegetarian Society feasts:
Susan B. Anthony
Amelia Bloomer
Lucy Stone

The society spawned other groups, such as the Vegetarian Society of America, a health-oriented group whose publications in the 1880s heartily endorsed an important new diet reformer named Dr. J. H. Kellogg. Dr. Kellogg and his family were the founders of the Kellogg's cereal company of Battle Creek, Michigan, and it was he who originated peanut butter, corn flakes, high-protein meat substitutes such as Protose, a certain form of granola, and other "health foods."

An assortment of vegetarian communes sprang up in the nineteenth century from various convictions and for different purposes. Perhaps the most notable yet shortest-lived vegetarian community was Fruitlands, established in 1843 by Bronson Alcott and Dr. William Alcott on an eleven-acre tract in Massachusetts. While William's stance against meat consumption was health-oriented, Bronson's was rigorously ethical. Apart from the Alcott family, including Louisa May (who later wrote of the Fruitlands experiment in a rather satirical piece entitled "Transcendental Wild Oats"), the society counted among its members other writers and reformers of the day. Family conflicts, the members' inadequate farming abilities, and other causes forced Fruitlands to disband after only seven months.

Henry David Thoreau (1817–1862), the author of *Walden,* a chronicle of simplicity in a solitary life, chose to experiment with vegetarianism in solitude rather than as part of the general movement. Long an advocate of vegetarianism but at best an inconsistent practitioner of it, he nevertheless wrote eloquently of vegetarian ideals:

One farmer says to me, "You cannot live on vegetable food solely, for it furnishes nothing to make bones with," and so he religiously devotes a part of his day to supplying his system with the raw material of bones; talking all the while he walks behind his oxen, which, with vegetable made bones, jerk him and his lumbering plow along in spite of every obstacle.

(*Walden,* 1854)

Turning back to the eighteenth century, we find another fascinating American who experimented with vegetarianism. Benjamin Franklin (1706–1790) gave up meat at the age of sixteen and seemed primarily to enjoy the thriftiness of such a diet. He convinced his employer, a printer whom he called a "great glutton," to enter upon the experiment with him:

He agreed to try the practice if I would keep him company. I did so, and we held it for three months. We had our victuals dress'd, and brought to us regularly by a woman in the neighborhood, who had from me a list of forty dishes, to be prepar'd for us at different times, in all which there was neither fish, flesh, or fowl, and the whim suited me the better at this time from the cheapness of it, not costing us above eighteen pence sterling per week.

(*The Autobiography of Benjamin Franklin*)

The employer tired of the experiment, and soon Franklin gave in to his love of fresh fish, "returning only now and then occasionally to a vegetarian diet."

SKEWERING VEGETARIANS

During vegetarianism's heyday in England, several writers took up their pens to poke fun at vegetarians. In many cases, the barbs were not exactly gentle, as in G. K. Chesterton's sarcastic essays or in some fictional pieces in which vegetarians are depicted as either gullible or simplistic, as in the works of Charles Lamb or Thomas Holcroft. Today, when we have strength in numbers, it is easy to laugh at these less than flattering depictions.

One that I found particularly amusing can be found in *Erewhon,* a novel written in 1872 by Samuel Butler (1835–1902). The people of Erewhon (an anagram of *nowhere,* and the name of a mock-Utopian society) give up eating meat, and after a time, one of their thinkers, the professor, postulates that vegetables are only animals under another name, and that if meat is not allowed, it is equally sinful to eat vegetables and their seeds:

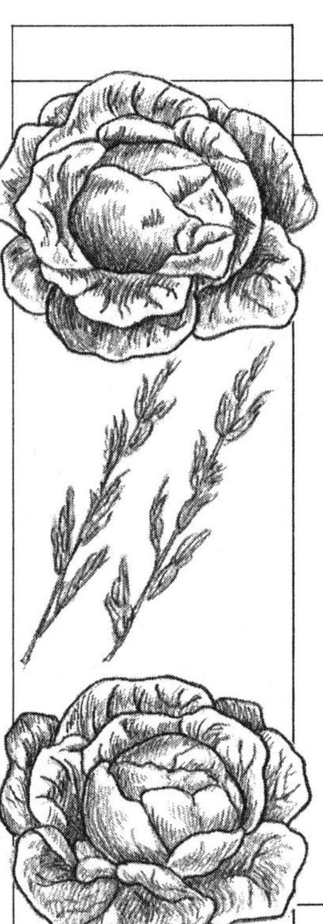

None such, he said, should be eaten, save what had died a natural death, such as fruit that was lying on the ground and about to rot, or cabbage-leaves that had turned yellow in late autumn. These and other like garbage he declared the only food that might be eaten with a clear conscience. Even so the eater must plant the pips of any apples or pears that he may have eaten, or any plum-stones, cherry stones, and the like, or he would come near to incurring the guilt of infanticide. The grain of cereals, according to him, was out of the question, for every such grain had a living soul as much as man had, and had as good a right as man to possess that soul in peace.

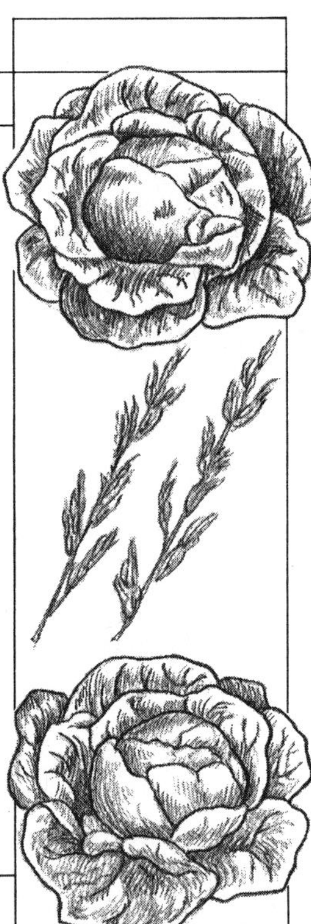

VEGETARIANISM IN UTOPIA

Vegetarianism in literature, when it was not being satirized, was often seen as an ideal concept and incorporated into the beliefs of Utopian societies by writers from Ovid to H. G. Wells. In a charming Utopian legend written by Voltaire (1694–1778), a beautiful princess, Formosanta, pursues a godlike young man, Amazan, around the world, frequently guided by a magical phoenix. She finally catches him on the banks of the Ganges, the site of the Utopia to which he belongs. Voltaire makes it clear that meat is not eaten in this society, whose people follow the "Pythagorean philosophy" because they revere all life. When Formosanta enters the house of Amazan and his mother, she encounters this scene:

> ***The Phoenix, who was not without influence in the house, introduced the Princess of Babylon into a saloon, the walls of which were covered with orange-tree wood and inlaid with ivory. The inferior shepherds and shepherdesses, who were dressed in long white garments, with gold colored trimmings, served up, in a hundred plain porcelain baskets, a hundred various delicacies. . . . They consisted of rice, sago, vermicelli, macaroni, omelettes, milk, eggs, cream, cheese, pastry of every kind, vegetables, fruits, particularly fragrant and grateful to the taste of which no idea can be formed in other climates; and they were accompanied with a profusion of refreshing liquors superior to the finest wine.***

Voltaire's wonderful banquet of one hundred vegetarian delicacies leads perfectly back to the subject of *Vegetariana*—a celebration of the rich variety and colorful legacy of the vegetarian treats that await you in the chapters ahead.

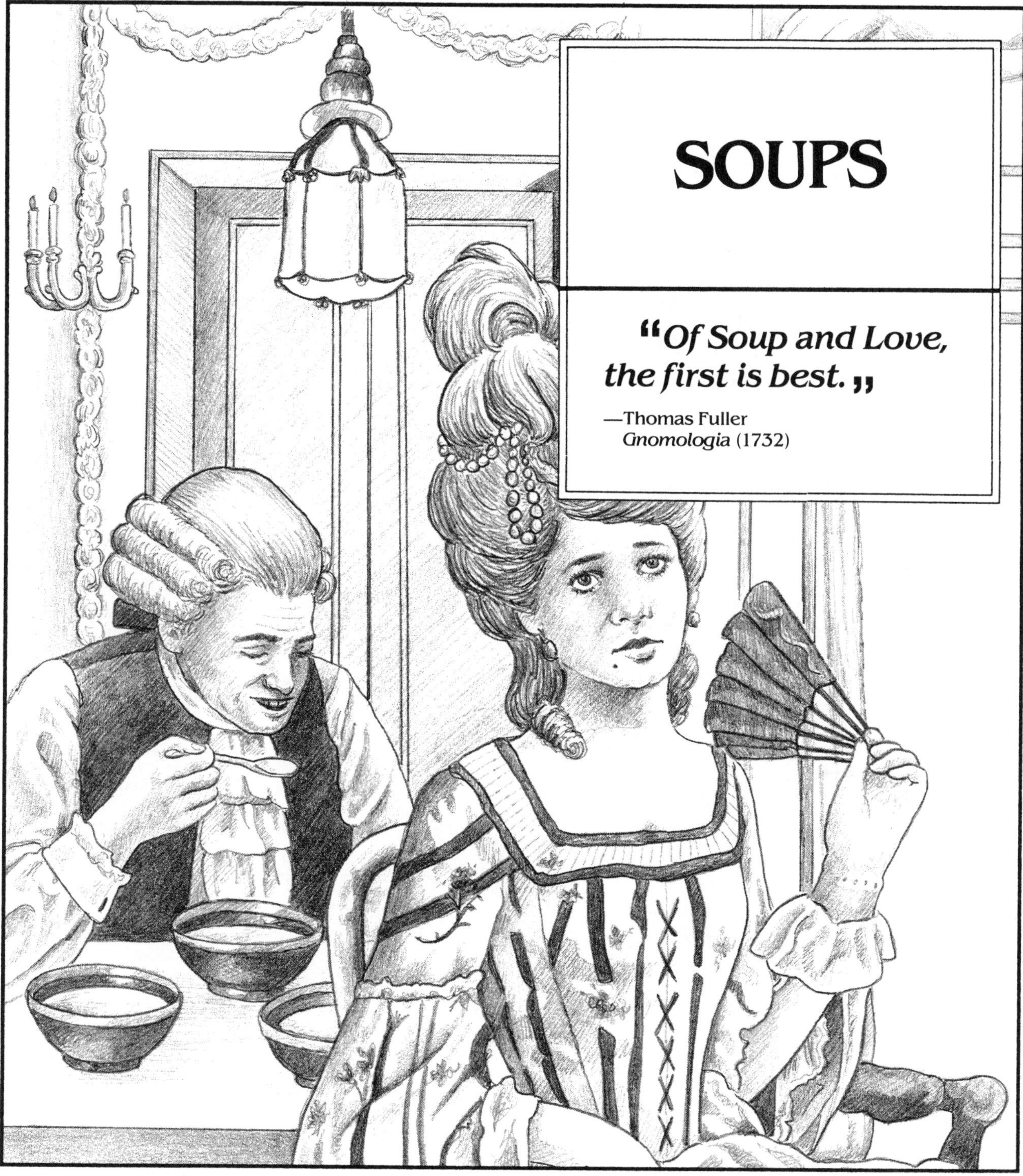

SOUPS

"Of Soup and Love, the first is best."

—Thomas Fuller
Gnomologia (1732)

So much lore and literature exist on soup that it can only be concluded that soup touches something basic in us all.

Soup can be a clear broth full of tender-crisp vegetables, an elegant blended liquid garnished with dumplings, or a thick, stewlike combination of leftover vegetables, grains, and legumes. It can be light enough to just take the edge off the appetite, or substantial enough to be a meal. Hot, it warms you through on a chilly day; cold, it refreshes you in the summer.

The special problem of vegetarian soups is that you can't use a rich meat stock to give the soup depth of flavor. Seasonings are therefore particularly important. The amounts given here are a guideline: Taste your soups as you cook them and adjust the herbs and spices to your liking.

Many would agree that it was the French who made soup cookery an art form, and it was a Frenchman who had the following to say about soup:

"It is to a dinner what a portico or a peristyle is to a building; that is to say, it is not only the first part of it, but it must be devised in such a manner as to set the tone of the banquet, in the same way as the overture of an opera announces the subject of the work."

—Grimod de la Reynière

AVOCADO GAZPACHO

Serves 4 to 6

The addition of an avocado gives this classic summer soup a rich, substantial base.

Base:
1 medium ripe avocado, peeled and quartered
⅔ medium cucumber, peeled and coarsely chopped
¾ medium green pepper, coarsely chopped
2 to 3 tablespoons chopped fresh parsley
1½ cups chopped ripe tomatoes
2 scallions, chopped
3 cups tomato juice
Juice of 1 lemon
1 tablespoon each minced fresh dill and minced fresh parsley
¼ teaspoon chili powder
Salt and freshly ground pepper to taste
1 tablespoon olive oil

Garnish:
⅓ cucumber, finely chopped
1 medium tomato, finely chopped
¼ green pepper, minced
¼ cup sliced green olives
Garlic Croutons (page 30), optional

Place the first 6 base ingredients in the container of a food processor. Process until smooth, then transfer to a serving bowl. Stir in all remaining base and garnish ingredients and mix thoroughly. Chill before serving. If you like, you can also garnish each serving of the soup with Garlic Croutons.

HOT OR COLD TOMATO-LEEK SOUP

Serves 6

2 pounds ripe tomatoes
⅓ cup firmly packed fresh parsley
1 large or 2 medium leeks
2 cloves garlic, minced
1 tablespoon olive oil
1 cup tomato sauce
2 tablespoons dry red wine
1 tablespoon minced fresh dill or 1 teaspoon dried dill
1½ teaspoons paprika
¼ teaspoon dried thyme
Salt and freshly ground pepper to taste
Garlic Croutons (page 30) or yogurt for garnish

Cut 1½ pounds of the tomatoes into quarters and place them in the container of a food processor. Add the parsley and process until well pureed. Dice the remaining tomatoes and set aside.

Chop the white and palest green parts of the leek into small, ¼-inch-wide strips. Rinse thoroughly, removing all the grit, and put them into a large soup pot along with the garlic and olive oil. Cover with 4 cups of water, bring to a boil, then lower heat and simmer for 5 minutes. Add both the pureed and the diced tomatoes and all the remaining ingredients and continue to simmer on low heat for 25 to 30 minutes, or until the leek rings are tender. If serving hot, let stand for 30 minutes, then heat through before serving. If not, let cool and serve at room temperature. Garnish the hot soup with Garlic Croutons, and the cold soup with a spoonful or two of yogurt in each serving.

"Leeks impart brilliance to the voice."

—Pliny the Elder (A.D. 23–79)
Natural History

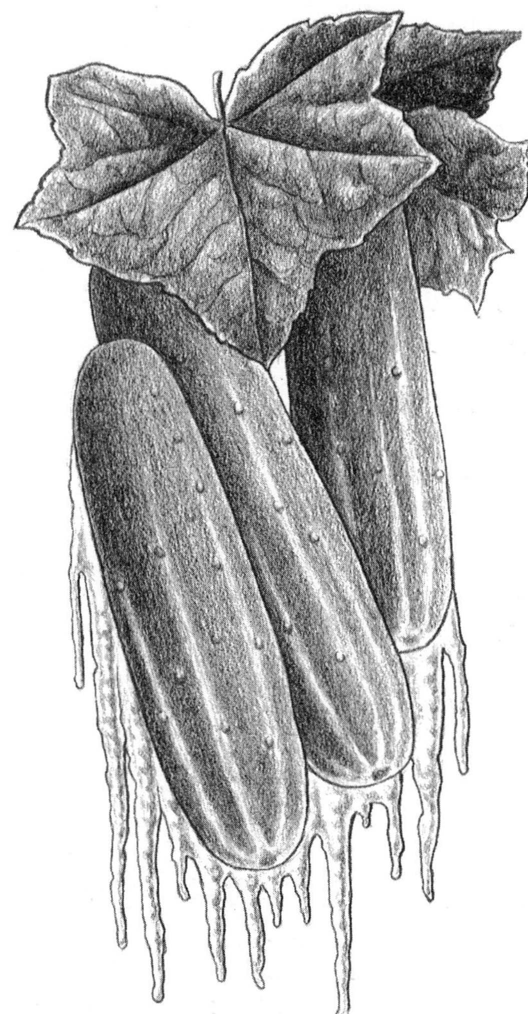

The expression "cool as a cucumber" has basis in fact—on a hot day, the inside of a cucumber stays about 20 degrees cooler than the air temperature. This cool quality is appreciated by today's cooks, but once caused great apprehension. The herbalist Nicolas Culpeper (1616–1654) said in his Herbal, *"they are under the dominion of the moon, though they are much cried out against for their coldness..."*

QUICK CHILLED CUCUMBER-SPINACH SOUP

Serves 4 to 6

This is practically an instant soup, especially if you're using frozen spinach, although I recommend using fresh spinach if possible. If you're in a hurry to eat, you need not even chill the soup.

¾ pound fresh spinach, stemmed, well washed, and chopped, or 1 10-ounce package frozen chopped spinach, thawed
1 quart buttermilk
1 large cucumber, peeled, seeded, and grated
Juice of ½ lemon
2 to 3 tablespoons minced fresh dill or 2 teaspoons dried dill
1 teaspoon good curry powder or Home-Mixed Curry (page 207)
Salt and freshly ground pepper to taste

If using fresh spinach, steam it until wilted. Transfer to a serving container along with any liquid that may have formed. If using frozen spinach, make sure it is thoroughly thawed, and place it in your serving bowl without draining it.

Combine the buttermilk with the spinach, then add the remaining ingredients and mix thoroughly. If the soup seems too dense, adjust the consistency with milk or water as needed. Let stand 10 minutes, then mix again. Chill, if desired, or serve at once.

RUSSIAN BEET BORSCHT

Serves 6 to 8

Beets are not exactly a maligned vegetable, but they are certainly a fairly ignored one, whether in cookery, lore, or literature. They are not by any means a versatile food, but in borscht, they are at their best, with a magnificent color and so much flavor that little seasoning is needed. A food processor is almost a must for the preparation—grating by hand is tedious and messy.

4 medium beets, peeled and grated
1 medium apple, peeled and grated
2 medium carrots, grated
1 medium onion, grated
Juice of 1 lemon, or more to taste
3 tablespoons light brown sugar, or more or less to taste
2 tablespoons minced fresh dill or 2 teaspoons dried dill
Freshly ground pepper to taste
Sour cream or yogurt for garnish

Place all the ingredients, except the garnish, in a large soup pot with enough water to cover. Bring to a boil, lower the heat, and simmer, covered, for about 45 minutes, or until all the vegetables are tender. Allow to cool, then cover and refrigerate until chilled. Top each serving with a dollop of sour cream or yogurt.

CHILLED POTATO SOUP

Serves 6

Start this refreshing yet substantial summer soup several hours before serving so that the potatoes in their cooking liquid can cool down thoroughly. For a light summer supper full of fresh herbs, serve this with a good bread, followed by Tabouleh (page 48), Kuku Sabzi (page 145), and a fruit dessert.

6 medium potatoes, peeled and diced
1 small onion, minced
1 bay leaf
1 tablespoon margarine
Basic Vegetable Stock (page 30) or water to cover
¼ cup chopped fresh parsley
2 cups string beans, cut into 1-inch pieces and steamed until crisp-tender
½ cup low-fat milk
1 cup plain yogurt or sour cream, or a combination
2 tablespoons minced fresh dill or 2 teaspoons dried dill
Salt and freshly ground pepper to taste

Place the potatoes, onion, bay leaf, and margarine in a large soup pot and add just enough vegetable stock or water to cover. Bring to a boil, then simmer, covered, over low heat until the potatoes are tender, taking care not to overcook them. Allow the potatoes to cool at room temperature, or refrigerate them overnight. When they have cooled, remove ½ cup of the diced potatoes with a slotted spoon, mash well, and return to the pot.

Add the remaining ingredients. Mix thoroughly and adjust the consistency with more milk, if desired. Chill before serving.

SWEET AND SOUR CABBAGE SOUP

Serves 6 to 8

⅓ cup raw barley
1 large carrot, sliced
1 large celery stalk, chopped
1 medium onion, chopped
2 tablespoons margarine
2 bay leaves
4¼ cups Basic Vegetable Stock (page 30) or water
3 cups coarsely shredded green cabbage
14-ounce can imported plum tomatoes with liquid, chopped
3 tablespoons dry red wine
3 tablespoons red wine vinegar
3 tablespoons light brown sugar
2 teaspoons paprika
½ teaspoon dried thyme
Salt and freshly ground pepper to taste

Place the barley, carrot, celery, onion, margarine, and bay leaves in a large soup pot and cover with the vegetable stock or water. Bring to a boil, then add all the remaining ingredients. Cover and simmer over low heat for 30 to 35 minutes, or until the vegetables and barley are tender but not overcooked. Allow the soup to stand for an hour before serving, then heat through. This is also a good soup to make a day ahead.

In times past, a child's inquiry as to where babies come from was met with a variety of quaint responses. Do you remember being told that the stork brought you, or that you came from the cabbage patch?

MUSHROOM BARLEY SOUP

Serves 6 to 8

I couldn't resist including my version of this warming, comforting classic soup that is so good in the winter.

¾ cup raw barley
1 large onion, chopped
2 large celery stalks, finely chopped
1 large carrot, sliced
2 bay leaves
2 tablespoons margarine
6 cups Basic Vegetable Stock (page 30) or water
1 teaspoon dried dill
1 teaspoon seasoned salt
½ teaspoon dried summer savory
Salt and freshly ground pepper to taste
10 to 12 ounces white mushrooms, coarsely chopped
2 cups low-fat milk or soymilk, or more or less as needed

Place the barley, onion, celery, carrot, bay leaves, and margarine in a large soup pot with vegetable stock or water and the seasonings. Bring to a boil and simmer, covered, over moderately low heat for 30 minutes. Add the mushrooms and simmer another 20 minutes, or until the vegetables are tender. Stir in enough milk to achieve a slightly thick consistency. Allow the soup to stand for 30 minutes off the heat before serving. The soup thickens quite a bit if it is refrigerated. Add more milk or vegetable stock as needed and adjust the seasonings.

In parts of Southeast Asia, it was believed that coming across mushrooms at the outset of a journey foretold good fortune.

MEDITERRANEAN BROCCOLI AND MUSHROOM SOUP

Serves 6 to 8

This is one of those soups that develop more and more flavor as they stand. It's a good soup to make a day ahead, and will keep very well for up to four days.

1 tablespoon olive oil
1 medium onion, chopped
1⁄3 cup raw barley or 1⁄3 cup raw orzo (rice-shaped pasta)
2 bay leaves
2 cloves garlic, minced
2½ to 3 cups finely chopped broccoli
½ pound coarsely chopped mushrooms
1 small turnip, peeled and diced
14-ounce can imported plum tomatoes with liquid, chopped
3 tablespoons minced fresh parsley
¼ cup dry red wine
1 teaspoon paprika
2 teaspoons Italian seasoning mix
Salt and freshly ground pepper to taste
Grated Parmesan cheese for topping, optional

Heat the oil in a soup pot. Add the onion and sauté until golden. Cover with 6 cups of water, then add the barley, bay leaves, and garlic. Bring to a boil, cover, and simmer over low heat for 15 minutes. (If you use the orzo instead of the barley, cook it separately until it is al dente, drain, and set aside. Add it to the soup just before serving.)

Add all the remaining ingredients to the pot. Cover and simmer over low heat for about 35 minutes, or until the vegetables and barley are tender. Let the soup stand at least an hour before serving, then heat through as needed. Sprinkle each serving with grated Parmesan cheese, if desired.

CURRIED SPINACH AND CHICK-PEA SOUP

Serves 8

This mildly curried soup is an inviting mixture of interesting flavors, textures, and colors.

2 tablespoons margarine
2 cloves garlic, minced
1 medium carrot, coarsely grated
¼ cup raw couscous
1 bay leaf
4 cups cooked or canned chick-peas (about 1⅔ cups raw, cooked using the directions on page 215)
10-ounce package frozen chopped spinach, thawed
1 small zucchini, diced
2 scallions, minced
1½ teaspoons good curry powder or Home-Mixed Curry (page 207), or more to taste
¼ teaspoon dried thyme
2 cups low-fat milk or soymilk
2 tablespoons lemon juice
Salt and freshly ground pepper to taste

Heat the margarine in a soup pot. Add the garlic and sauté for 1 minute. Add 3 cups of water along with the carrot, couscous, and bay leaf. Bring to a boil, cover, and simmer over moderate heat for 15 minutes.

Mash half of the chick-peas. Add them to the pot along with the remaining chick-peas and the spinach, zucchini, scallions, and seasonings. Simmer, covered, for 15 minutes longer.

Add the milk or soymilk and lemon juice. Simmer over very low heat for 15 minutes longer, or until the couscous is tender and the flavors are well integrated. Adjust the consistency with more liquid if the soup is too dense. Season to taste with salt and pepper. Let the soup stand off the heat for an hour before serving, then heat through.

I saw a famous man eating soup.
I say he was lifting a fat broth
Into his mouth with a spoon.
His name was in the newspapers
that day
Spelled out in tall black headlines
And thousands of people were
talking about him.

When I saw him,
He sat bending his head over a plate
Putting soup in his mouth with
a spoon.

—Carl Sandburg
Smoke and Steel (1920)

MUNG DAL

Serves 4 to 6

This traditional recipe is adapted from Julie Sahni's Classic Indian Vegetarian and Grain Cooking. *It's almost a cross between a soup and a sauce; soft Indian breads are often used to scoop it up.*

1 cup mung beans, rinsed and sorted
2 tablespoons safflower or peanut oil
1 teaspoon cumin seeds
1 teaspoon freshly grated ginger
1 or 2 green chilies, mild or hot, seeded and minced
Juice of ½ lemon
3 to 4 tablespoons minced cilantro
Salt to taste

Cook the mung beans in 3½ cups of water until they are soft, about 1 hour. Heat the oil in a small skillet. Add the remaining ingredients and cook over moderate heat, stirring, until fragrant, about 5 to 7 minutes. Add to the mung beans and cook over low heat for 10 minutes. Serve hot as a side dish with vegetable curries or grain dishes.

JOHN DOUGH
EMBEZZLES
$1.2 MILLION
FROM ORPHANAGES

BAROMETER SOUP

I knew, by my scientific reading, that either thermometers or barometers ought to be boiled to make them accurate; I did not know which it was, so I boiled both. There was still no result... I hunted up another barometer; it was new and perfect. I boiled it half an hour in a pot of bean soup which the cooks were making. The result was unexpected: the instrument was not affected at all, but there was such a strong barometer taste to the soup that the head cook, who was a most conscientious person, changed its name in the bill of fare. The dish was so greatly liked by all, that I ordered the cook to have barometer soup every day.

—Mark Twain
A Tramp Abroad (1880)

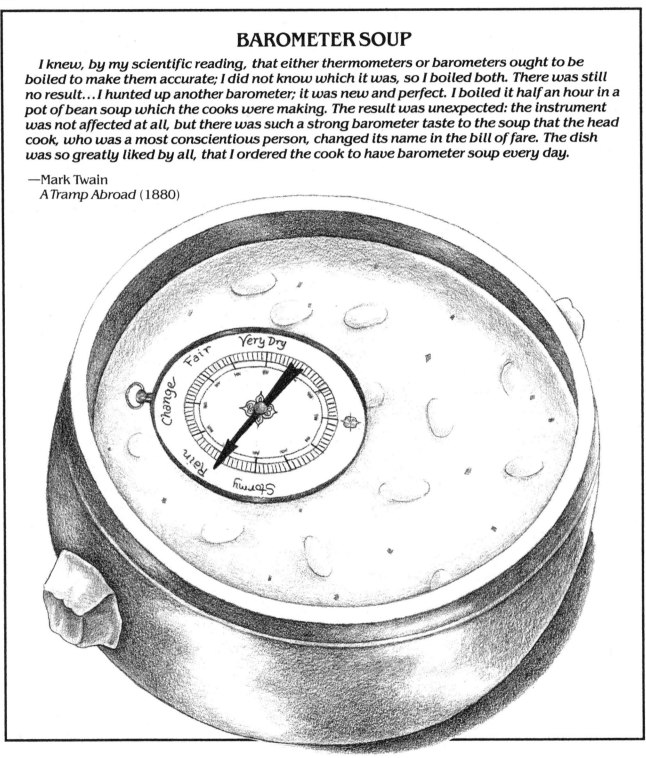

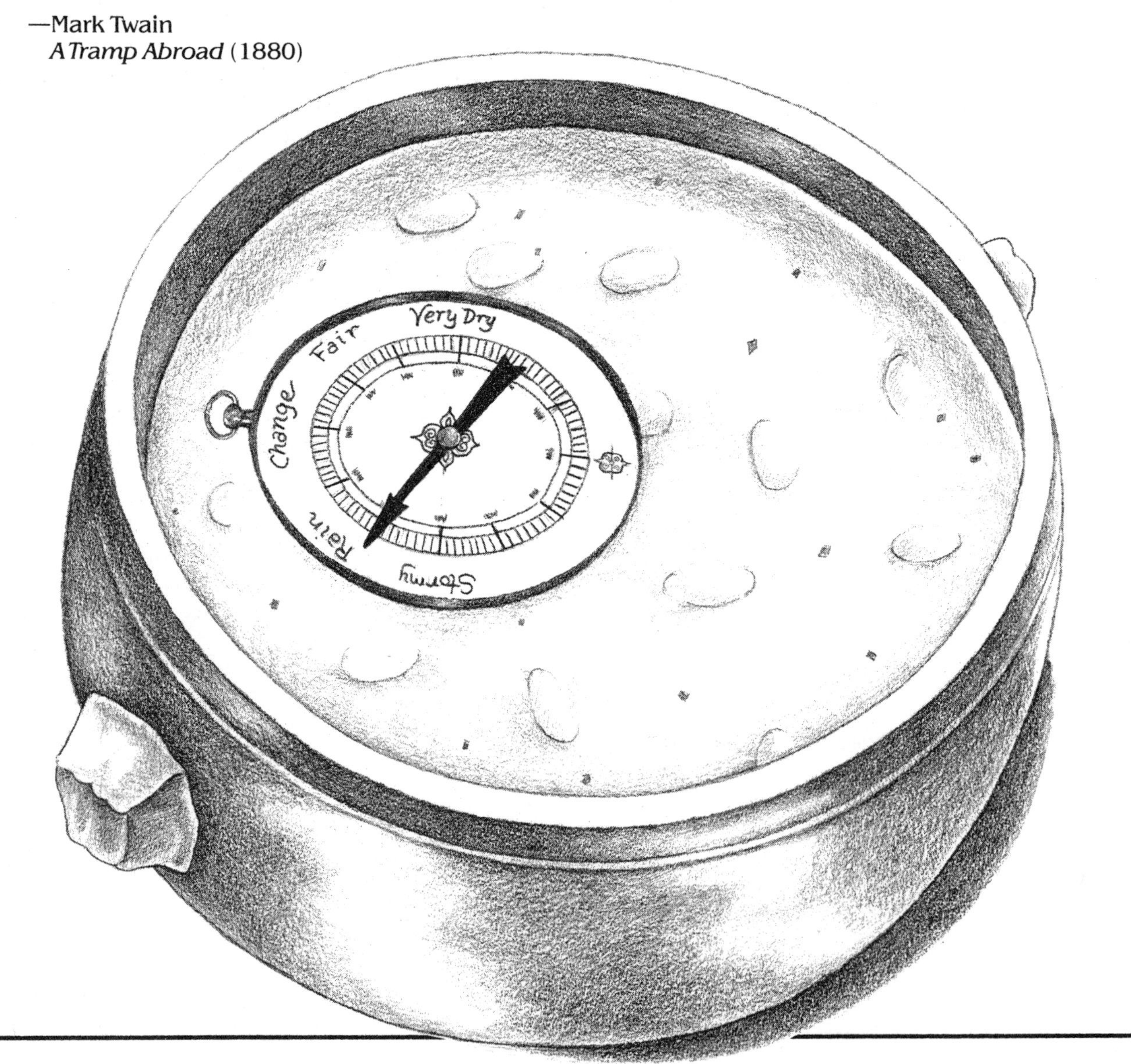

HEARTY BEAN SOUP

Serves 8

The filling and flavorful bean soups on this page are good to make a day ahead and will keep well for several days, developing flavor as they stand. Although you can use canned beans, raw beans work best in these soups.

2 cups cooked or canned great northern beans (about ¾ cup raw)
2 cups cooked or canned kidney or red beans (about ¾ cup raw)
2 tablespoons olive oil
1 medium onion, chopped
2 large celery stalks, chopped
1 medium potato, scrubbed and diced (don't peel)
1 cup string beans, cut into 1-inch pieces
14-ounce can imported plum tomatoes with liquid, chopped
¼ cup dry red wine
1 teaspoon each dried summer savory and paprika
½ teaspoon each ground coriander and ground cumin
Salt and freshly ground pepper to taste

Cook the beans following the directions on page 215. Use extra water in cooking them so it can be used as stock.

Heat the olive oil in a soup pot. Add the onion and celery and sauté until golden. Add the potato and string beans along with just enough water or cooking liquid from the beans to cover. Bring to a boil, then simmer, covered, over moderate heat until the vegetables are just tender, about 20 to 25 minutes. Add the beans and all the remaining ingredients plus 2 more cups of water or cooking liquid from the beans. Simmer, covered, over low heat for another 20 to 25 minutes. Taste to be sure that everything is done to your liking.

WHITE BEAN AND ZUCCHINI SOUP

Serves 8

2½ cups cooked or canned white beans such as navy or great northern beans (about 1 cup raw)
1 large onion, chopped
¼ cup raw barley
2 tablespoons margarine
2 bay leaves
1 heaping cup shredded white cabbage
2 medium zucchini, diced
1 small turnip, peeled and diced
1 teaspoon each ground cumin and dried dill
½ teaspoon each dry mustard and ground coriander
¼ cup minced fresh parsley
Salt and freshly ground pepper to taste
1 cup low-fat milk or soymilk, or more as needed

Cook the beans following the directions on page 215. Do not drain any of their cooking liquid.

Place the onion, barley, margarine, and bay leaves in a soup pot and cover with 4 cups total of water and cooking liquid from the beans. Bring to a boil, then simmer, covered, over moderate heat for 15 minutes. Add the cabbage and simmer for 10 minutes longer. Add the beans and remaining ingredients and simmer for another 20 to 30 minutes, or until the vegetables and barley are tender. Adjust the consistency with more milk or soymilk as needed to achieve a slightly thick consistency.

CHEDDAR CHEESE GARLIC SOUP

Serves 6

Melting the cheese before adding the smoothly pureed vegetables assures a wonderfully velvety texture. This rich soup is a special-occasion treat.

2 tablespoons safflower oil
8 cloves garlic, crushed or minced
1 small onion, chopped
2 medium celery stalks, finely chopped
14-ounce can imported plum tomatoes with liquid, chopped
1 tablespoon margarine
1 pound mild cheddar cheese, cut into small dice
3 tablespoons dry white wine
1½ cups low-fat milk, or more or less as needed
1 teaspoon paprika
½ teaspoon dry mustard
Salt and freshly ground pepper to taste

Garnish:
Broccoli florets, finely chopped and steamed crisp-tender

Heat the oil in a soup pot. Add the garlic, onion, and celery and sauté over very low heat, stirring frequently, until the onion is translucent. Cover with 1 cup of water and simmer, covered, over moderate heat until the onion and celery are tender. Transfer to the container of a food processor along with the cooking liquid and process until thoroughly pureed. Add the tomatoes and puree again until smooth. Set aside.

In the same soup pot, heat the margarine. Add the cheese and stir constantly over very low heat until melted to a velvety texture. If the cheese seems to be sticking to the pot, add tiny amounts of water.

Slowly stir in the pureed mixture until everything is thoroughly blended. Add the remaining ingredients, using enough milk to achieve a slightly thick consistency. Simmer, uncovered, over low heat until just heated through, stirring frequently. Serve at once. Garnish each serving with a few freshly steamed broccoli florets.

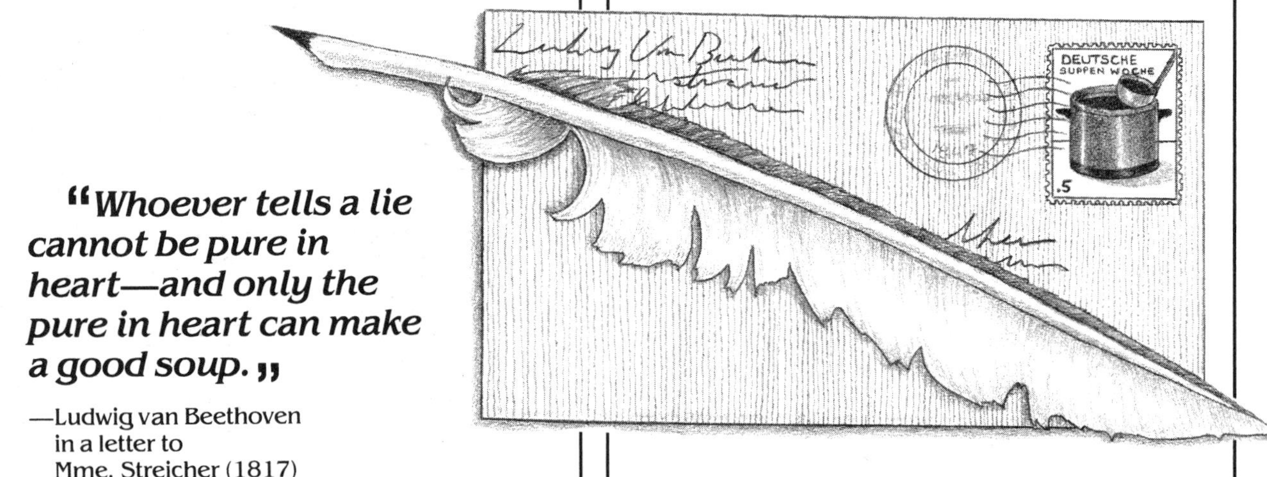

"Whoever tells a lie cannot be pure in heart—and only the pure in heart can make a good soup."

—Ludwig van Beethoven
in a letter to
Mme. Streicher (1817)

DILLED POTATO AND DUTCH CHEESE SOUP

Serves 6 or more

Warming and soothing as this soup is when served hot, it is also excellent chilled.

6 medium-large potatoes, peeled and diced
1 large onion, chopped
2 cloves garlic, minced
2 bay leaves
2 tablespoons margarine
Basic Vegetable Stock (page 30) or water
1 cup low-fat milk
1½ cups grated Edam or Gouda cheese
2 tablespoons unbleached white flour
2 tablespoons dry white wine
3 tablespoons minced fresh dill
½ teaspoon dry mustard
Salt and freshly ground pepper to taste

Place the potatoes, onion, garlic, bay leaves, and margarine in a soup pot and add just enough vegetable stock or water to cover. Bring to a boil, then simmer, covered, over moderate heat until the potatoes are done, about 15 to 20 minutes.

Use a slotted spoon to remove 1 cup of the potato dice. Mash well and return to the pot. Stir in the milk, then the cheese, a little at a time. Dissolve the flour in just enough water to make a smooth, flowing paste, and whisk it into the soup.

Add the remaining ingredients and simmer, covered, over very low heat for 10 to 15 minutes. Remove from the heat and let stand for about 30 minutes before serving. Adjust the consistency by adding more milk as needed, then heat through and serve.

"I had rather live with Cheese and Garlicke in a windmill."

—William Shakespeare
1st *Henry IV* (ca. 1597)

ALMOND CREAM OF BROCCOLI SOUP

Serves 6

The flavors of broccoli and almonds are sometimes wonderfully compatible. The almonds and the apple add a subtly sweet touch to this soup.

1½ pounds broccoli
2 tablespoons safflower oil
1 large onion, chopped
1 large celery stalk, chopped
1 medium apple, peeled, cored, and diced
Basic Vegetable Stock (page 30) or water
½ cup almonds
1 tablespoon minced fresh parsley
½ teaspoon dried basil
¼ teaspoon dried thyme
Salt and freshly ground pepper to taste
Juice of ½ lemon
1 cup low-fat milk or soymilk, or more or less as needed
Chopped almonds for garnish

Remove and discard the tough ends of the broccoli stems, and chop the remaining broccoli into 1- to 2-inch pieces. Set aside.

Heat the oil in a soup pot. Add the onion and celery and sauté over moderately low heat until golden. Add the broccoli and apple and just enough vegetable stock or water to cover. Bring to a boil, then simmer, covered, for 5 minutes. Use a slotted spoon to remove about a cup of the smaller broccoli florets, and set them aside. Cover and continue to simmer until the vegetables are quite tender, about 20 to 25 minutes, then remove from the heat.

Place the almonds in the container of a food processor and process until finely ground. Transfer the cooked vegetables to the processor with a slotted spoon, half at a time if necessary, and process with the almonds until well pureed.

Stir the puree back into the liquid in the soup pot. Return to low heat and stir in the seasonings, lemon juice, milk or soymilk, and reserved broccoli pieces and simmer until just heated through. Adjust the consistency with more stock or milk if necessary. Let the soup stand off the heat for an hour or so before serving, then heat through as needed. Garnish each serving with a sprinkling of chopped almonds.

Broccoli is native to Italy (it means "little sprouts" in Italian), and its cookery dates back to the epicure of classical Rome, Apicius, who gave the world one of its first recorded cookbooks. The controversial Roman emperor Tiberius was reported to have seriously scolded his son Drusus for overindulging in broccoli.

CREAM OF ASPARAGUS AND STRING BEAN SOUP

Serves 6

1 pound asparagus, cut into 1-inch pieces
1 pound string beans, cut into 1-inch pieces
1 medium onion, chopped
2 cloves garlic, minced
1 medium potato, scrubbed and diced (don't peel)
2 tablespoons margarine
2 bay leaves
1 teaspoon each dried basil and dried dill
Basic Vegetable Stock (page 30) or water
1 cup low-fat milk, or more or less as needed
Salt and freshly ground pepper to taste
Garnish of choice (page 30, Soup Extras)

Cut the tips off the asparagus and set them aside; while the soup is cooking, steam them until they are crisp-tender.

Combine the remaining ingredients, except the milk, salt, pepper, and garnish, in a soup pot with just enough vegetable stock or water to cover. Bring to a boil, then simmer, covered, on moderately low heat until the vegetables are quite tender, about 25 to 30 minutes.

With a slotted spoon, transfer the vegetables to the container of a food processor, half at a time, and process until very smoothly pureed. Stir back into the pot and return to low heat. Add enough milk to achieve a slightly thick consistency, followed by the steamed asparagus tips and salt and pepper, and simmer until just heated through. Serve at once, garnished with any of the Soup Extras.

Beautiful Soup, so rich and green,
Waiting in a hot tureen!
Who for such dainties would not
stoop?
Soup of the evening, beautiful Soup!
Soup of the evening, beautiful Soup!
Beau—ootiful Soo—oop!
Beau—ootiful Soo—oop!
Soo—oop of the e–e–vening,
Beautiful, beautiful Soup!

Beautiful Soup! Who cares for fish,
Game, or any other dish?
Who would not give all else for two
Pennyworth only of beautiful Soup?
Pennyworth only of beautiful Soup?
Beau—ootiful Soo—oop!
Beau—ootiful Soo—oop!
Soo—oop of the e–e–vening,
Beau—ootiful, beautiFUL SOUP!

—Lewis Carroll
Alice's Adventures in Wonderland (1865)

LENTIL AND BROWN RICE SOUP

Serves 6 or more

With its complementary proteins, lentils and rice, and its savory flavors, this is one of the "everyday" soups I like best. It's a good choice when you want to serve soup as the main course; a good bread, a hearty salad such as Colorful Cabbage Salad (page 34), and a fruit dessert would round out this meal nicely.

⅔ cup raw lentils, sorted and rinsed
⅓ cup raw brown rice
2 tablespoons olive oil
2 cloves garlic, minced
2 tablespoons soy sauce
2 bay leaves
1 small onion, finely chopped
2 medium carrots, thinly sliced
1 large celery stalk, finely chopped
Handful of chopped celery leaves
14-ounce can imported plum tomatoes with liquid, chopped
¼ cup dry red wine or dry sherry
1 teaspoon each dried basil and paprika
½ teaspoon each dried oregano and dried thyme
Salt and freshly ground pepper to taste

Place the first 6 ingredients in a soup pot and cover with 6 cups of water. Bring to a boil and simmer, covered, over moderate heat for 10 minutes.

Add all of the remaining ingredients except salt and pepper. Simmer over low heat for 40 to 45 minutes, or until the vegetables, rice, and lentils are done to your liking. Add salt and pepper to taste.

CREAM OF CELERY AND CORN SOUP

Serves 6

8 large celery stalks
Handful of chopped celery leaves
1 medium onion, chopped
2 medium potatoes, peeled and diced
1 teaspoon dried dill
½ teaspoon dried thyme
¼ teaspoon ground coriander
3 cups cooked fresh or thawed frozen corn kernels
Salt and freshly ground pepper to taste
1 to 1½ cups low-fat milk or soymilk, or more or less as needed
2 tablespoons margarine

Garlic Croutons (page 30) for garnish

Cut 6 of the celery stalks into 1-inch pieces. Place them in a soup pot along with the celery leaves, onion, potatoes, and seasonings. Add just enough water to cover. Bring to a boil, then simmer, covered, until the vegetables are quite tender, about 25 to 30 minutes. Remove from the heat.

Using a slotted spoon, transfer the vegetables to a container of a food processor. Process in batches until fairly smooth. Then process 2 cups of the corn kernels with a little of the cooking liquid until well pureed. Stir the pureed corn and vegetables into the soup pot. Return to moderately low heat. Add the milk and remaining corn kernels and allow to simmer, uncovered.

Chop the 2 remaining celery stalks into small dice. Heat the margarine in a small skillet. Add the celery and sauté over low heat until lightly browned. Stir the celery into the soup and simmer just until the soup is thoroughly heated through. Allow the soup to stand off the heat for an hour or so, then heat through again. Garnish each serving with Garlic Croutons.

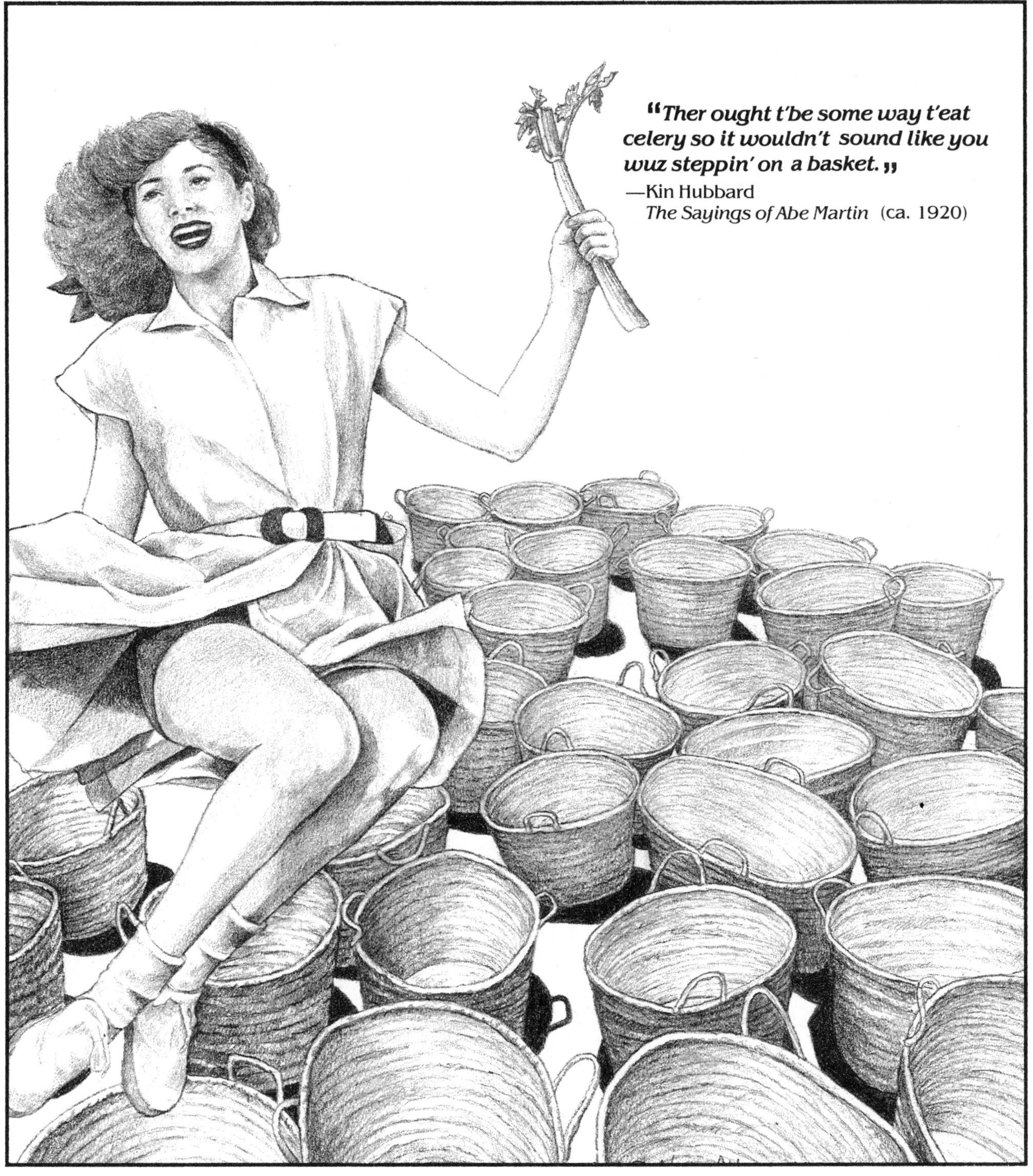
"Ther ought t'be some way t'eat celery so it wouldn't sound like you wuz steppin' on a basket."
—Kin Hubbard
The Sayings of Abe Martin (ca. 1920)

PUMPKIN SOUP

Serves 6

Once you have the cooked beans ready, this slightly eccentric soup can be made in about half an hour.

2 cups cooked or canned navy beans (about ¾ cup raw)
2 tablespoons margarine
1 medium onion, minced
2 cloves garlic, minced
1 medium zucchini, quartered lengthwise and sliced
1½ cups coarsely chopped white mushrooms
2 bay leaves
2 cups cooked, pureed pumpkin or 1 16-ounce can plain, unsweetened pumpkin
½ cup sliced black olives
Juice of ½ lemon
½ teaspoon each ground nutmeg, ground allspice, and ground coriander
Salt and freshly ground pepper to taste

Cook the beans following the directions on page 215. Cook them in extra water so it can be used as stock.

Heat the margarine in a large soup pot. Add the onion and garlic and sauté until golden. Cover with 4 cups total of cooking liquid from the beans and water. Add the zucchini, mushrooms, and bay leaves, then simmer, covered, over moderate heat just until the zucchini and mushrooms are tender, about 10 minutes. Add the remaining ingredients. Adjust the consistency with more cooking liquid from the beans or water as needed to achieve a slightly thick consistency. Allow the soup to stand off the heat for an hour or so before serving, then heat through.

Nowadays, we don't eat very much pumpkin except in pie, but it was a staple food for the Pilgrims of Plymouth Colony. They were so innundated with it that they invented this little song:

We have pumpkin at morning
And pumpkin at noon
If it were not for pumpkin
We would be undoon.

POTATO-CORN CHOWDER

Serves 8

2 tablespoons safflower oil
1 medium onion, chopped
3 medium potatoes, scrubbed well and diced (don't peel)
2 medium carrots, sliced
1 large celery stalk, chopped
2 bay leaves
3 cups cooked fresh or thawed frozen corn kernels
14-ounce can imported plum tomatoes with liquid, chopped
1½ teaspoons ground coriander
1 teaspoon dried summer savory
½ teaspoon dried thyme
Salt and freshly ground pepper to taste
1 cup low-fat milk or soymilk, or more or less as needed

Heat the oil in a soup pot. Add the onion and sauté until golden. Add the potatoes, carrots, celery, and bay leaves, and just enough water or vegetable stock to cover. Bring to a boil and simmer, covered, over low heat for 15 minutes. Add the corn kernels, tomatoes, and seasonings. Simmer, covered, over moderately low heat for about 20 to 25 minutes, or until all the vegetables are cooked to taste. Use a slotted spoon to remove 1 cup of the potatoes. Mash well and stir into the soup. Add enough milk or soymilk to achieve your desired consistency and stir well. Cover and simmer for 5 minutes longer. Let the soup stand off the heat for an hour before serving, then heat through.

CHINESE VEGETABLE-MISO SOUP

Serves 6

Miso is a concentrated high-protein paste made from soybeans. Its salty flavor is reminiscent of soy sauce. Look for it in health-food stores or in Oriental groceries. This soup is best eaten on the same day it's made.

1 tablespoon sesame oil
2 celery stalks, sliced diagonally
1 medium carrot, thinly sliced
2 cloves garlic, minced
1 medium turnip, peeled and diced
2 or 3 scallions, chopped (white and green parts kept separate)
1½ cups chopped mushrooms
¾ cup snow peas, cut into 1-inch pieces
1 cup firmly packed fresh mung bean sprouts
2 tablespoons dry sherry
1 tablespoon white wine or rice vinegar
½ pound tofu, diced
4 tablespoons miso, or more or less to taste

Bring 5 cups of water to a boil in a soup pot. Add the sesame oil, celery, carrot, and garlic. Simmer, covered, over moderate heat for 10 minutes.

Add the turnip and the white parts of the scallions to the soup pot, cover, and simmer for 5 minutes. Then add all the remaining ingredients except the tofu and miso, and simmer until all the vegetables are cooked to a crisp-tender texture. Add the tofu and remove from heat.

Dissolve the miso in ½ cup of warm water. Stir into the soup. If you've never had miso before, try pouring half in and tasting it before you add the rest. Serve at once.

BASIC VEGETABLE STOCK

Makes about 6 cups

This basic stock may be used in place of water in most any vegetable soup to give added depth of flavor. It's also a good way to use up vegetables that are limp or less than perfectly fresh.

1 large onion, chopped
1 large carrot, sliced
2 large celery stalks, sliced
1 medium potato, scrubbed and diced
1 cup coarsely shredded white cabbage
2 teaspoons mixed dried herbs of your choice
1 teaspoon salt

Place all the ingredients in a large soup pot with 7 cups of water. Bring to a boil, then simmer, covered, over low heat for 40 to 45 minutes, or until the vegetables are quite tender. Strain the stock through a colander lined with 3 layers of cheesecloth.

"In taking soup, it is necessary to avoid lifting too much into the spoon, or filling the mouth so full as to almost stop the breath."

—St. John the Baptist de la Salle
The Rules of Christian Manners and Civility (1695)

SOUP EXTRAS

GARLIC CROUTONS

Simply take as many slices of whole-grain bread as needed, preferably several days old, and rub them with the inside of a clove of garlic. Cut the bread into small cubes and arrange on a baking sheet. Bake at 300° F, stirring occasionally, until brown and crisp.

WHEAT BERRIES

The nutty taste and chewy texture of whole wheat berries make for an offbeat soup garnish. Cook following the directions on page 214. If you like, you can sauté them in a little margarine or safflower oil and soy sauce before adding them to soup.

CORNMEAL DUMPLINGS

½ cup cornmeal
½ cup whole wheat flour
1 teaspoon salt
1 tablespoon safflower oil

Combine the first 3 ingredients, then work in the oil and ½ cup of water to form a stiff batter. Shape into 1-inch balls. Bring a large pot of water to a rolling boil. Drop the dumplings into the water and cook for 15 minutes. Drain. Makes about 12 to 14 dumplings.

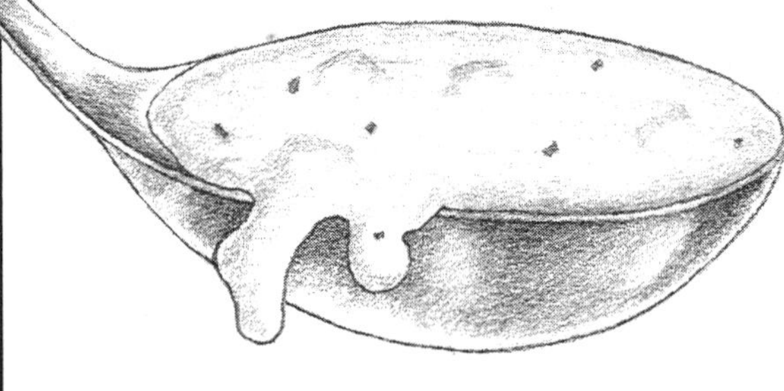

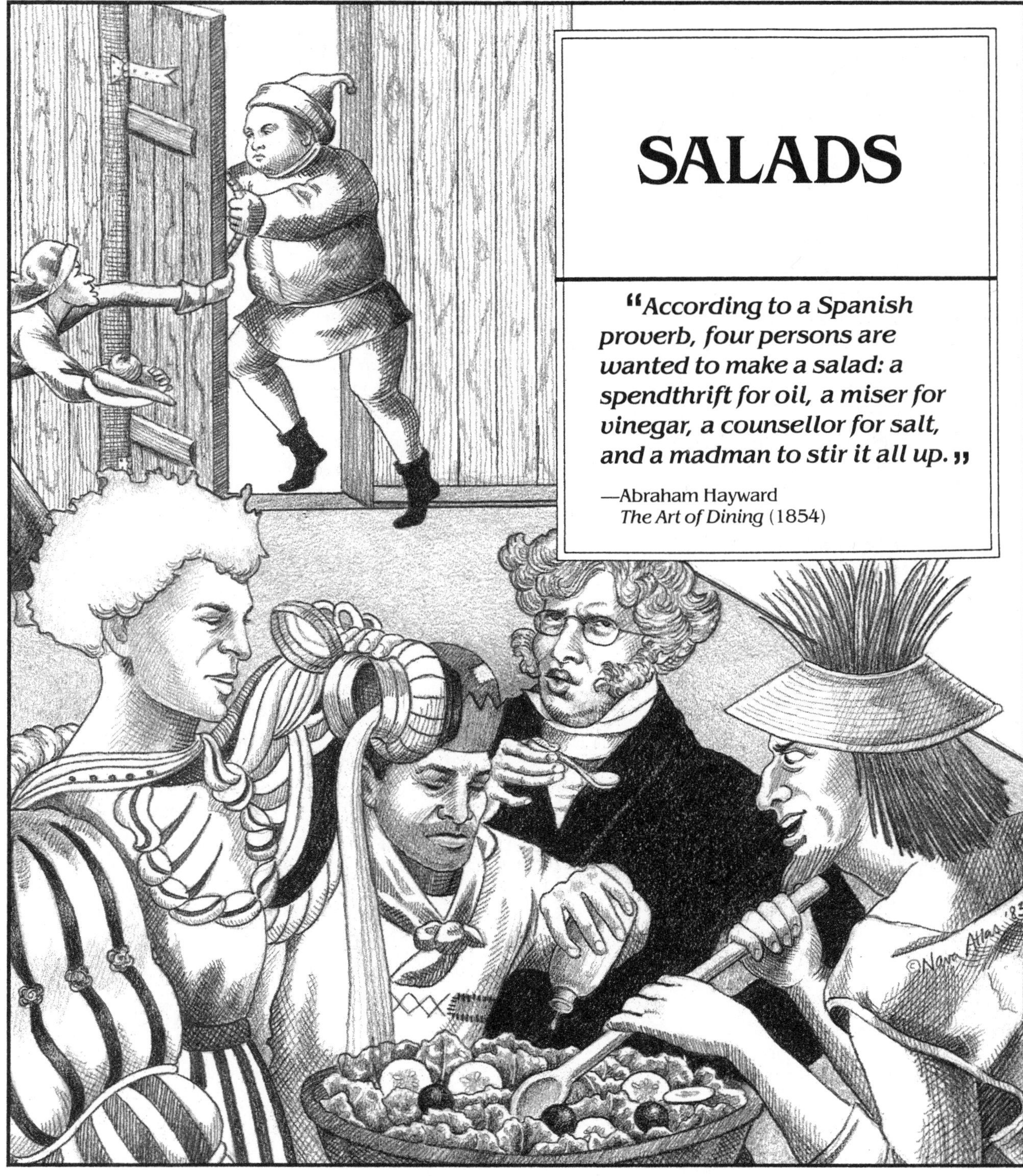

SALADS

"According to a Spanish proverb, four persons are wanted to make a salad: a spendthrift for oil, a miser for vinegar, a counsellor for salt, and a madman to stir it all up."

—Abraham Hayward
The Art of Dining (1854)

Preparations of fresh, raw, or semi-cooked vegetables, mixed with herbs and spices and dressed in oils, vinegars, and juices, have been made since time immemorial. Salad-making is recorded in the Bible and in various writings of ancient Greece and Rome and medieval Europe, among others. In some ways, the salad of yesteryear may have been more sophisticated than today's, due to the greater awareness of usable herbs and even flowers.

Rather than going into ways of combining seasonal greens, which most salad-lovers do as a matter of course, this chapter takes a more offbeat approach to the salad. Some, which utilize grains, beans, and cheeses, are hearty enough to constitute the main dish of a summer meal. Others present vegetables better known for their use in hot dishes with an unusual twist.

LENTIL AND FETA CHEESE SALAD

Serves 6 to 8

A substantial, high-protein salad with a Greek flavor, this is a good choice when you want salad to be the main dish for lunch or supper.

1 cup raw lentils, sorted, rinsed, and cooked following the directions on page 215
1 medium green pepper, sliced into long strips
2 medium firm, ripe tomatoes, diced
1 small red or white onion, chopped, optional
½ pound feta cheese, crumbled
¼ cup olive oil
Juice of 1 large lemon, or more to taste
1 teaspoon each dried basil and dried dill
Freshly ground pepper to taste
Dark green lettuce leaves

Garnish:
Greek black olives
Lemon wedges

Allow the cooked lentils to cool to room temperature. Transfer them to a mixing bowl and combine with all of the remaining ingredients except the lettuce and garnishes. Although this salad may be served immediately, ideally it should be allowed to stand, refrigerated, for 1 to 2 hours.

Prepare a bed of lettuce for each serving and garnish with the olives and lemon wedges.

BLACK BEAN SALAD WITH FETA CHEESE

Serves 4 to 6

3 cups cooked black beans (about 1¼ cups raw)
¼ cup olive oil
2 to 3 tablespoons, to taste, red wine vinegar
¼ cup chopped fresh parsley
1 teaspoon dried oregano
1 small green bell pepper, cut into narrow strips
2 scallions, minced
¼ pound feta cheese, crumbled
2 medium tomatoes, diced
Freshly ground pepper to taste

In a serving bowl, combine the black beans with all but the last 3 ingredients. Mix thoroughly and allow to marinate for 1 to 2 hours. Just before serving, add the feta cheese, tomatoes, and pepper. Toss well and serve at once.

"*A wise man is the proper composer of an excellent sallet, and how many transcendancies belong to an accomplish'd sallet-dresser, so as to emerge an exact critic indeed.*"

—John Evelyn
Acetaria: A Discourse of Sallet (1699)

O Sallet!
With how many
exactitudes have
I dressed thee?

COLORFUL CABBAGE SALAD

Serves 4 to 6

If cabbages really did have feelings, they'd be somewhat hurt, because they are frequently maligned in modern literature. This was not so in classical Greece and Rome, where cabbage was praised by Pliny and others for its nutritive qualities and its ability to prevent drunkenness. Cabbage gives salads such crispness and substance that I'm devoting these two pages to it—start crunching!

2½ cups thinly shredded cabbage
1 cup halved cherry tomatoes
1 large carrot, coarsely grated
⅓ cup chopped or sliced black olives
¾ cup diced mozzarella cheese, optional
2 scallions, finely chopped
2 tablespoons finely chopped fresh parsley
Freshly ground pepper to taste
Yogurt-Dill Dressing (page 66)

Combine all the ingredients except the dressing in a serving bowl. Pass the Yogurt-Dill Dressing around with the salad.

"When I tell people that I am a vegetarian, I am always told that cabbages also have feelings."

—George Bernard Shaw

CABBAGE-APPLE COOLER

Serves 6

Cabbage and apple in yogurt combine to make a refreshing, palate-cooling salad that's perfect with spicy dishes.

3 cups thinly shredded red or white cabbage
1 medium apple, peeled and diced
¼ cup raisins
1 small carrot, coarsely grated
1 tablespoon sesame or poppy seeds
1 to 2 tablespoons minced fresh mint leaves or 1 to 2 teaspoons dried mint
1 cup plain yogurt
Juice of ½ lemon
1 teaspoon sesame oil
2 tablespoons honey

Combine the first 6 ingredients in a large bowl.

Combine the yogurt, lemon juice, sesame oil, and honey in a small bowl. Mix thoroughly and pour over the cabbage mixture. Toss until well combined. Chill before serving.

SUNFLOWER COLESLAW

Serves 6

Sunflower seeds add a nice nutty flavor to this coleslaw.

3 cups thinly shredded white or red cabbage
2 medium carrots, coarsely grated
Juice of 1 lemon
3 tablespoons finely chopped fresh parsley
¼ cup toasted sunflower seeds
Freshly ground pepper to taste
1 cup Tofu "Mayonnaise" (page 58) or 1 cup Parsley Dressing (page 67)

Combine all the ingredients in a bowl and mix thoroughly. If you're using the Parsley Dressing, eliminate the fresh parsley listed above. Chill before serving.

"The Floure of the Sunne is called in Latin Flos Solis; for that some have reported it to turn with the Sunne. . . but I rather think it was so called because it resembles the radiant beams of the Sunne. . . "

—John Gerarde
The Herball (1636)

GREEK SALAD

Serves 6 to 8

1 small cucumber, peeled and thinly sliced
1 medium green bell pepper, cut into julienne strips
2 large ripe tomatoes, diced
1 cup thinly shredded red cabbage
1 small red onion, sliced into thin rings
½ cup cured black olives, such as Kalamatas
Herb Marinade (page 65), as needed
Dark green lettuce leaves, as needed
4 to 6 ounces feta or crumbly goat cheese, crumbled
Dried oregano

Combine the first 6 ingredients in a mixing bowl. This may be done ahead of time. Just before serving, add enough Herb Vinaigrette to coat the vegetables, and toss well. Arrange the salad on a large platter lined with lettuce leaves. Sprinkle the crumbled feta cheese over the top, followed by a sprinkling of dried oregano. Serve at once.

"You can put everything, and the more things the better, into salad, as into a conversation; but everything depends upon the skill of mixing."

—Charles Dudley Warner
My Summer in a Garden (1871)

GREENS AND ENDIVES WITH ORANGE VINAIGRETTE

Serves 6

This elegant salad is easy to make and has a lively and lilting citrus flavor.

6 cups washed and torn mixed green lettuce leaves, such as a combination of romaine, chicory, and red-leaf lettuce
2 Belgian endives, thinly sliced
1 small red onion, thinly sliced
2 small sweet seedless oranges, such as Sweet Minneolas or clementines, sectioned
⅓ cup sliced almonds

Vinaigrette:
¼ cup light olive oil
2 tablespoons red wine or balsamic vinegar
2 tablespoons fresh orange juice

Combine the salad ingredients in a salad bowl and toss together. Combine the vinaigrette ingredients in a small bowl and stir together. Just before serving, dress the salad with enough dressing to moisten, but not drench, the greens.

'Twas a good lady; we may pick a thousand salads, ere we light on such another herb.

Indeed, sir, she was the sweet marjoram of the salad, or rather the herb of grace.

—William Shakespeare
All's Well That Ends Well (ca. 1602)

MARINATED SPROUTS AND STRING BEANS

Serves 4 to 6

If you like fresh bean sprouts, this is an attractive way to serve them in a salad. Beware of tough-skinned string beans; choose small, tender ones.

3 heaping cups string beans, cut into 1-inch pieces
2½ cups (about ½ pound) fresh mung bean sprouts
1 medium carrot, coarsely grated
2 tablespoons finely minced onion
½ cup Herb Marinade (page 65)
Salt and freshly ground pepper to taste
Dark green lettuce leaves

Steam the string beans and bean sprouts separately to a crisp-tender texture. When they are done, rinse them under cool water until they stop steaming and then drain them thoroughly. Combine in a mixing bowl. Add the remaining ingredients, except lettuce, to the bowl and mix thoroughly. Marinate for several hours, refrigerated, stirring occasionally to distribute the marinade.

Place each serving on a bed of dark green lettuce leaves.

HEARTY PASTA AND RED BEAN SALAD

Serves 6

Pasta salads make a satisfying yet surprisingly light lunch or supper offering in the summer, but there is no reason not to have them year-round.

2 cups raw, medium-sized pasta, such as rotelle or sea shells
2 cups cooked or canned kidney beans (about ¾ cup raw, cooked following the directions on page 215)
1 cup diced zucchini (approximately 1 medium zucchini)
1 small green pepper, finely chopped
1 medium ripe tomato, chopped
⅓ cup chopped green olives
¼ cup grated Parmesan cheese or Parmesan-style soy cheese
1 cup plain yogurt or 1 cup Tofu "Mayonnaise" (page 58)
1 teaspoon Dijon-style mustard
½ teaspoon each chili powder and ground coriander
Salt and freshly ground pepper to taste

Cook the pasta al dente. Rinse with cool water, drain well, and place in a mixing bowl. Add the remaining ingredients and mix thoroughly. Serve at room temperature or chilled.

"To make a good salad is to be a brilliant diplomat: one must know exactly how much oil one must put with one's vinegar."

—Oscar Wilde (1856–1900)

PASTA SALAD WITH ARTICHOKES AND SPROUTS

Serves 4 to 6

The artichoke hearts provide an instant marinade, and the alfalfa sprouts lend an interesting texture.

2 cups raw small pasta, such as small shells or elbows
¾ pound marinated artichoke hearts, either 2 6-ounce jars or bought by weight with liquid
¾ cup firmly packed alfalfa sprouts
1 small green pepper, finely chopped
½ cup sliced or chopped black olives
2 tablespoons red wine vinegar, or more to taste
1 tablespoon minced fresh basil or ½ teaspoon dried basil
Salt and freshly ground pepper to taste

Cook the pasta al dente. Rinse with cool water, drain well, and place in a mixing bowl.

Chop the artichokes into bite-sized pieces and add them to the pasta. Add the alfalfa sprouts, separating the strands as much as possible with a fork, and the remaining ingredients. Mix well and allow to stand for 1 to 2 hours, either at room temperature or refrigerated, before serving.

Variation:

To serve as a main-dish salad, garnish with hard-boiled eggs or add some diced mozzarella cheese or mozzarella-style soy cheese.

COLD JAPANESE NOODLES WITH DAIKON AND CARROTS

Serves 4 to 6

The cold noodle dishes of Japan make for lively, savory salads. The hearty and flavorful noodles are nice and filling.

4 shiitake mushrooms
1 medium daikon radish, cut into matchsticks (if unavailable, substitute a crisp white turnip)
2 large carrots, cut into matchsticks
8 ounces Japanese noodles such as buckwheat, udon, somen, or jinenjo

Dressing:
2 tablespoons natural soy sauce
1 to 2 tablespoons rice vinegar, to taste
1 tablespoon peanut oil
1 tablespoon sesame seeds
1 teaspoon honey

Garnish:
2 scallions, chopped

Soak the shiitakes in hot water for 15 minutes. Pat them dry, remove and discard the tough stems, and slice the caps. Reserve the liquid for another use.

Have the vegetables cut as directed above before cooking the noodles. Cook the noodles al dente. Rinse with cold water, drain well, and place in a mixing bowl. Toss with the daikon, carrots, and mushrooms.

Combine the dressing ingredients in a small bowl and stir together until blended. Pour over the noodle mixture and toss to combine thoroughly. Garnish with scallions. Chill until needed or serve at once.

"In the composure of a sallet every plant should come in to bear its part, without being overpower'd by some herb of a stronger taste, so as to endanger the native sapor and virtue of the rest, but fall into their places, like the notes in music, in which there should be nothing harsh or grating: and tho' admitting some discords (to distinguish and illustrate the rest), striking in the more sprightly, and sometimes gentler notes, reconcile all dissonance and melt them into an agreeable composition."

—John Evelyn
Acetaria: A Discourse of Sallet (1699)

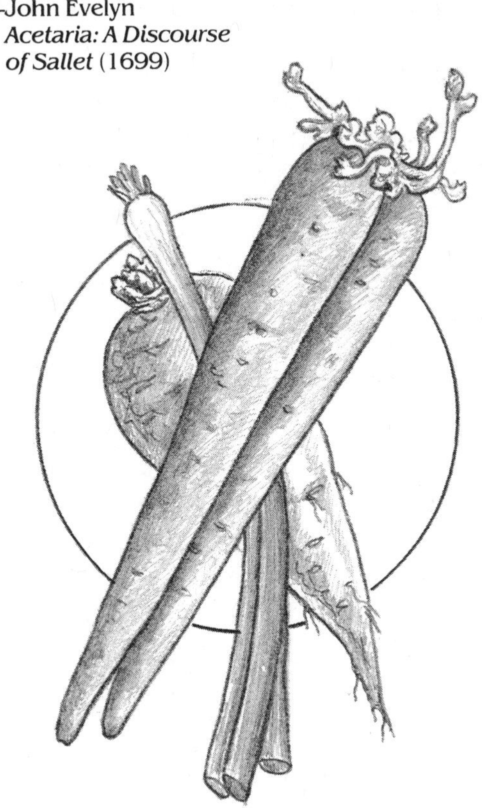

MARINATED CAULIFLOWER AND BROCCOLI

Serves 6 to 8

I have found this salad to be a favorite at parties; it looks as appealing as it tastes, especially if you are able to use red peppers. It complements Italian-style pasta dishes very nicely.

4 heaping cups cauliflower, cut into bite-sized pieces and florets
4 heaping cups broccoli, cut as above
1 medium sweet red or green bell pepper, cut into julienne strips
1 or 2 scallions, minced
⅔ cup Herb Marinade (page 65)
2 tablespoons lemon juice
Salt and freshly ground pepper to taste
½ teaspoon each dill seed and dried tarragon, optional

Fill a large pot with enough water to immerse all the cauliflower and broccoli and bring to a full, rolling boil. Drop the cauliflower and broccoli pieces into the boiling water and cook over high heat for no longer than 3 minutes, or to a crisp-tender texture. Drain (reserve the liquid to use as vegetable stock for soup) and rinse with cool water until the vegetables stop steaming.

Place the cauliflower and broccoli in a large mixing bowl and add all the remaining ingredients. Toss well to combine. Refrigerate for several hours, stirring occasionally to distribute the marinade.

AVOCADOS STUFFED WITH CURRIED EGG SALAD

Serves 4

Not only are avocados among the most sensuous additions to a salad, they are also great receptacles for one. This delicious and substantial presentation of avocado, with its appealing colors and textures, is high on my list of favorites.

2 large avocados, ripe but not mushy
4 hard-boiled eggs
2 tablespoons minced chives or scallion
1 small carrot, coarsely grated
½ cup plain yogurt or Tofu "Mayonnaise" (page 58)
½ cup chopped cucumber
2 tablespoons lemon juice
2 teaspoons good curry powder or Home-Mixed Curry (page 207), or more or less to taste
Salt and freshly ground pepper to taste
Paprika for garnish

Cut the avocados in half lengthwise. Remove the pit and scoop out the pulp, leaving a ¼-inch shell all around.

Place the pulp in a mixing bowl and add the eggs. Mash them together with a fork. Add the remaining ingredients except paprika and mix together thoroughly. Stuff the avocado halves and sprinkle the paprika over the stuffing.

MULTICOLORED AVOCADO-RAISIN SALAD

Serves 4 to 6

1 sweet red bell pepper, cut into julienne strips
1 cup finely shredded red cabbage
1 medium bunch broccoli, cut into bite-sized pieces and steamed crisp-tender
1 medium avocado, quartered and thinly sliced
½ cup raisins
¼ cup toasted sunflower seeds

Dressing:

½ cup plain yogurt or pureed soft tofu
Juice of ½ lemon
3 tablespoons safflower oil
½ teaspoon each dried dill and dry mustard

Combine the salad ingredients in a serving bowl. Combine the dressing ingredients in a small mixing bowl, stir well, and pour onto the salad. Toss well and serve at once.

The ancient Maya and Aztec Indians developed and cultivated many varieties of avocado ages before the Europeans descended upon the Americas. These ancient races evidently had high regard for the avocado, as its depiction is to be found on their pottery and sculpture. The avocado has been known by its native names of ahuacatl *and* aguacate, *as well as the descriptive terms alligator pear and midshipman's butter.*

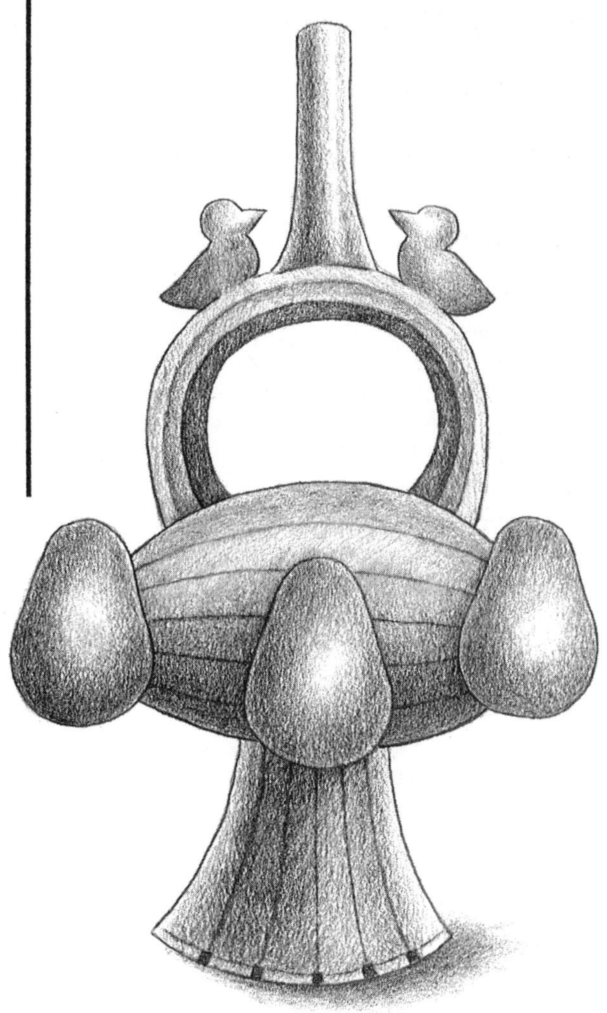

CUCUMBER RAITA

Serves 4 to 6

Raitas are relishlike, yogurt-based salads that are served with curries to cool the palate. Cucumber is a traditional ingredient since it has cooling properties of its own.

1 large cucumber, chopped
1 cup plain yogurt
1 teaspoon safflower or vegetable oil
2 tablespoons chopped cilantro, optional
1 tablespoon minced fresh mint or 1 teaspoon dry mint
Dash ground cumin
Salt and freshly ground pepper to taste

Combine all the ingredients in a bowl and mix thoroughly. Chill well before serving. You can also serve this with chili and other spicy dishes.

In folklore, dreaming of cucumbers had several meanings. If one was ill, a cucumber dream meant a speedy recovery. If one was in love, it meant that marriage was impending. If a sailor dreamt of cucumbers, it meant that his next voyage would be a pleasant one.

SUMMER POTATO SALAD

Serves 6

6 medium potatoes, well scrubbed
2 medium celery stalks, finely chopped
1 cup steamed fresh or thawed frozen green peas
½ cup minced green bell pepper
⅓ cup chopped black or green olives
1 scallion, minced
2 tablespoons finely chopped fresh parsley
1 tablespoon minced fresh dill
2 tablespoons toasted sunflower seeds
1 cup plain yogurt or ½ cup each plain yogurt and sour cream, mixed, or 1 cup Tofu "Mayonnaise" (page 58)
2 tablespoons safflower oil
1 to 2 teaspoons Dijon mustard, to taste
Salt and freshly ground pepper to taste

Cook or microwave the potatoes in their skins until they are tender but still firm. When they are cool enough to handle, dice them, leaving the skins on, and place them in a large mixing bowl. Allow to cool to room temperature.

Add the remaining ingredents to the potatoes and mix thoroughly. Serve chilled or at room temperature.

WINTER POTATO SALAD WITH SNOW PEAS

Serves 6

6 medium potatoes, well scrubbed
6 ounces snow peas, trimmed and steamed until crisp-tender
1 small zucchini, quartered and very thinly sliced
3 tablespoons minced fresh parsley
1 tablespoon minced fresh dill or 1 teaspoon dried dill
2 scallions, minced
Herb Marinade (page 65), as needed to moisten (about ½ cup)
Salt and freshly ground pepper to taste

Cook or microwave the potatoes in their skins until they are tender but still firm. Cool to room temperature and then cut them in half lengthwise, then into ½-inch slices. Place in a mixing bowl along with the remaining ingredients and toss well. Let stand for an hour or more. If you are making this salad ahead of time, bring it to room temperature before serving.

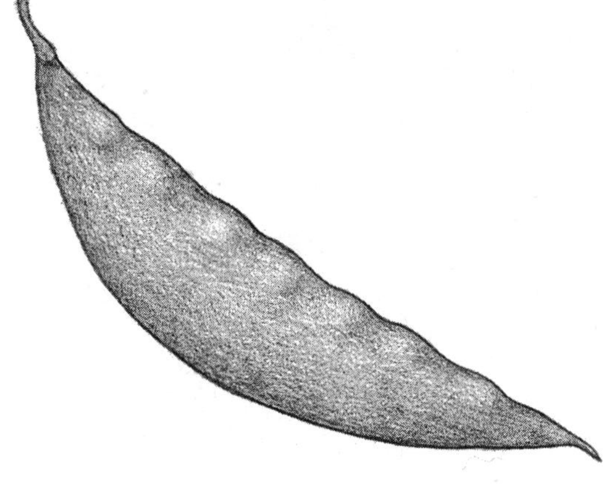

OPEN SESAME! And while you're at it, bring me some of this sesame salad!

Say the word "sesame" and it may bring to mind the phrase "Open, Sesame!" which comes to us from the story of "Ali Baba and the Forty Thieves." This magical command enabled Ali Baba to enter the secret cave of treasure.

CRISP SESAME VEGETABLES

Serves 4 to 6

The sesame dressing and sesame seeds give this crunchy salad a pleasant Oriental accent. This salad enhances Oriental-style rice or noodle dishes.

Choose several of the following fresh, raw vegetables:
Bok choy or celery, sliced diagonally
Broccoli florets
Cauliflower florets
Snow peas (steamed briefly, if you prefer)
Cabbage, coarsely shredded
Carrot, sliced diagonally
White turnip, peeled and diced
Green bell pepper, julienned or diced

Prepare 5 heaping cups of the vegetables of your choice, as described above, for 4 large or 6 smaller servings. Combine them in a mixing bowl, and add:

1 cup alfalfa sprouts
2 or 3 scallions, chopped
Sesame-Soy Salad Dressing (page 68), as needed to moisten and flavor

Toss together, separating the sprouts with a fork. Serve at once.

PISTACHIO-APPLE SALAD

Serves 4

3 medium tart apples, cored, and sliced
¼ cup raisins or other dried fruit
¼ cup unsalted pistachios, coarsely chopped
1 medium celery stalk, finely diced

Dressing:
½ cup yogurt
1 tablespoon safflower oil
2 teaspoons honey
½ teaspoon dried mint
¼ teaspoon cinnamon
¼ teaspoon curry powder

Dark green lettuce leaves, as needed

Combine the first 4 ingredients in a serving bowl. Combine the ingredients for the dressing in a small bowl and stir together. Pour the dressing over the salad and toss well. Serve at once, placing each serving on a bed of dark green lettuce leaves.

He that will not a wife wed Must eat an apple on going to bed.

—Old English Proverb

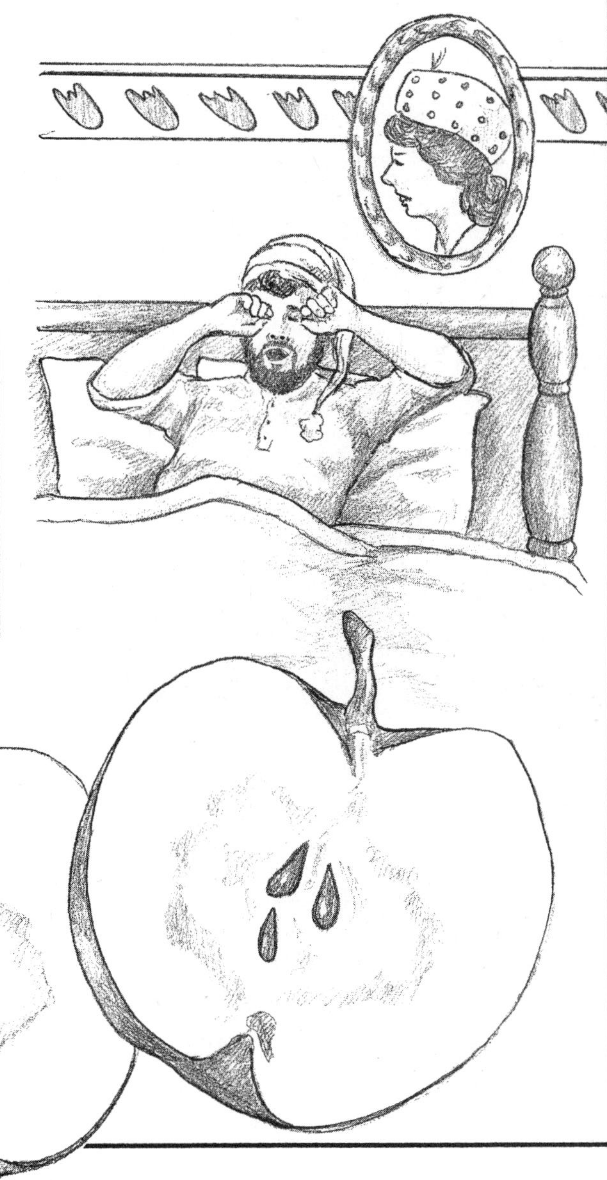

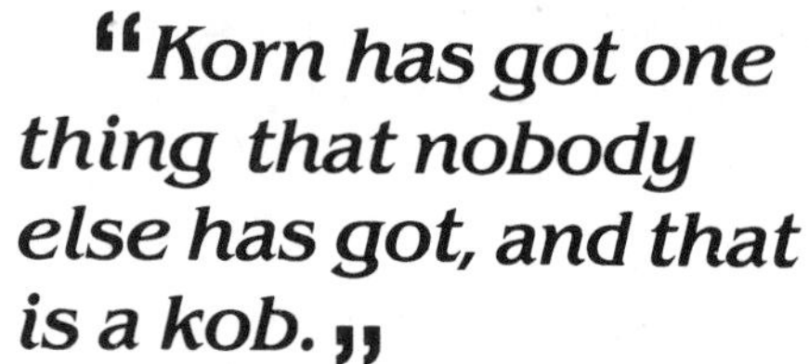

"Korn has got one
thing that nobody
else has got, and that
is a kob."

—Josh Billings
His Works, Complete (1876)

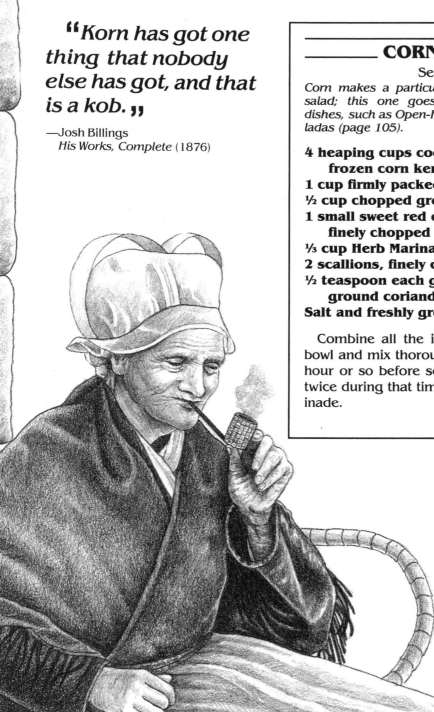

CORN SALAD

Serves 6

Corn makes a particularly pleasant base for a salad; this one goes well with chili-flavored dishes, such as Open-Faced Avocado Bean Enchiladas (page 105).

4 heaping cups cooked fresh or thawed frozen corn kernels
1 cup firmly packed grated zucchini
½ cup chopped green olives
1 small sweet red or green bell pepper, finely chopped
⅓ cup Herb Marinade (page 65)
2 scallions, finely chopped
½ teaspoon each ground cumin and ground coriander
Salt and freshly ground pepper to taste

Combine all the ingredients in a mixing bowl and mix thoroughly. Refrigerate for an hour or so before serving, stirring once or twice during that time to distribute the marinade.

MIDDLE EASTERN EGGPLANT SALAD

Serves 6 to 8

Eggplant is a wonderful basis for a salad when baked whole in its own skin. It develops a distinctive, slightly smoked flavor. On this page are two possibilities that use this baking method. This Middle Eastern classic is a favorite with anyone who loves eggplant.

2 medium eggplants (about 2½ pounds total)
2 tablespoons olive oil
1 medium onion, chopped
2 or 3 cloves garlic, minced
Juice of ½ lemon, or more to taste
¼ cup tahini (sesame paste)
Salt and freshly ground pepper to taste

Garnish:

Pita bread, warmed
Crisp raw vegetables
Black olives

Preheat the oven to 400° F. Place the whole, unpeeled eggplants on a foil-lined baking sheet. Bake for about 40 minutes, or until the eggplant is very tender and has collapsed.

When it is cool enough to handle, peel and coarsely chop the eggplant and place the pieces in a colander to drain.

In the meantime, heat the olive oil in a small skillet. Sauté the onion and garlic over moderately low heat until the onion is lightly browned.

Transfer the eggplant to the container of a food processor. Add the onion mixture and the remaining ingredients. Pulse on and off until coarsely pureed. Serve at room temperature with warm pita bread to scoop it up with, and with a garnish of crisp raw vegetables and black olives.

ITALIAN-STYLE EGGPLANT AND PEPPER SALAD

Serves 6 or more

1 large eggplant
2 large green bell peppers, or 1 green and 1 red bell pepper
2 large celery stalks
Olive or vegetable oil for sautéing
2 cloves garlic, minced
¼ cup olive oil
¼ cup red wine vinegar
1 teaspoon dried oregano
Salt and freshly ground pepper to taste
¼ cup chopped black olives, optional

Preheat the oven to 400° F.

Place the whole, unpeeled eggplant on a foil-lined baking sheet. Wrap the peppers and celery stalks individually in aluminum foil and place them on a rack in the oven. Bake the eggplant and the other vegetables for 30 minutes, or until the peppers can be easily pierced with a fork. Remove them and the celery and allow them to cool. Bake the eggplant an additional 15 to 20 minutes, or until it is very tender and has collapsed.

When the vegetables are cool enough to handle, peel the eggplant, cut it into several pieces and allow them to drain in a colander for about 20 minutes, and then chop them into small dice. Chop the peppers into large dice, removing the stems and seeds. Chop the celery into ½-inch pieces. Combine all the vegetables in a mixing bowl.

Heat a few drops of oil in a small skillet and sauté the garlic until golden. Add it to the vegetable mixture along with the remaining ingredients and mix thoroughly. Cover and let stand at room temperature for an hour or so before serving. Serve at room temperature.

TABOULEH

Serves 6

As a base for salads, grains lend texture, substance, and protein. Tabouleh, a classic grain salad using bulgur (presteamed cracked wheat), is of Middle Eastern origin. The addition of chick-peas is not traditional, but they add a great deal of flavor and make the salad substantial enough to serve as a main dish in a light meal.

1 cup raw bulgur
2 large firm, ripe tomatoes, chopped
1½ cups cooked or canned chick-peas (about ½ cup raw, cooked following the directions on page 215)
¼ to ½ cup chopped fresh parsley, to taste
2 or 3 scallions, finely chopped
2 or 3 tablespoons minced fresh mint leaves or 2 teaspoons dried mint
¼ cup olive oil
Juice of 1 large lemon
Salt and freshly ground pepper to taste

Prepare the bulgur according to the directions in Cooking Grains (page 214). Allow it to cool until just warm, then add the remaining ingredients. Mix thoroughly and chill for 1 to 2 hours before serving.

"Bread, wine, and wholesome salads you may buy. What nature adds besides, is luxury."

—Horace

BULGUR SALAD WITH FRUITS AND NUTS

Serves 6 to 8

This sweet and crunchy concoction makes a nice change of pace from tabouleh when you're in the mood for a hearty grain salad.

1 cup raw bulgur
⅔ cup coarsely chopped walnuts
½ cup raisins or currants
1 large celery stalk, finely diced
¼ cup toasted sunflower seeds
2 tablespoons minced chives
1 medium apple, cored and finely diced (don't peel)
Juice of ½ lemon
¼ cup (scant) safflower oil
1 tablespoon honey, or to taste
½ teaspoon cumin
¼ teaspoon cinnamon
Dash nutmeg

Prepare the bulgur according to the directions in Cooking Grains (page 214). Cool to room temperature.

In a serving bowl, combine the bulgur with the walnuts, raisins or currants, celery, sunflower seeds, and chives. Toss the diced apple with half of the lemon juice, then add it, along with the remaining lemon juice and the rest of the ingredients, to the bulgur mixture. Toss until thoroughly combined. Serve at once or chill until needed.

NUTTY BROWN RICE SALAD

Serves 4 to 6

1 cup raw brown rice
1 cup chopped nuts, such as almonds, walnuts, cashews, or a combination
1 scallion, finely chopped
1 cup seeded, chopped cucumber
1 small green bell pepper, finely chopped
1 tablespoon soy sauce, or to taste
Juice of ½ lemon
Freshly ground pepper to taste
½ teaspoon ground cumin
¾ cup Tofu Dijon or Tofu Garlic "Mayonnaise" (page 58)

Cook the rice according to the directions in Cooking Grains (page 214) and allow it to cool to room temperature.

Combine the rice with the next 5 ingredients in a mixing bowl and toss together. In a small bowl, combine the soy sauce, lemon juice, pepper, and cumin with the tofu dressing of your choice. Mix well, pour over the salad, and toss together thoroughly.

"My salad days, when I was green in judgement."

—William Shakespeare
Antony and Cleopatra (ca. 1607)

BARLEY PILAF SALAD

Serves 6

The combination of barley and beans makes for a high-protein grain salad with refreshing, lightly marinated flavor.

¾ cup raw barley
1 tablespoon soy sauce
1 bay leaf
1½ cups cooked or canned navy beans (about ½ to ⅔ cup raw, cooked following the directions on page 215)
½ medium cucumber, peeled, seeded, and diced
1 cup string beans, cut into 1-inch pieces and steamed
⅓ cup chopped black or green olives
2 tablespoons minced scallion or chives
2 tablespoons minced fresh dill
2 tablespoons minced fresh parsley
3 tablespoons olive oil
3 tablespoons red wine vinegar
½ teaspoon each dried basil and dried oregano
Salt and freshly ground pepper to taste

Cook the barley according to the directions in Cooking Grains (page 214), adding the soy sauce and bay leaf to the cooking water. When the barley is done, remove the bay leaf and allow the barley to cool to room temperature.

Transfer the barley to a mixing bowl. Add the beans, cucumber, string beans, olives, scallion or chives, dill, and parsley and mix well.

Combine the remaining ingredients in a small bowl and mix thoroughly. Pour over the salad and toss until everything is evenly coated. Let stand for an hour or so at room temperature before serving.

COUSCOUS SALAD WITH ROASTED VEGETABLES

Serves 6

Couscous, or presteamed and cracked semolina, combined with fresh herbs and the smoky flavors of the roasted vegetables, makes a great base for an unusually savory salad.

1 medium eggplant
1 large green or red bell pepper
2 medium firm, ripe tomatoes
1 cup uncooked couscous
¼ cup chopped fresh parsley
2 tablespoons minced fresh dill
2 scallions, chopped
1 medium celery stalk, minced
¼ cup olive oil
Juice of ½ lemon, or more to taste
½ teaspoon each ground cumin and ground turmeric
Salt and freshly ground pepper to taste

Preheat the oven to 375° F.

Place the eggplant on a foil-lined baking sheet. Bake for 35 to 45 minutes, or until it has collapsed. Roast the pepper and the tomatoes under a broiler, turning on all sides until their skin is quite blistered. Place them in a paper bag to cool. Place the couscous in an ovenproof bowl. Pour 2 cups of boiling water over it and cover. After 15 minutes, fluff with a fork.

When all of the vegetables have cooled to room temperature, slip their skins off and chop them into bite-sized pieces.

Combine the couscous, the vegetables, and all the remaining ingredients in a serving bowl and toss thoroughly to mix. Serve at room temperature.

SAUCES AND DRESSINGS

"Homer has not, if I remember correctly, ever said a word about sauces."

—Plato (ca. 427–347 B.C.)

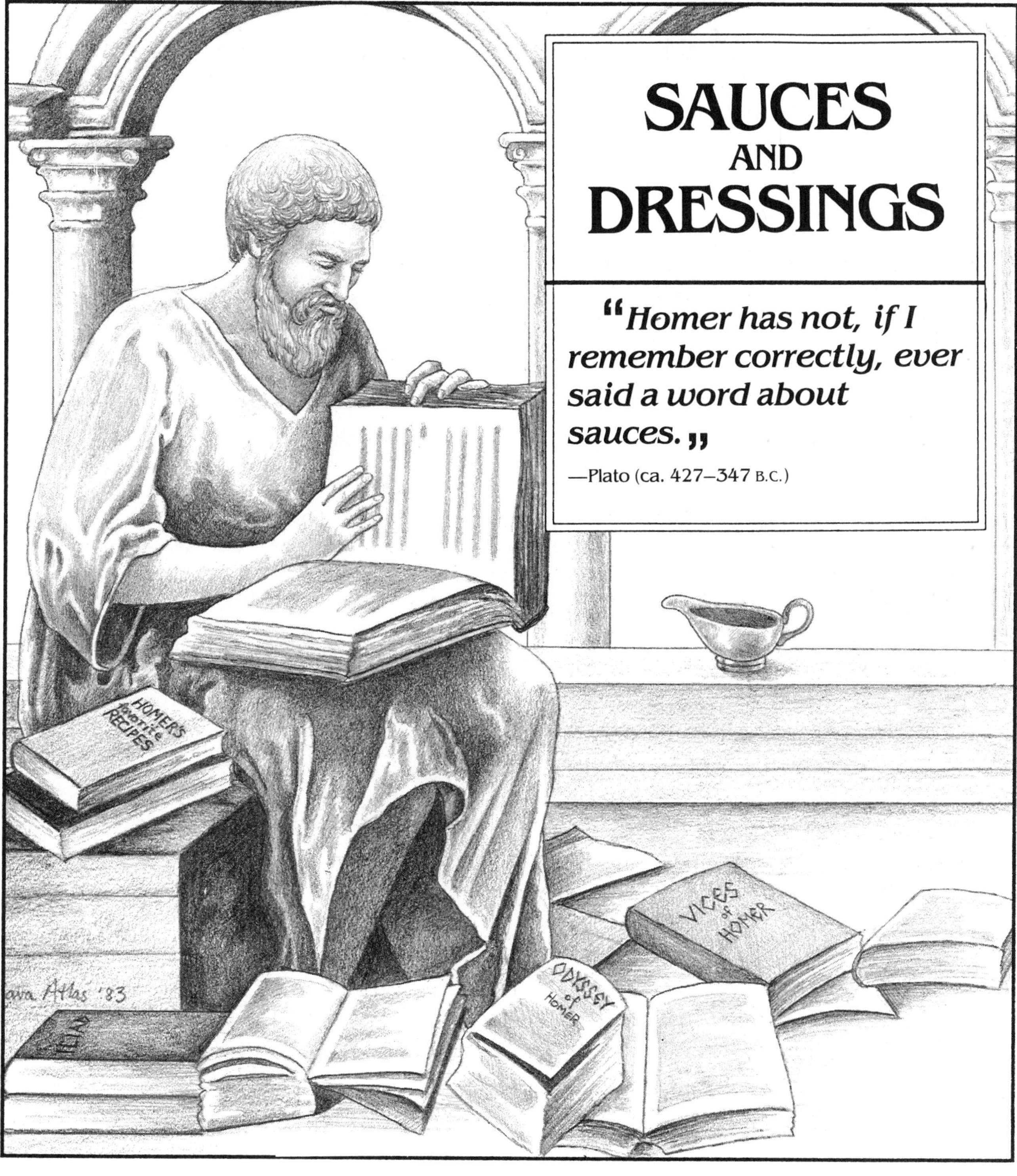

Once relegated to the realm of gourmet cookery, making good sauces and dressings can be a very simple and basic task. Just about every sauce and dressing in this chapter can be made in minutes, and can give new life to an otherwise uninspired dish or even add a new dimension to leftovers.

The dictionary tells us that "sauce," as a verb, means "to add zest to," and that the word "sauce" also gives us "saucy," meaning alternatively, "pert" or "impudent." This interpretation aside, sauce must be associated with something worth reaching for, as we are told that "what is sauce for the goose is sauce for the gander."

BASIC CHINESE SAUCE

Makes about 2 cups

This sauce is called for in several Oriental-style recipes given in this book.

1 tablespoon sesame oil
2 or 3 cloves garlic, minced
1½ cups Basic Vegetable Stock (page 30) or water, or a combination
4 tablespoons soy sauce, or more or less to taste
3 tablespoons dry sherry
½ to 1 teaspoon freshly grated ginger, or more or less to taste
2½ tablespoons cornstarch

Heat the sesame oil in a heavy saucepan. Add the garlic and sauté over low heat until golden.

If you are using water instead of vegetable stock, you can include liquid from any canned Chinese vegetables you may be including, such as bamboo shoots or baby corn. Pour the stock over the garlic, then add the soy sauce, sherry, and ginger and cook over moderate heat.

Dissolve the cornstarch in just enough water to make it smooth and pourable. When the liquid in the saucepan is just under the boiling point, lower the heat and whisk in the cornstarch. Let the sauce simmer slowly until thickened, stirring almost continuously.

MISO-GINGER SAUCE

Makes about 1½ cups

This sauce is excellent over tofu, tempeh, seitan, grains, noodles, or root vegetables such as turnips, daikon radish, and even potatoes.

1 tablespoon sesame oil
1 large onion, quartered and thinly sliced
1 clove garlic, minced
1½ tablespoons unbleached white flour
1 to 2 teaspoons freshly grated ginger, to taste
3 tablespoons miso, or more or less to taste
1 tablespoon sesame seeds
Dash cayenne pepper, optional

Heat the oil in a saucepan. Add the onion and sauté over low heat until translucent. Add the garlic and continue to sauté until the onion is lightly browned. Sprinkle in the flour and stir until it dissolves. Stir in the ginger. Combine the miso with ¾ cup of water in a small bowl and stir until dissolved, then slowly pour into the saucepan. Simmer over very low heat for 3 to 4 minutes; do not boil. Add the sesame seeds and the optional cayenne. Serve at once.

This is ev'ry Cooks Opinion,
No sav'ry Dish without an
Onyon;
But lest your kissing should be
spoyl'd,
Your Onyons must be th'roughly
boyl'd...

—Jonathan Swift (1667–1745)

ONION AND GARLIC SAUCE

Makes about 2 cups

I can promise you that this flavorful sauce will not spoil your kissing—and in fact, it may improve it, since onions and garlic are reputed to be aphrodisiacs. This is especially good served over green vegetables such as string beans or broccoli.

2 tablespoons margarine
2 large onions, chopped
4 large cloves garlic, minced
2 tablespoons unbleached white flour
3 tablespoons soy sauce
1 tablespoon dry red wine
Freshly ground pepper to taste

Heat the margarine in a saucepan, then add 1 tablespoon of water and the onions and garlic. Sauté over low heat until lightly browned, stirring frequently. Sprinkle in the flour slowly and stir until it dissolves. Slowly add 1¼ cups of water, raise the heat, and bring to a boil. Add the soy sauce, wine, and pepper. Lower the heat and simmer for 10 to 15 minutes, until the sauce has thickened.

WHITE CHEESE SAUCE

Makes about 2 cups

This multipurpose sauce is called for in several of the recipes in this book; it is quick and practically goof-proof. Use the suggested soy substitutions if you want to make it dairy-free.

1 cup firmly packed grated mild white cheese, such as brick, Monterey Jack, mozzarella, or mozzarella-style soy cheese
2 tablespoons unbleached white flour
1⅓ cups low-fat milk or soymilk
2 tablespoons margarine
½ teaspoon salt

Before starting the sauce, have the grated cheese ready and set aside. In a small bowl, combine the flour with enough cold water to make it smooth and flowing.

In a small saucepan, warm the milk, margarine, and salt over moderately low heat. When it is just under the boiling point, whisk in the cheese, a little at a time. Then whisk in the flour paste and continue to whisk until the sauce is smooth and thick.

Variation:

CURRY CHEESE SAUCE

Simply stir 2 teaspoons (or more or less to taste) of good curry powder or Home-Mixed Curry (page 207) into the White Cheese Sauce as soon as it is done.

SWEET AND SAVORY GRILLING SAUCE

Makes about 2 cups

This strong-flavored sauce is excellent for broiling or simmering tofu, tempeh, or seitan.

1 tablespoon safflower oil
1 small onion, finely chopped
1 clove garlic, minced
1½ cups thick tomato sauce
¼ cup molasses
3 tablespoons natural soy sauce, or more or less to taste
½ teaspoon freshly grated ginger
1 teaspoon chili powder
½ teaspoon each dry mustard and paprika

In a heavy saucepan, heat the safflower oil. Add the onion and garlic and sauté over moderate heat until golden. Add the remaining ingredients and stir to mix. Simmer over low heat, uncovered, for 15 minutes.

"There are in England sixty different religious sects, but only one sauce."

—Francesco Caraccioli (1752-1799)

MUSHROOM GRAVY

Makes about 1½ cups

This richly flavored sauce is good over meatless burgers and cutlets (such as Tempeh Burgers, page 124), green vegetables, or mashed potatoes.

2 tablespoons margarine
½ pound small white mushrooms, sliced
1 cup Basic Vegetable Stock (page 30), soymilk, or water
1½ tablespoons cornstarch
1 tablespoon soy sauce
2 to 3 tablespoons nutritional yeast (see note below), to taste

Heat the margarine in a saucepan. Add the mushrooms, cover, and cook over medium-low heat until wilted. Use a little of the stock, soymilk, or water to dissolve the cornstarch in a small container, then pour that and the remaining liquid into the saucepan and bring to a simmer. Simmer, uncovered, until thickened, then stir in the soy sauce and yeast. Simmer over low heat for another 2 to 3 minutes. Serve at once or cover and reheat when ready to use.

NOTE: Nutritional yeast, available in natural food stores, is nourishing as well as tasty. It can be used as a nondairy substitute for Parmesan cheese on pasta, sprinkled into casseroles, and stirred into many types of dips and sauces.

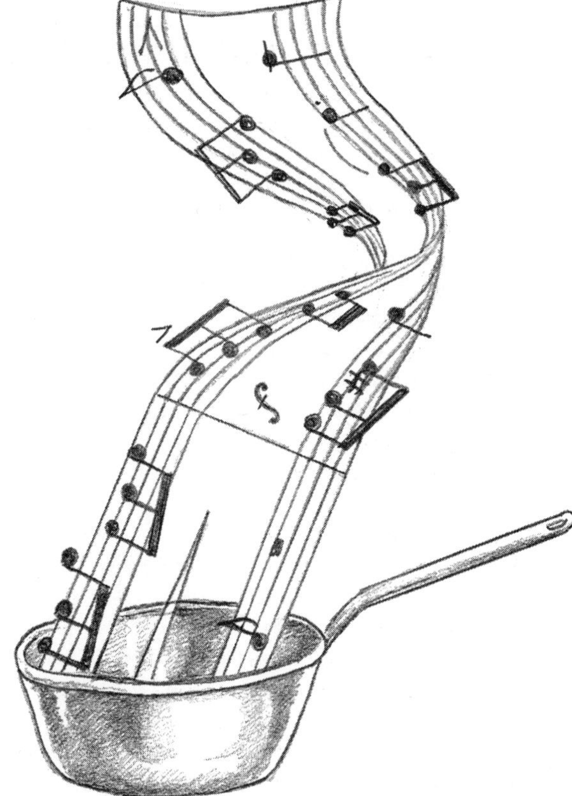

"Sauces are to cookery what the gamut is to the composition of music; as it is by the arrangement of notes that harmony is produced, so should the ingredients in the sauce be nicely blended, and that delightful concord should exist, which would equally delight the palate, as a masterpiece of a Mozart or a Rossini should delight the ear."

—Alexis Soyer
The Modern Housewife (1851)

AVOCADO-TAHINI DIP

Makes about 1½ cups

Tahini is an unexpected flavor complement to avocado in this rich dip, and an interesting change of pace from guacamole for using up ripe avocados. Serve with crisp tortillas, pita bread, or raw vegetables.

1 large, ripe avocado, peeled and diced
⅓ cup sesame paste (tahini)
Juice of 1 lemon
½ teaspoon ground cumin
2 tablespoons minced fresh parsley or cilantro
Salt and freshly ground pepper to taste

You can make this in a food processor by placing all of the ingredients except the parsley or cilantro in the container and processing until smooth. Add ¼ to ½ cup of water, as needed, to achieve a medium-thick consistency. Pour into a serving bowl and stir in the herbs.

To make the dip by hand, put the avocado in a mixing bowl and mash it thoroughly. Add the remaining ingredients and stir until well mixed.

TAHINI MAYONNAISE

Makes about 1½ cups

This simple, tangy sauce is excellent as a dip for raw vegetables or as a dressing for pita sandwiches.

¼ cup sesame paste (tahini)
¼ cup safflower or no-cholesterol mayonnaise
1 cup plain yogurt
Juice of ½ lemon

Combine all the ingredients in a small mixing bowl. Whisk to blend thoroughly.

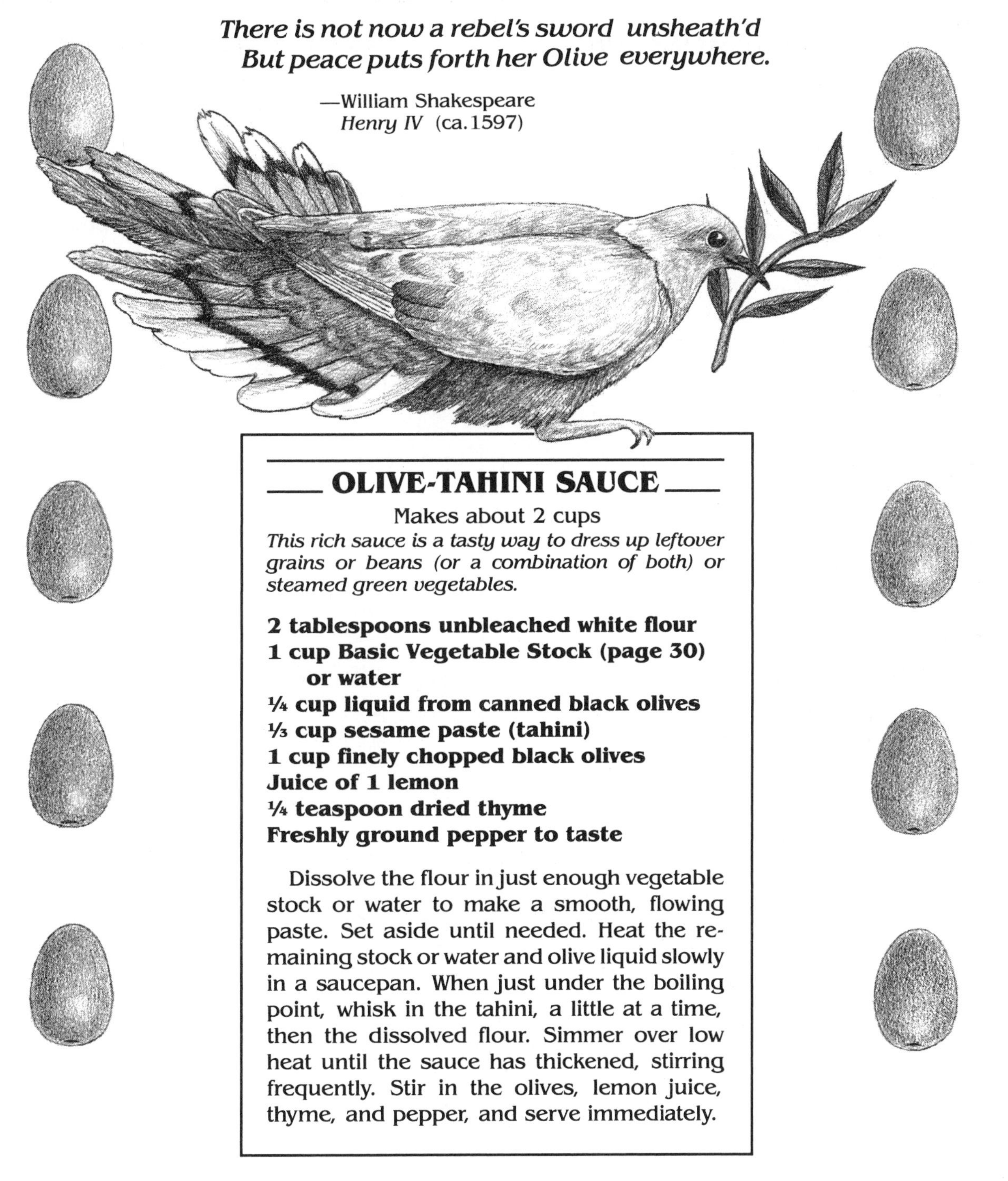

There is not now a rebel's sword unsheath'd
But peace puts forth her Olive everywhere.

—William Shakespeare
Henry IV (ca. 1597)

OLIVE-TAHINI SAUCE

Makes about 2 cups

This rich sauce is a tasty way to dress up leftover grains or beans (or a combination of both) or steamed green vegetables.

2 tablespoons unbleached white flour
1 cup Basic Vegetable Stock (page 30) or water
¼ cup liquid from canned black olives
⅓ cup sesame paste (tahini)
1 cup finely chopped black olives
Juice of 1 lemon
¼ teaspoon dried thyme
Freshly ground pepper to taste

Dissolve the flour in just enough vegetable stock or water to make a smooth, flowing paste. Set aside until needed. Heat the remaining stock or water and olive liquid slowly in a saucepan. When just under the boiling point, whisk in the tahini, a little at a time, then the dissolved flour. Simmer over low heat until the sauce has thickened, stirring frequently. Stir in the olives, lemon juice, thyme, and pepper, and serve immediately.

DILLED MISO-TOFU DIP

Makes about 1½ cups

Serve this dip with crisp cucumber spears, Belgian endives, radishes, or any sort of hearty whole-grain flatbread or cracker.

½ pound soft tofu
2 to 3 tablespoons mild miso, such as genmai, shiro, or mellow white, to taste
1 tablespoon lemon juice
3 tablespoons chopped fresh dill
¼ cup low-fat milk or soymilk

Place all the ingredients in the container of a food processor. Process until smooth.

"Sauce: The one infallible sign of civilization and enlightenment. A people with no sauces has one thousand vices; a people with one sauce has only nine hundred and ninety nine. For every sauce invented and accepted a vice is renounced and forgiven."

—Ambrose Bierce (1842–1914)

TOFU "MAYONNAISE"

Makes about 1½ cups

This is a creamy dressing that has the consistency of mayonnaise but a lighter, less oily flavor. Use it wherever you might use ordinary mayonnaise, or as a high-protein salad dressing. It will keep in the refrigerator for up to a week.

½ pound soft or medium-firm tofu
¼ cup safflower oil
Juice of ½ lemon
½ teaspoon salt

Place all the ingredients in the container of a food processor. Process to a velvety texture.

Variations:

TOFU DIJON MAYONNAISE

Add 1 to 2 teaspoons, to taste, of Dijon mustard before processing.

TOFU GARLIC MAYONNAISE

Sauté 3 cloves of minced garlic in a little oil, until golden, and add before processing.

TOFU TARTAR SAUCE

Add 2 teaspoons of prepared mustard before processing, and after processing, stir in ¼ cup of sweet pickle relish, or more or less to taste.

TOFU-SESAME DRESSING OR SAUCE

Makes about 2 cups

Not only does this versatile blend give a pleasant Oriental flavor to salads, it is also a nice way to enhance leftover grains or noodles when it is warmed up with them.

½ pound soft or medium-firm tofu
⅓ cup tahini (sesame paste)
1 tablespoon sesame oil
1 or 2 cloves garlic, crushed or minced
2 tablespoons rice vinegar or white wine vinegar
½ cup Basic Vegetable Stock (page 30) or water
3 tablespoons soy sauce, or more or less to taste
2 tablespoons honey
½ teaspoon freshly grated ginger, or to taste
Dash cayenne pepper

Place all of the ingredients in the container of a food processor and process until completely smooth. If you prefer a less pronounced garlic flavor, sauté the garlic in a small amount of oil, until golden, before processing.

There are three bean curd gods in Chinese folklore. They are Chiao Kuan, whose role is obscure, Huai Nan Tzu, who invented bean curd, and Kuan Yu, depicted here, who was a bean curd seller when he was young, and grew up to be the great war god.

"Cook, see all your sauces be sharp and poynant in the palate, that they may commend you."

—Francis Beaumont (1584–1616)

SALSA RANCHERA

Makes about 2 cups

It's always handy to have a basic recipe for this popular Southwestern relish. Use it as a dip with crisp tortilla chips or to spice up tortilla dishes as a topping. Use jalapeños for a hot flavor, and mild chilies for a tamer one.

2 cups chopped ripe tomatoes or 14-ounce can imported tomatoes, lightly drained
1 small onion, quartered, optional
1 or 2 jalapeño peppers, seeded and chopped, or 1 6-ounce can mild green chilies
1 tablespoon lemon juice
½ teaspoon ground cumin
Dash salt

To prepare in a food processor, simply place all the ingredients in the container and pulse on and off until coarsely pureed. Transfer to a serving container. To prepare by hand, mince the tomatoes, onion, and jalapeños or chilies as finely as possible and combine in a serving container. Stir in the remaining ingredients. Store whatever is not used up immediately in an airtight jar, where it will keep for several days in the refrigerator.

GREAT NORTHERN PÂTÉ

Makes about 2 cups

Serve this as an appetizer with whole-grain crackers, rye bread, or crisp vegetables.

1 tablespoon safflower oil
1 medium onion, chopped
2 cloves garlic, minced
1 medium celery stalk, chopped
2 tablespoons miso, or more or less to taste
Juice of ½ lemon
1 sprig parsley
1½ cups well-cooked great northern beans (about ⅔ cup raw, cooked following the directions on page 215)
Freshly ground pepper to taste
Paprika for garnish

Heat the oil in a small skillet. Add the onion, garlic, and celery and sauté over moderate heat until all are tender and golden. Transfer to the container of a food processor with all of the remaining ingredients except the paprika, plus 2 tablespoons of water. Process until creamy and smooth. Pour into a shallow serving container and sprinkle with paprika. This may be made ahead of time and refrigerated, but bring it to room temperature before serving.

CHICK-PEA SANDWICH SPREAD

Makes about 2 cups

This easy preparation is good as an appetizer spread on whole-grain crackers, or as a sandwich spread on a hearty bread such as dark rye.

2 cups well-cooked or canned chick-peas (about ¾ cup raw, cooked following directions on page 215)
¼ cup minced green bell pepper
2 tablespoons minced fresh parsley
1 tablespoon minced scallion or chives
Juice of ½ lemon
2 tablespoons sesame paste (tahini)
½ teaspoon dried dill
½ teaspoon ground cumin
Salt and freshly ground pepper to taste

Mash the chick-peas well and combine them with the remaining ingredients in a mixing bowl. Mix thoroughly and pat into an attractive serving container. Serve at once or cover and refrigerate until needed.

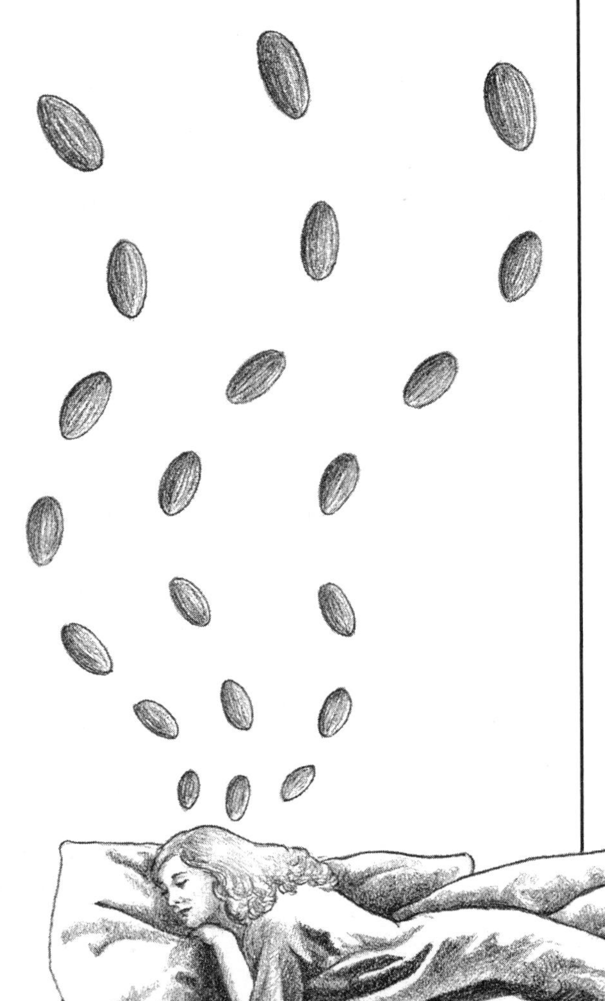

ROASTED EGGPLANT AND ALMOND-BUTTER SPREAD

Makes about 2 cups

1 large eggplant (about 1½ pounds)
¼ cup almond butter
2 tablespoons safflower or peanut oil
1 clove garlic, crushed
Juice of ½ lemon
2 tablespoons finely minced parsley
½ teaspoon cumin
½ teaspoon coriander
Salt and freshly ground pepper to taste

Preheat the oven to 400° F. Place the eggplant on a foil-lined baking sheet and bake for about 40 minutes, or until it has collapsed. Allow it to cool.

When the eggplant is cool enough to handle, peel it, cut it into several large pieces, and place them in a colander for about 10 minutes to drain. Mash them well with a mashing implement and place them in a serving container. Add the remaining ingredients and stir together thoroughly. Serve with whole-grain crackers as an appetizer.

Should you dream of almonds, according to folk-belief, it means that you will embark on a journey. If the dream-almonds taste sweet, the journey will be a prosperous one.

PEANUT SAUCE

Makes about 1½ cups

Use this sauce for stir-fries or noodle or rice dishes. See one interesting use for it in Tofu and Eggs in Peanut Sauce (page 124).

½ cup peanut butter
3 to 4 tablespoons soy sauce, to taste
1 small onion, chopped
1 teaspoon freshly grated ginger
2 tablespoons honey
2 tablespoons rice vinegar or white wine vinegar
1 teaspoon chili powder
Cayenne pepper to taste

Place all the ingredients in the container of a food processor, along with ½ cup of water. Process until smooth. Pour the sauce into a small heavy saucepan and heat over low heat until warm, or simply toss with hot noodles, rice, or vegetables.

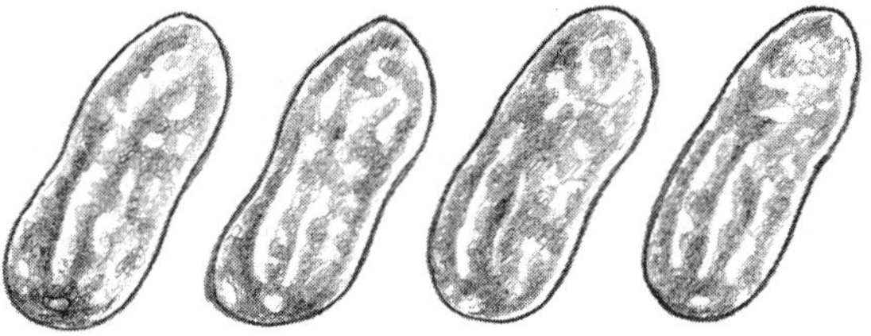

CASHEW BUTTER SAUCE

Makes about 2 cups

Cashew butter, which is readily available in natural food stores, is the basis of a heavenly sauce that is great over steamed green vegetables, noodles, grains, or whole wheat toast.

1 tablespoon margarine
1 small onion, finely chopped
½ small green or red bell pepper, finely chopped
1 medium tomato, finely chopped
1 tablespoon unbleached white flour
½ cup cashew butter
1 cup Basic Vegetable Stock (page 30) or water
¼ teaspoon chili powder
Salt and freshly ground pepper
3 tablespoons finely chopped cashews, optional

Melt the margarine in a saucepan. Add the onion and sauté over moderate heat until translucent. Add the chopped bell pepper and sauté until the onion is golden. Add the tomato and cook, stirring occasionally, until it has softened, about 5 minutes. Sprinkle in the flour and stir until it dissolves. Add the cashew butter and stock or water and simmer for 5 to 7 minutes, stirring until the cashew butter is smoothly blended in. Stir in the chili powder and season to taste with salt and pepper. Add the optional chopped cashews and serve at once.

Herbs, too, she knew, and well of
each could speak
That in her garden sip'd the silv'ry
dew;
Where no vain flow'r disclosed a
gaudy streak
But herbs for use, and physic, not a
few,
Of grey renown within these
borders grew...

—William Shenstone (1714–1764)
"The School Mistress"

FRESH HERB SAUCE

Makes about 2 cups

Herbs add the flavor interest to this and the remaining recipes in this chapter. If you can use any or all fresh herbs, so much the better; substitute using a 3-to-1 ratio of fresh herbs to dried. Serve this sauce over freshly steamed or sautéed summer vegetables or over grains.

2 tablespoons unbleached white flour
1 cup low-fat milk
½ teaspoon salt
½ cup minced fresh herbs of your choice (use a mix, including such herbs as parsley, dill, thyme, basil, and oregano)
½ cup reduced-fat sour cream or plain yogurt

Dissolve the flour in just enough water to make it smooth and flowing. Set aside until needed.

In a saucepan, heat the milk and salt over moderate heat. When it is just under the boiling point, whisk in the dissolved flour. Allow the sauce to simmer slowly, stirring constantly until it is thickened.

Remove the sauce from the heat and let it stand for a minute or so, then stir in the herbs and sour cream or yogurt. Serve at once.

Come sweetheart, come,
Dear as my heart to me,
Come to the room
I have made fine for thee.
Here be the couches spread
Tapestries tented,
Flowers for thee to tread,
Green herbs, sweet scented.

—Medieval Love Song

HERB MARINADE

Makes about 1 cup

This is a basic dressing for marinating steamed or parboiled vegetables. It can also be used as an Italian-style salad dressing, with a little less oil and more pungency than a vinaigrette.

½ cup olive oil or ¼ cup olive oil and ¼ cup safflower oil
½ cup red or white wine vinegar
½ teaspoon Dijon mustard
2 to 2½ teaspoons mixed dried herbs (choose several among oregano, dill, marjoram, savory, basil, thyme, and tarragon)
Freshly ground pepper to taste

Combine all the ingredients in a jar with a tight-fitting lid, or a cruet, and shake well. This will keep well for at least two weeks if refrigerated.

YOGURT-DILL DRESSING

Makes about 1¼ cups

Yogurt, which is fermented from milk by live cultures, has long been valued for its nutritional properties and is a staple food in several societies renowned for their members' longevity. Methusela, who is famous for supposedly having lived for nine hundred years, was reportedly a big fan of yogurt. Likewise, the wise King Solomon enjoyed it, and it was a great favorite of the biblical patriarch Abraham, who was particularly fond of goat's-milk yogurt. Genghis Khan, the Mongol conqueror, also ate great quantities of it but preferred the yak's-milk variety.

This quick and simple dressing is very refreshing with any mixed green salad.

1 cup plain yogurt
¼ cup olive oil
2 to 3 tablespoons minced fresh dill or 1 to 1½ tablespoons dried dill
Juice of ½ lemon

Combine all the ingredients in a small bowl and mix until thoroughly blended. Refrigerate the unused portion in an airtight container and use it within two days.

CUCUMBER-SCALLION DRESSING

Makes about 1½ cups

John Evelyn, a seventeenth-century writer, said of cucumbers, "The pulp in broth is greatly refreshing, and may be mingl'd in most sallets." Combined with a "broth" of yogurt, another great refresher, cucumbers make an excellent base for a light and low-calorie dressing.

1 medium cucumber, peeled, seeded, and chopped
2 scallions
¼ cup safflower oil
½ cup plain yogurt
Juice of ½ lemon
½ teaspoon dried tarragon, optional
¼ teaspoon each dried summer savory and dried basil
Freshly ground pepper to taste

Place all of the ingredients in the container of a food processor and process until smooth. Refrigerate the unused portion in an airtight container and use it within two days.

PARSLEY DRESSING

Makes 2 cups

This dressing, which is pale green with tiny specks of darker green, tastes as refreshing as it looks. A little goes a long way.

1 cup firmly packed fresh parsley
¼ cup safflower oil
¼ cup olive oil
½ cup peeled, seeded, and chopped cucumber
2 tablespoons lemon juice
1 teaspoon dried dill
½ teaspoon salt
Freshly ground pepper to taste

Place all the ingredients in the container of a food processor. Process until all that remains of the parsley is tiny flakes. Refrigerate the unused portion in an airtight container and use it within two days.

"There is no garden hearb comes neare unto parsley, as well for toothsomenesse as for health."

—William Vaughn
Directions for Health (1617)

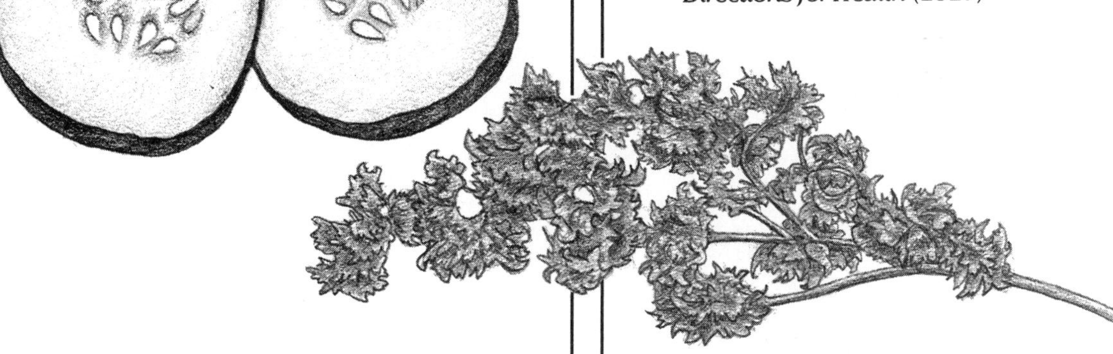

MISO SALAD DRESSING

Makes about 1 cup

Like the previous recipe, this pungent dressing works nicely with crisp, characteristically Oriental vegetables. Try it with winter roots, too—it's a splendid dressing for warm, crisp-tender parsnips, carrots, daikon radish, and rutabagas.

1 to 3 tablespoons miso, to taste
¼ cup safflower or peanut oil
3 tablespoons rice vinegar
1 tablespoon honey
½ teaspoon dry mustard

Stir the miso with ⅓ cup of water in a small bowl until smooth. Add the remaining ingredients and whisk together until well blended. Refrigerate the unused portion in an airtight container and use it within a week.

SESAME-SOY SALAD DRESSING

Makes about ¾ cup

This is a very tasty, offbeat dressing for crisp salads, especially those containing cabbage, sprouts, snow peas, and other characteristically Oriental vegetables.

3 tablespoons sesame oil
4 tablespoons safflower or peanut oil
2 to 3 tablespoons soy sauce
3 tablespoons rice or white wine vinegar
1 teaspoon honey
2 teaspoons sesame seeds
½ teaspoon chili powder

Combine all the ingredients in a small bowl or cruet. Shake or stir well before each use.

EGGS AND CHEESES

"Don't touch me please," she said softly. "I am part egg-shell. Or perhaps I had better put it in a safe place." She began unfastening the collar of her gown.

"What is it?" said her lover.

"An egg—a Cochin's egg. I am hatching a very rare sort. I carry it everywhere with me, and it will get hatched in less than three weeks."

"Where do you carry it?"

"Just here." She put her hand into her bosom and drew out the egg...

—Thomas Hardy
Jude the Obscure (1885)

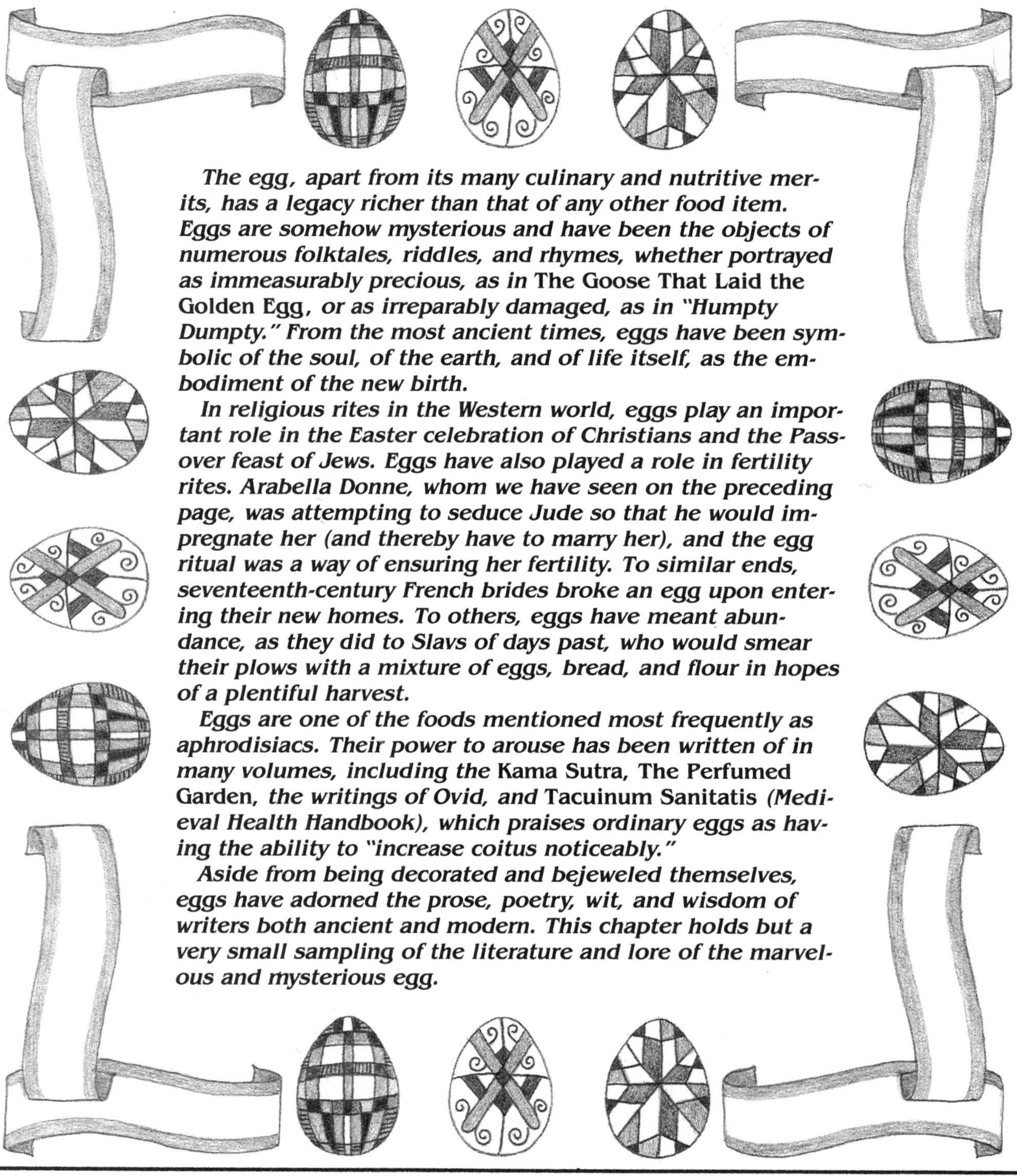

The egg, apart from its many culinary and nutritive merits, has a legacy richer than that of any other food item. Eggs are somehow mysterious and have been the objects of numerous folktales, riddles, and rhymes, whether portrayed as immeasurably precious, as in The Goose That Laid the Golden Egg, or as irreparably damaged, as in "Humpty Dumpty." From the most ancient times, eggs have been symbolic of the soul, of the earth, and of life itself, as the embodiment of the new birth.

In religious rites in the Western world, eggs play an important role in the Easter celebration of Christians and the Passover feast of Jews. Eggs have also played a role in fertility rites. Arabella Donne, whom we have seen on the preceding page, was attempting to seduce Jude so that he would impregnate her (and thereby have to marry her), and the egg ritual was a way of ensuring her fertility. To similar ends, seventeenth-century French brides broke an egg upon entering their new homes. To others, eggs have meant abundance, as they did to Slavs of days past, who would smear their plows with a mixture of eggs, bread, and flour in hopes of a plentiful harvest.

Eggs are one of the foods mentioned most frequently as aphrodisiacs. Their power to arouse has been written of in many volumes, including the Kama Sutra, The Perfumed Garden, the writings of Ovid, and Tacuinum Sanitatis (Medieval Health Handbook), which praises ordinary eggs as having the ability to "increase coitus noticeably."

Aside from being decorated and bejeweled themselves, eggs have adorned the prose, poetry, wit, and wisdom of writers both ancient and modern. This chapter holds but a very small sampling of the literature and lore of the marvelous and mysterious egg.

BAKED EGGS AND CHEESE WITH VEGETABLES

Serves 6

This is a good way to use up any odds and ends of vegetables that you may have on hand, and it's bound to please even the most finicky palate.

Choose 4 to 6 of the following vegetables:

String beans
Zucchini
Broccoli
Cauliflower
Carrots
Mushrooms
Asparagus
Sweet red or green bell peppers
Cooked fresh or thawed frozen peas

Cut the vegetables into bite-sized pieces and steam or stir-fry them until they are done to a texture a bit softer than crisp-tender. Use 6 cups total of vegetables.

2 tablespoons margarine
1 large onion, chopped
8 eggs, well beaten
¼ cup low-fat milk or soymilk
Salt and freshly ground pepper to taste
1 to 2 teaspoons mixed dried herbs of your choice
2 cups grated cheese or soy cheese of your choice
Sesame seeds for topping

Preheat the oven to 350° F.

Heat the margarine in a small skillet. Add the onion and sauté over moderate heat until lightly browned.

In a large mixing bowl, combine the beaten eggs with the milk or soymilk; add salt and pepper. Combine the cooked vegetables with the sautéed onion in a separate bowl and season with salt and pepper and the herbs.

Oil a deep, 2-quart casserole and layer it as follows: one third of the eggs, one third of the vegetables, and one third of the cheese; repeat twice. Sprinkle the top with sesame seeds. Bake for 35 to 40 minutes or until the eggs are set and the top is lightly browned.

SPROUT-FILLED EGG PANCAKES

Serves 4 to 6

These are a nice accompaniment (and a good protein supplement) to steamed or stir-fried vegetables with rice.

1 tablespoon sesame oil
2 cloves garlic, peeled and minced
2 celery stalks, finely chopped
2 tablespoons soy sauce or tamari
2½ cups firmly packed alfalfa sprouts
2 tablespoons wheat germ
6 eggs
6 tablespoons low-fat milk or soymilk
Freshly ground pepper
Safflower oil for frying

Heat the sesame oil in a large skillet. Add the garlic and celery and sauté over moderate heat until golden. If you need extra moisture in the skillet, add a tablespoon or two of water. Add the soy sauce or tamari and the alfalfa sprouts, separating them with a fork, and cook, covered, just until the sprouts are a bit wilted. Stir in the wheat germ and remove from the heat.

Beat the eggs with the milk or soymilk and grind in some pepper. Stir in the sprout mixture. Heat enough oil to coat the bottom of a 9- or 10-inch nonstick skillet. When the skillet is hot enough to make a drop of water sizzle, pour in half of the egg mixture and tip the pan to distribute it. Keep tipping, lifting the edges of the egg with a spatula so the loose egg runs underneath. When the bottom is lightly browned and the top is fairly set, flip according to the directions on page 216, How to Fry and Flip a Skillet Pie or Frittata, and let the second side brown lightly. Slide the pancake out onto a plate, cover to keep it warm, and repeat with the remaining egg mixture. Cut each pancake into 4 or 6 wedges and serve at once.

CURRIED EGGS

Serves 6

This savory and versatile dish can be served over toast, rice, or noodles, or on its own with vegetable curries.

1 tablespoon margarine
1 medium sweet red or green bell pepper, cut into julienne strips
2 tablespoons chopped cilantro or fresh parsley
Dash cayenne pepper
¼ teaspoon ground turmeric, optional
Salt to taste
1 recipe Curry Cheese Sauce (page 54)
8 large hard-boiled eggs, thinly sliced

Heat the margarine in a small skillet. Add the bell pepper and sauté over moderate heat until tender. Add the cilantro or parsley and continue to sauté until it is slightly wilted. Remove from the heat.

Combine the sautéed pepper mixture and seasonings with the Curry Cheese Sauce in the saucepan in which you are cooking the sauce. Gently fold in the eggs and cook over low heat until nicely heated through. Serve at once.

> *"A hen is only an egg's way of making another egg."*
>
> —Samuel Butler
> *Life and Habit* (1877)

EASY EGGS FOO YONG

Serves 4

A great vehicle for lots of fresh bean sprouts. Try serving this with Cold Sesame Noodles (page 140) and Sunflower Coleslaw (page 35) for a tasty, Oriental-flavored meal. Or for a simple meal, serve it with hot cooked rice.

1 recipe Basic Chinese Sauce (page 52)
2 tablespoons sesame oil
1 tablespoon soy sauce
4 cups (about 1 pound) fresh mung bean sprouts
4 scallions, chopped
½ pound mushrooms, sliced
8 eggs
Freshly ground pepper to taste
Oil for frying

Prepare the sauce according to the recipe, up to the point before heating it, and set it aside.

Heat the sesame oil and soy sauce in a large skillet or wok. Add the sprouts, scallions, and mushrooms and stir-fry over moderate heat just until all are slightly wilted. Remove from the heat.

Beat 2 of the eggs in a small bowl. Grind in a little pepper and stir in one quarter of the stir-fried vegetables. Heat just enough oil to coat the bottom of a 6- or 7-inch nonstick skillet. When the skillet is hot enough to make a drop of water sizzle, pour in the egg mixture, cover, and cook over moderate heat until the bottom is nicely browned and the eggs are fairly set on top. Flip with a wide spatula and brown the other side, uncovered. Repeat the process three more times with 2 eggs and one quarter of the vegetables. Keep the cooked pancakes hot in a covered container while the others cook. While the last pancake is cooking, finish preparing the sauce. Serve at once, topping each pancake with a generous helping of sauce.

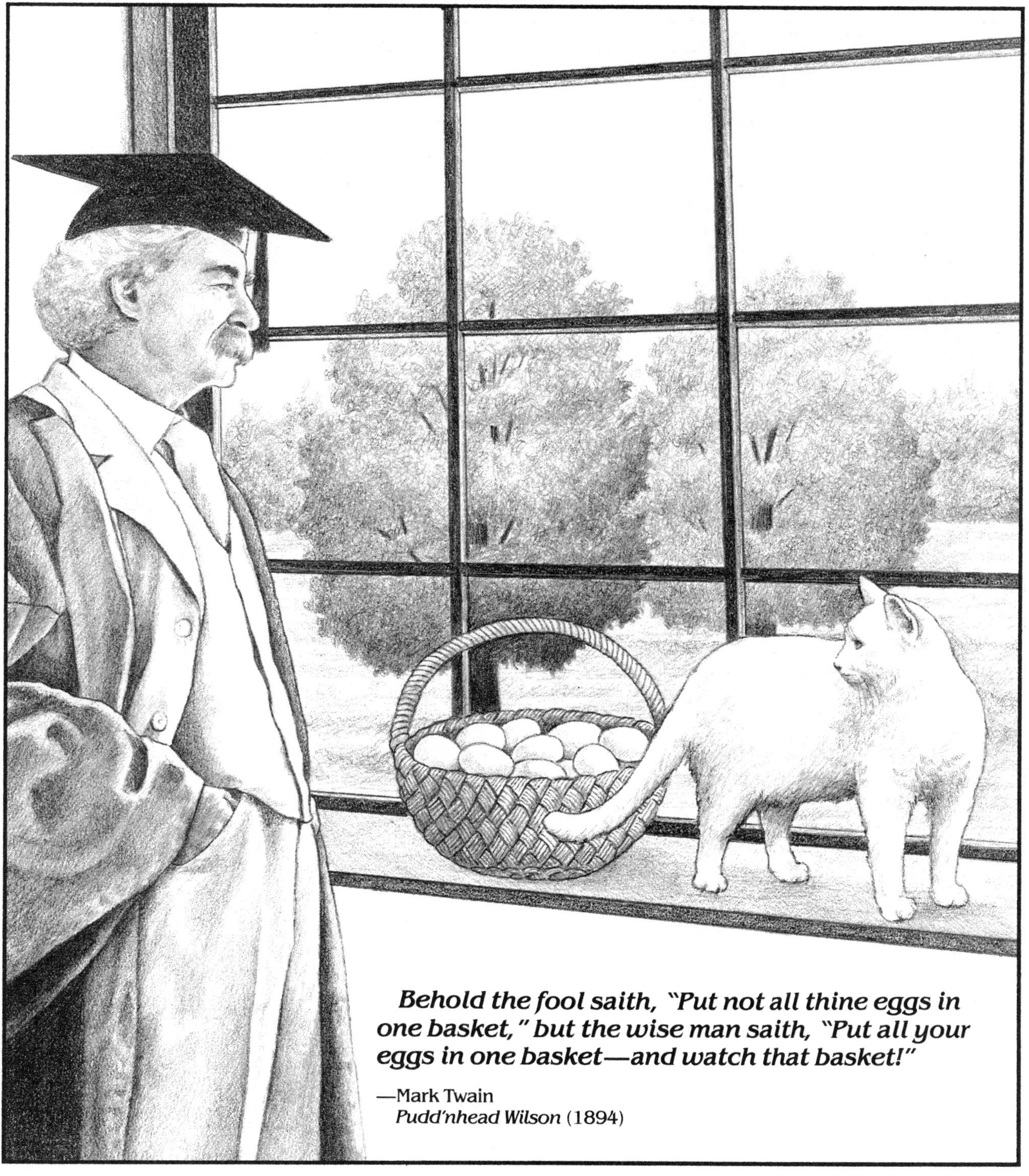

Behold the fool saith, "Put not all thine eggs in one basket," but the wise man saith, "Put all your eggs in one basket—and watch that basket!"

—Mark Twain
Pudd'nhead Wilson (1894)

HERBED POTATO-BRIE OMELET

Makes 2 omelets

1 large potato, cooked, baked, or microwaved in its skin
1 tablespoon safflower oil
1 small onion, minced
2 tablespoons minced fresh parsley
1 tablespoon minced fresh dill or 1 teaspoon dried dill
1 tablespoon minced fresh basil or ½ teaspoon dried basil
Salt and freshly ground pepper to taste
4 eggs
2 tablespoons low-fat milk
2 tablespoons margarine
¼ pound Brie cheese, thinly sliced

Peel and slice the cooked or baked potato when it is cool enough to handle. Heat the oil in a large skillet. Add the onion and sauté over moderate heat until translucent. Add 2 tablespoons of water to the skillet, then add the potato and continue to sauté until the onion and potato are lightly browned. Add the herbs and a little salt and pepper, stir together, and remove from the heat.

Combine 2 of the eggs in a small bowl with 1 tablespoon of the milk and beat until bubbly. Heat 1 tablespoon of the margarine in an 8- or 9-inch nonstick skillet. When the skillet is hot enough to make a drop of water sizzle, pour in the beaten eggs. Tip the skillet so that the eggs coat it evenly. Keep tipping, lifting the omelet's edge so that the loose egg runs underneath. When the eggs are fairly set on top but still moist, quickly arrange half of the potato mixture on one side of the omelet or in the middle third, followed by half of the Brie slices. Fold the omelet in half or fold the outside edges over the middle, according to where you arranged the potato mixture. Slide the omelet out onto a plate and cover it carefully with foil or a matching plate to keep it warm while you repeat the process with the second omelet. Serve at once.

"Be content to remember that those who can make omelettes properly can do nothing else. And thank the Lord that you have other talents... There is nothing made by man, no, not even his false religions, which for full success requires so complete a conduct of the affair as the making of an omelette."

—Hilaire Belloc
A Conversation with a Cat (1931)

PERFUMED GARDEN ASPARAGUS OMELET

Makes 2 omelets

2 tablespoons margarine
1 clove garlic, minced
2 medium firm, ripe tomatoes, finely chopped
2 tablespoons minced fresh parsley
¼ cup grated Parmesan cheese
¼ teaspoon dried basil
½ pound asparagus, cut into 1-inch pieces and steamed crisp-tender
Salt and freshly ground pepper to taste
4 eggs
2 tablespoons low-fat milk
1 teaspoon good curry powder or Home-Mixed Curry (page 207)

Heat 1 tablespoon of the margarine in a medium-sized skillet. Add the garlic and sauté over low heat until golden. Add the tomatoes and sauté until softened. Add the parsley, Parmesan cheese, basil, steamed asparagus, and salt and pepper. Remove from the heat and cover.

Combine 2 of the eggs with 1 tablespoon of the milk in a small bowl and beat until bubbly, then stir in ½ teaspoon of the curry.

Heat half of the remaining margarine in an 8- or 9-inch nonstick skillet. Prepare the omelets according to the directions given in the previous recipe, filling each with half of the asparagus mixture. Serve at once.

"He who boils asparagus, and then fries them in fat, and then pours upon them the yolks of eggs with pounded condiments, and eats every day of this dish, will grow very strong for coitus, and find in it a stimulant for his amorous desires."

—Shaykh Nefzawi
The Perfumed Garden (ca. 1400)

A kiss without a moustache is like an egg without salt.

—Old Spanish saying

FRITTATA OF PEPPERS AND FINE NOODLES

Makes 2 frittatas, serves 4 to 6

A frittata sounds fancy, but it is simply a flat omelet. Precede this with Avocado Gazpacho (page 12), add some good bread and some crisp raw vegetables, and you've got a light summer repast.

2 heaping cups raw fine egg noodles
2 tablespoons olive oil
1 medium onion, chopped
1 large sweet red bell pepper, cut into julienne strips
1 large green bell pepper, cut into julienne strips
2 medium ripe tomatoes, chopped
6 eggs, well beaten
½ cup small-curd cottage cheese or ricotta cheese
½ teaspoon each dried oregano and chili powder
Salt and freshly ground pepper to taste

Cook the noodles al dente, then drain them, cover them, and set them aside.

In the meantime, heat the olive oil in a medium-sized skillet. Add the onion and sauté over moderate heat until translucent. Add the peppers and tomatoes and sauté until the peppers are crisp-tender and the tomatoes have softened.

In a mixing bowl, combine the beaten eggs with the cottage cheese or ricotta. Add the noodles, the pepper mixture, and the seasonings and mix thoroughly. Divide the mixture into 2 parts and prepare following the directions on page 216, How to Fry and Flip a Skillet Pie or Frittata. Cut each frittata into 4 or 6 wedges and serve at once.

EASY CORN FRITTATA

Makes 2 frittatas, serves 4 to 6

This frittata can be whipped up very quickly. Try serving it with Linguini Aglio Olio (page 132), which is also quick to fix, and a big salad of seasonal greens.

1 tablespoon safflower oil
1 large onion, chopped
6 eggs
⅓ cup low-fat milk
3 cups cooked fresh or thawed frozen corn kernels
½ cup cornmeal or matzo meal
1 cup grated cheese of your choice, optional
Salt and freshly ground pepper to taste

Heat the oil in a medium-sized skillet. Add the onion and sauté over moderate heat until lightly browned.

In a mixing bowl, beat the eggs well with the milk. Add the remaining ingredients, including the sautéed onion, and mix well.

Divide the mixture into 2 parts and prepare following the directions on page 216 for How to Fry and Flip a Skillet Pie or Frittata. Cut each frittata into 4 or 6 wedges and serve at once.

According to folk-belief, if you dream of eggs it is an omen of luck, money, or marriage.

I can't see you tonight—I have a deadline...

"Promises and Pie-Crust are made to be broken."

—Jonathan Swift (1667–1745)
Polite Conversation

PUFFED SPINACH AND FETA CHEESE QUICHE

Serves 6

Quiches are such a tasty and relatively easy way to use eggs and cheeses that they've become almost a vegetarian cliché. The two recipes on these pages are pleasantly offbeat. This one is lightened by using only the egg whites and has a nice tang from the lemon, fresh herbs, and feta cheese.

1 tablespoon margarine
1 small onion, finely chopped
⅓ cup minced fresh herbs (combine parsley with small amounts of dill and/or basil)
10-ounce package frozen chopped spinach, thawed and well drained
Juice of ½ lemon
3 tablespoons low-fat milk
¼ pound feta cheese, finely crumbled
1 cup grated mild white cheese of your choice, such as mozzarella
½ teaspoon ground cumin
Dash nutmeg
Salt and freshly ground pepper to taste
3 egg whites
1 regular unbaked 9-inch pie crust

Preheat the oven to 325° F.

Heat the margarine in a small skillet. Add the onion and sauté until translucent. Add the herbs and sauté only until they are slightly wilted. In a mixing bowl, combine the onion and herb mixture with the spinach, lemon juice, milk, the two cheeses, and the seasonings. Mix well.

Beat the egg whites until they form stiff peaks. Fold them gently into the spinach mixture, then pour the mixture into the pie crust. Bake for 35 to 40 minutes, or until the quiche is puffed and lightly browned. Let stand for 10 minutes, then cut into 6 wedges to serve.

CURRIED QUICHE WITH CHICK-PEAS AND STRING BEANS

Serves 6

Eggs taste wonderful when they're curried, so why not curry a quiche? Chick-peas are an unusual ingredient in a quiche, but they add to the exotic flavor.

1 tablespoon olive oil
1 medium onion, chopped
2 cloves garlic, minced
3 eggs, well beaten
1 tablespoon minced fresh parsley or cilantro
1½ cups cooked or canned chick-peas (about ⅔ cups raw, cooked following the directions on page 215)
1 cup string beans, steamed and cut into 1-inch pieces
1½ teaspoons good curry powder or Home-Mixed Curry (page 207)
Salt and freshly ground pepper to taste
1 regular unbaked 9-inch pie crust
1 cup firmly packed grated mild cheese
Wheat germ and paprika for topping

Preheat the oven to 350° F.

Heat the olive oil in a small skillet. Add the onion and garlic and sauté over moderate heat until golden.

In a mixing bowl, combine the beaten eggs with the parsley, chick-peas, string beans, seasonings, and sautéed onion and garlic. Mix thoroughly. Pour half of this mixture into the pie shell and top it with half of the grated cheese. Pour in the remaining egg mixture and top with the remaining cheese. Sprinkle with wheat germ and paprika.

Bake for 45 minutes, or until the top is golden and the eggs are set. Let the quiche stand for 5 to 10 minutes before serving.

In marble walls as white as milk,
Lined with a skin as soft as silk;
Within a fountain crystal clear,
A golden apple doth appear.
No doors there are to this stronghold,
Yet thieves break in and steal the gold.

—Old English Riddle

"One cheese differs from another, and the difference is in sweeps, and in landscapes, and in provinces, and in countrysides, and in climates, and in principalities, and in realms, and in the nature of things. Cheese does most gloriously reflect the multitudinous effect of earthly things. . ."

—Hilaire Belloc
First and Last (1931)

SWISS CHEESE PANCAKES

Makes about 12 pancakes

These crepelike pancakes are a nice accompaniment to fresh vegetable dishes such as Summer Harvest Squash Sauté (page 161). They may also be stuffed with chopped and steamed vegetables such as spinach or zucchini, or served with a sauce such as Onion and Garlic Sauce (page 53).

3 eggs, well beaten
1 cup low-fat milk
½ cup unbleached white flour
¼ cup wheat germ
½ teaspoon each salt, paprika, and dry mustard
1 teaspoon caraway seeds, optional
2 cups firmly packed grated Swiss cheese
Safflower oil for frying

In a mixing bowl, combine the beaten eggs with the milk. Stir in the flour, wheat germ, and seasonings, then add the cheese and mix thoroughly.

Heat just enough oil to coat the bottom of a 6- or 7-inch nonstick skillet. When the skillet is hot enough to make a drop of water sizzle, turn the heat to moderate and pour in a scant ¼ cup of the batter. Tip the skillet quickly to distribute the batter. Cook until the bottom of the pancake is nicely browned and the top is fairly set; flip with a wide spatula and brown the other side. Repeat with the remaining batter. The first one may not come out perfectly, but the rest will fare better as the skillet gets hotter.

Serve flat and stacked, or roll up each pancake and close it securely with a toothpick. If you stuff them, fold one side over the other in the center.

VEGETABLE CHEESE KNISHES

Makes about 10 knishes

This recipe is actually a composite of a Jewish dairy specialty, cheese knishes, and a vegetarian favorite, Russian vegetable pie.

1 recipe Potato Dough (page 177)
2 cups ricotta cheese
½ teaspoon salt
2 tablespoons safflower oil
1½ cups finely shredded cabbage
1 medium carrot, grated
1 medium onion, finely chopped
4 or 5 medium mushrooms, chopped
¼ cup beer
1 tablespoon red wine vinegar
2 teaspoons dried dill
1 teaspoon poppy or dill seeds
Salt and freshly ground pepper to taste

Prepare the Potato Dough as directed in the recipe and let it rest. Preheat the oven to 350° F.

In a small mixing bowl, combine the ricotta and salt. Mix well and set aside.

Heat the oil in a large skillet. Add the cabbage, carrot, and onion. Cover and sauté until the onion is translucent. Add the mushrooms, beer, vinegar, and seasonings and cook, covered, until all the liquid has been absorbed and the vegetables are crisp-tender.

Roll out the dough for filling as directed in the Potato Dough recipe. Place about 2 heaping tablespoons of the ricotta mixture in the center of each square of dough, followed by a bit of the vegetable mixture. Fold each corner toward the center, overlapping each just a little, and pinch the corners shut. Arrange on an oiled and floured baking sheet and bake for 35 minutes, or until the dough is lightly browned.

COTTAGE CHEESE AND BLUEBERRY PANCAKES

Makes about 16 pancakes

These pancakes are nice for a leisurely weekend breakfast.

3 eggs, well beaten
1 cup low-fat milk
1 cup small-curd cottage cheese
3 tablespoons honey
⅔ cup whole wheat pastry flour
4 tablespoons wheat germ
1 teaspoon cinnamon
1 cup blueberries (preferably fresh; if frozen, thawed and well drained)
Oil for frying
Applesauce or maple syrup

In a mixing bowl, blend the beaten eggs with the milk, cottage cheese, and honey. Add the flour, stirring it in half at a time, followed by the wheat germ, cinnamon, and blueberries.

Since this batter is somewhat sticky, you will need a good nonstick skillet or griddle. Heat just enough oil to coat the bottom of a large skillet. When the oil is hot enough to make a drop of water sizzle, pour in enough batter to make 3- to 4-inch pancakes. Cook on each side until lightly browned; flip gently. Keep the first batch warm in a covered container while the rest cook. Serve with applesauce or maple syrup.

"Cheese: Milk's leap toward immortality."

—Clifton Fadiman (1904–

THE FOX AND THE CROW

A Crow had snatched a goodly piece of cheese out of a window and flew with it into a high tree, intent to enjoy her prize. A Fox spied the dainty morsel, and thus he planned his approaches. "O Crow," said he, "how beautiful are thy wings, how bright thine eye! how graceful thy neck! thy breast is the breast of an eagle! thy claws—I beg pardon—thy talons, are a match for all the beasts of the field. O! that such a bird should be dumb, and want only a voice!" The Crow, pleased with the flattery, and chuckling to think how she would surprise the Fox with her caw, opened her mouth—down dropped the cheese! which the Fox snapping up, observed, as he walked away, "that whatever he had remarked of her beauty, he had said nothing yet of her brains."

Men seldom flatter without some private end in view; and they who listen to such music may expect to have to pay the piper.

—The Fables of Aesop

TOMATO AND ZUCCHINI RAREBIT

Serves 4

An easy cheese and bread dish, this vegetable variation of Welsh rarebit is zesty and superquick.

1 tablespoon safflower oil
1 small onion, minced
1 medium zucchini, grated
2 medium tomatoes, finely chopped
2 tablespoons flour
½ pound sharp cheddar cheese, diced
1 teaspoon dry mustard
Dash cayenne pepper
½ cup beer
8 slices toasted whole-grain bread

Heat the oil in a large saucepan. Add the onion and sauté over moderate heat until translucent. Add the zucchini and tomatoes and continue to sauté, stirring often, until they soften and the onion is golden. Sprinkle in the flour slowly, stirring until it dissolves.

Stir in the cheese, mustard, and cayenne. Cook over low heat, stirring almost constantly, until the cheese has melted. Add the beer, stirring it in until it is completely blended with the cheese. Simmer on very low heat for 2 minutes. For each serving, spread 2 slices of toasted bread on a plate and pour the cheese mixture over them.

Variation:
Although rarebit is traditionally served over bread, you can also serve this over grains or noodles.

CHEESE AND BREAD PUDDING

Serves 4 to 6

A tasty and easy combination of cheese, bread, and eggs, this dish is nice served with freshly steamed vegetables and Italian-Style Eggplant and Pepper Salad (page 47).

2 tablespoons margarine
1 medium onion, chopped
1 clove garlic, minced
4 eggs
¾ cup low-fat milk
¼ cup dry white wine
6 average slices soft whole-grain bread
1½ cups firmly packed grated cheese of your choice
¼ cup grated Parmesan cheese
½ teaspoon Dijon mustard
½ teaspoon paprika
Dash cayenne pepper
Salt and freshly ground pepper to taste
1 teaspoon caraway seeds, optional

Preheat the oven to 325° F.

Heat the margarine in a small skillet. Add the onion and garlic and sauté over moderately low heat until lightly browned.

Beat the eggs in a large mixing bowl until bubbly. Stir in the milk and wine. Tear the bread into small pieces and add it to the egg mixture. Let it soak for about 5 minutes, then add all the remaining ingredients, including the onion and garlic, and mix thoroughly.

Pour the mixture into an oiled 1½-quart casserole dish and bake for 35 minutes or until the top is lightly browned.

"Bachelor's fare: Bread and cheese, and kisses."

—Jonathan Swift (1667–1745)
Polite Conversation

BASIC PIZZA DOUGH

Makes enough crust for two 12- to 14-inch pizzas

There's something remarkably fun and festive about homemade pizza. Those of you on dairy-free diets will find that two of the three following recipes can be adapted to your needs by the substitution of soy cheese for cheddar or Monterey Jack.

2 envelopes active dry yeast
¼ cup safflower oil
2 tablespoons granulated sugar
3 cups whole wheat flour
2 cups unbleached white flour
1 teaspoon salt
Cornmeal

Combine the yeast with 2 cups of warm water. Let stand for 10 minutes to dissolve. Stir in the oil and sugar.

In a large mixing bowl, combine the flours and the salt. Make a well in the center and pour in the yeast mixture. Work everything together, first with a wooden spoon and then with your hands, to form a dough. Turn it out onto a well-floured board and knead it for 8 minutes, adding flour until the dough loses its stickiness. Place the dough in a floured bowl, cover it with a tea towel, and put it in a warm place. Let rise until doubled in bulk, 1 to 1½ hours.

Punch the dough down, divide it, and form it into two rounds. Roll out each round on a well-floured board and stretch it to fit a 12- or 14-inch round pizza pan. Lightly oil the two pans and sprinkle them with cornmeal. Lay the rounds on the pans and make a lip of dough around the edge. Arrange the topping on the dough and prepare it according to one of the following recipes.

BROCCOLI, RED ONION, AND CHEDDAR PIZZA

Serves 6

Basic Pizza Dough (preceding recipe)
2 tablespoons olive oil
2 medium red onions, quartered and thinly sliced
2 medium bunches broccoli, cut into bite-sized pieces and florets
2 cups canned crushed or pureed tomatoes
Dried oregano
Freshly ground pepper
¾ pound cheddar cheese or cheddar-style soy cheese

Have the dough ready as directed in the preceding recipe. Preheat the oven to 425° F.

Heat the oil in a large skillet. Add the onion and sauté over medium heat until it just begins to turn golden. Stir in the broccoli and cover. Sauté just until it is bright green and crisp-tender. Remove from the heat. Divide the mixture between the two pizza doughs. Spread the tomato puree over the vegetables with a ladle. Sprinkle with oregano and a grinding of pepper, followed by the cheese.

Bake for 15 minutes or until the crust is golden and the cheese is melted. Slice each pizza into 6 wedges and serve.

EGGPLANT AND RICOTTA PIZZA

Serves 6

Basic Pizza Dough (page 84)
1 tablespoon olive oil
2 to 3 cloves garlic, minced
2 medium eggplants, about 2 pounds total, sliced ½ inch thick, then peeled and diced
Salt and freshly ground pepper to taste
Cornmeal
2 cups canned crushed or pureed tomatoes
Ricotta cheese, as needed
Dried oregano
12 ounces part-skim mozzarella cheese
Minced scallions for garnish

Have the dough ready as directed in the recipe. Preheat the over to 425° F.

Heat the oil in a large skillet. Add the garlic and sauté over medium heat for not more than 1 minute. Stir in the eggplant dice along with ¼ cup of water. Cover and cook until the eggplant dice are tender, stirring occasionally. Season to taste with salt and pepper.

Sprinkle the tops of the two pizza doughs lightly with cornmeal, then divide the diced eggplant between them. Spread the tomato puree over the eggplant with a ladle. Arrange 6 rounded tablespoonfuls of ricotta cheese around the edges of each pizza. Sprinkle with oregano, then with the mozzarella. Sprinkle the minced scallions over the center of each pizza. Bake for 15 minutes or until the crust is golden and the cheese is melted. To serve, slice each pizza into 6 wedges, each containing a scoop of ricotta.

MEXICAN PIZZA

Serves 6

Basic Pizza Dough (page 84)
2 tablespoons olive oil
1 medium onion, minced
2 cloves garlic, minced
2 medium zucchini, about ¾ pound total, coarsely grated
½ teaspoon ground cumin
Salt and freshly ground pepper to taste
Cornmeal
2 cups canned crushed or pureed tomatoes
2 cups thawed frozen corn
Dried oregano
½ cup sliced black olives
12 ounces Monterey Jack cheese or cheddar-style soy cheese

Have the pizza dough ready as directed in the recipe and preheat the oven to 425° F.

Heat the oil in a large skillet. Add the onion and sauté until lightly golden. Stir in the garlic and zucchini and sauté until the zucchini is just wilted. Stir in the cumin and season to taste with salt and pepper.

Sprinkle the tops of the pizza dough lightly with cornmeal. Spread the tomato puree over them. Arrange the skillet mixture in the center of each pizza, leaving a 2-inch ring around the edge. Surround the zucchini mixture with the corn. Sprinkle everything with the oregano and olives, then top with the cheese. Bake for 15 minutes or until the crust is golden and the cheese is melted.

Slice each pizza into 6 wedges to serve.

"Many's the long night I've dreamed of cheese—toasted, mostly."

—Robert Louis Stevenson
Treasure Island (1883)

CHEDDAR-RICE WEDGES

Serves 6

This simple and tasty dish is reminiscent of spoonbread. It goes nicely with bean soups and pureed vegetable soups.

2 cups cooked small- or medium-grain brown rice (about ¾ cup raw, cooked following the directions on page 214)
2 egg whites, beaten
½ cup low-fat milk or soymilk
⅓ cup whole wheat pastry flour
½ teaspoon each salt and baking powder
2 tablespoons margarine, melted
¾ cup firmly packed grated cheddar or cheddar-style soy cheese

Preheat the oven to 400° F.

Combine the cooked rice with the remaining ingredients in a mixing bowl and mix thoroughly. Pour the mixture into an oiled 9-inch deep-dish pie pan. Bake for 20 to 25 minutes, or until the top is nicely browned. Allow to cool for 10 to 15 minutes, then cut into wedges to serve.

GRAINS AND LEGUMES

Rice, the grain that is the staff of life for half the world's population, has long been part of the wedding ritual in India and China, where it symbolizes abundance, fertility, and life itself. Most likely it was this use of rice in nuptial ceremonies in the East that influenced its adoption by the West. By the late nineteenth century, the practice of throwing rice at the bridal couple had become common both in Victorian England and in the United States. This ritual, having persisted to the present day, is now simply a way of say "Good Luck" to the newlyweds, sending them off with wishes of happiness.

Grains are the seeds or fruits of the cereal grasses, most of which are immeasurably ancient. That being the case, it is especially curious to note that many grains today are still struggling to emerge as everyday foods rather than just being labeled as "health foods." However, grains are definitely making a comeback, as more and more is being said about their good protein and fiber content and their versatility in cookery. This chapter will present sample recipes using the more common grains. For cooking specifics, see Cooking Grains, page 214.

The word "cereal" derives from the Latin adjective "cerealis," which means "of Ceres." Ceres was the Roman goddess of the harvest, the protector and overseer of the crops. Also known as Demeter in Greek mythology, Ceres is closely related in function to the conception of the Egyptian earth mother Isis. By whatever name, this powerful goddess was the benefactress of the fruitful earth, and it was her influence that ensured the bountiful yield of grain.

BULGUR BROCCOLI PILAF

Serves 4 to 6

Bulgur is presteamed, cracked whole wheat berries. Nutty and chewy, it's a good alternative to brown rice in casseroles and pilafs.

1 cup raw bulgur
2 tablespoons safflower oil
1 large onion, chopped
2 cloves garlic, minced
2 heaping cups finely chopped broccoli
14-ounce can imported plum tomatoes with liquid, chopped
2 cups cooked or canned kidney beans or chick-peas (about ¾ cup raw, cooked following the directions on page 215)
2 tablespoons soy sauce
1 teaspoon chili powder
½ teaspoon each ground coriander, ground cumin, and dried basil
Dash cayenne pepper

Cook the bulgur as directed in Cooking Grains (page 214).

Heat the oil in a large skillet. Add the onion and sauté over moderate heat until translucent. Add the garlic and broccoli. Sauté, stirring frequently, until the broccoli is crisp-tender. Add the tomatoes and then all the remaining ingredients, including the bulgur and beans. Stir together and cook over low heat, stirring occasionally, for 10 minutes.

BUCKWHEAT GROATS WITH VERMICELLI

Serves 6

Because of their assertive aroma and flavor, buckwheat groats, or kasha, are a grain that people either love or dislike intensely. If you fall into the former category, you will enjoy this dish, a sort of contemporary interpretation of the Jewish classic "kasha varnitchkes."

1 tablespoon safflower oil
1 cup buckwheat groats (kasha)
2 cups Basic Vegetable Stock (page 30) or 2 cups water with 1 dissolved vegetable bouillon cube
1 cup raw vermicelli (extra-thin spaghetti), broken into 2-inch lengths
2 tablespoons margarine
1 medium sweet red bell pepper, cut into 1½-inch-long julienne strips
1 medium turnip, cut into 1½-inch-long matchsticks
1 cup firmly packed finely shredded cabbage
1 medium celery stalk, finely diced
3 scallions, chopped
¼ cup finely chopped fresh parsley
Juice of ½ lemon
2 teaspoons poppy seeds
Salt and freshly ground pepper to taste

Heat the oil in a heavy skillet. Add the groats and stir quickly to coat them with the oil. Toast over moderate heat, stirring frequently, until they become darker and very aromatic. Pour the stock or water over the groats and bring to a simmer. Simmer, covered, over low heat until the liquid is absorbed, about 15 to 25 minutes depending on the grind of the groats.

While the groats are simmering, cook the vermicelli until just al dente, then immediately rinse with cool water.

Heat the margarine in a large heavy skillet or wok. Add the bell pepper, turnip, cabbage, and celery and stir-fry over moderate heat until they are crisp-tender. Stir in the cooked groats and vermicelli along with the remaining ingredients and cook over low heat, stirring frequently, for 10 to 12 minutes. If the mixture seems dry, add just a bit of water. Serve at once.

"The Goddess ov korn iz also the Goddess ov oats, and barley, and bukwheat. Her name is Series, she is a mithological woman, and like menny wimmen now a daze, she is hard tew lokate."

—Josh Billings
His Works, Complete (1876)

Rice cultivation probably originated in Eastern Asia and, as has already been mentioned, is the staff of life for half the human race. Rice has always been so highly regarded by the Chinese they have traditionally said "Have you eaten your rice today?" in the same way that we would say "How do you do?" According to Sir James Frazer, author of The Golden Bough, *other cultures, particularly the Indonesians, believed that rice contained a soul, and treated the rice in bloom with the same deference with which they may have treated a pregnant woman. Loud noises were not allowed in the rice field lest the rice-souls be frightened, and the growing rice would be fed the same foods that might be given an expectant mother.*

RICE SKILLET PIE WITH NUTS AND SPROUTS

Serves 4 to 6

This is a very good way to use up leftover rice.

3 eggs, lightly beaten
1½ cups cooked brown rice (about ½ cup raw, cooked following the directions on page 214)
⅓ cup finely chopped walnuts
½ cup firmly packed alfalfa sprouts, separated with a fork
1 cup firmly packed grated cheddar cheese or cheddar-style soy cheese
¼ cup finely chopped celery
2 tablespoons minced chives
3 tablespoons soy sauce, or more or less to taste
½ teaspoon each paprika and ground cumin
Dash cayenne pepper

In a mixing bowl, combine the lightly beaten eggs with the rice and all the remaining ingredients and mix thoroughly. Prepare as directed on page 216, How to Fry and Flip a Skillet Pie or Frittata.

TANGY BAKED RICE WITH STRING BEANS

Serves 4 to 6

Lemon and sour cream combine to give this casserole a zesty flavor.

2 tablespoons olive oil
1 medium onion, chopped
1 clove garlic, minced
1 cup sliced mushrooms
2¼ cups cooked brown rice (about ¾ cup raw, cooked following the directions on page 214)
3 cups string beans, cut into 1-inch pieces and steamed crisp-tender
1 cup firmly packed grated mild white cheese, such as Monterey Jack
¾ cup reduced-fat sour cream
Juice of 1 lemon
1 teaspoon dried dill
¼ teaspoon dried thyme
Salt and freshly ground pepper to taste
Wheat germ for topping

Preheat the oven to 375° F. Heat the oil in a small skillet. Add the onion and garlic and sauté until the onion is translucent. Add the mushrooms and sauté until they are wilted and the onion is golden.

Combine the rice with the steamed string beans and the mushroom mixture in a large mixing bowl. Add the remaining ingredients, except the wheat germ, and mix thoroughly. Pour into an oiled shallow 9-by-13-inch baking dish. Sprinkle with wheat germ. Bake for 25 to 30 minutes.

SAFFRON FRUITED RICE

Serves 4 to 6

In sixteenth-century England, if someone was in high spirits, he or she was often said to have slept in a bag of saffron—historically considered an exhilarating spice. Its color is gorgeous, but alas, saffron is extremely expensive. For a similar effect, substitute turmeric to color this exotic fruited rice dish.

2 tablespoons fragrant nut oil, such as almond, hazelnut, or unrefined peanut
1 medium onion, chopped
1 large sweet apple, peeled, cored, and diced
4 cups cooked brown rice (about 1⅓ cups raw, cooked following the directions on page 214)
⅓ cup chopped nuts of your choice
⅓ cup raisins or currants
⅓ cup chopped dried fruit (apricots, dates, or black figs, or a combination)
2 to 3 tablespoons honey, to taste
2 tablespoons wheat germ
½ teaspoon saffron threads, dissolved in 2 tablespoons warm water, or ½ teaspoon ground turmeric
¼ teaspoon each cinnamon and ground nutmeg
½ cup plain yogurt, optional

Heat the oil in a large skillet. Add the onion and sauté over moderate heat until translucent. Add the apple and sauté until it softens, about 3 or 4 minutes. Add the remaining ingredients, except the yogurt, and cook over low heat, stirring frequently, for 10 to 12 minutes. Stir in the yogurt, if desired, and serve at once.

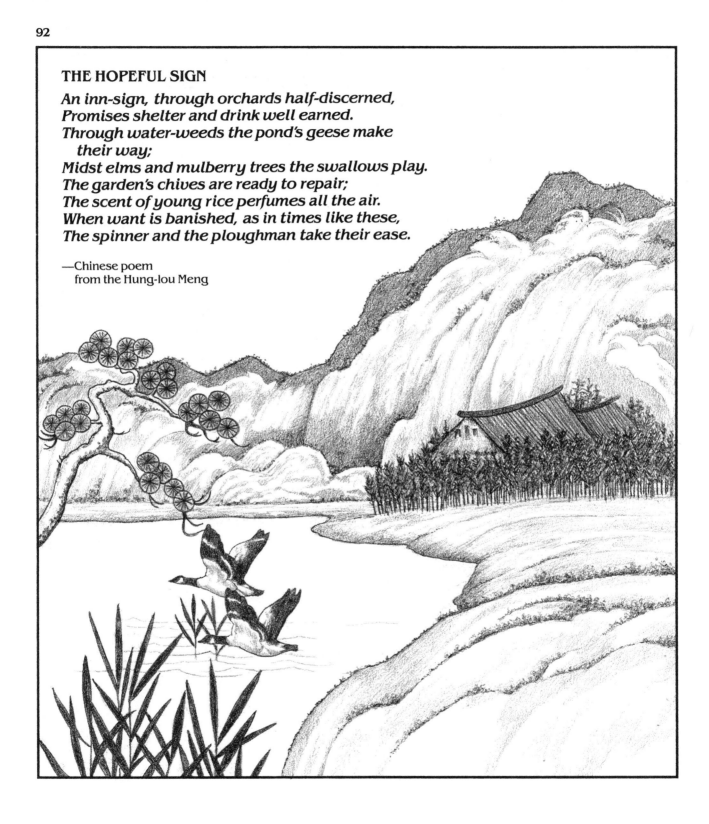

THE HOPEFUL SIGN

An inn-sign, through orchards half-discerned,
Promises shelter and drink well earned.
Through water-weeds the pond's geese make
their way;
Midst elms and mulberry trees the swallows play.
The garden's chives are ready to repair;
The scent of young rice perfumes all the air.
When want is banished, as in times like these,
The spinner and the ploughman take their ease.

—Chinese poem
from the Hung-lou Meng

BROCCOLI AND PARSLEY RICE

Serves 6

3 tablespoons margarine
3 cups finely chopped broccoli
1 medium onion, finely chopped
1 large celery stalk, finely chopped
½ cup chopped fresh parsley
4 cups cooked brown rice (about 1⅓ cups raw, cooked following the directions on page 214)
2 cups grated sharp cheddar cheese or cheddar-style soy cheese
1 cup low-fat milk or soymilk
1 teaspoon dried dill
½ teaspoon each dried marjoram and dried summer savory
Salt and freshly ground pepper to taste
Wheat germ or sesame seeds for topping

Preheat the oven to 375° F.

Heat the margarine in a large skillet. Add the broccoli, onion, and celery. Sauté over moderate heat until all are tender and the onion is just beginning to brown. Add the parsley and sauté just until slightly wilted.

In a mixing bowl, combine the cooked rice with the vegetable mixture and all the remaining ingredients except the wheat germ or sesame seeds. Mix thoroughly and pour into an oiled large shallow baking dish. Pat the mixture in smoothly and sprinkle the wheat germ or sesame seeds on top. Bake for 35 to 40 minutes, or until the top is golden brown.

PEANUT RICE AND TOFU

Serves 4 to 6

If you plan on having leftovers from this dish, add only half of the peanuts to the portion of the dish you will be using immediately, and save the rest to add when you reheat the remainder. Otherwise, the peanuts will absorb moisture and lose the texture that gives this dish its nice crunch.

2 tablespoons sesame oil
1 medium green bell pepper, diced
4 scallions, chopped
2 cloves garlic, minced
4 cups cooked brown rice (about 1⅓ cups raw, cooked following the directions on page 214)
3 tablespoons soy sauce, or more or less to taste
1 tablespoon honey
1 teaspoon freshly grated ginger
¾ pound tofu, diced
½ cup peanut halves

Heat the sesame oil in a large skillet or wok. Add the green pepper, scallions, and garlic and sauté over moderate heat until the pepper is tender. Add the cooked rice, soy sauce, honey, and ginger and mix together thoroughly. Stir in the tofu dice. Cook on very low heat for 7 to 8 minutes, stirring frequently. Just before serving, stir in the peanuts.

She who is the wife of one man cannot eat the rice of two.

—Chinese Proverb

CAULIFLOWER RICE PILAF

Serves 6 to 8

2 tablespoons safflower oil
3 to 4 cloves garlic, minced
1 small head cauliflower, cut into small florets
1 teaspoon freshly grated ginger
3 cups cooked brown rice (about 1 cup raw, cooked following the directions on page 214)
⅓ cup raisins or currants
1 teaspoon good curry powder or Home-Mixed Curry (page 207)
½ teaspoon ground coriander
¼ teaspoon each cinnamon and ground cloves
3 scallions, chopped
1 tablespoon soy margarine
½ cup yogurt, optional
2 tablespoons sesame seeds

Heat the oil in a very large skillet or wok. Add the garlic and sauté over moderate heat for 1 minute. Add the cauliflower and ginger and 3 tablespoons of water and sauté until the cauliflower is lightly browned. Add all the remaining ingredients except the last 3. Stir together and cook, covered, over very low heat for 15 minutes. Stir in the soy margarine, yogurt (if desired), and sesame seeds. Remove from the heat and serve at once.

BASMATI AND WILD RICE PILAF WITH CASHEWS

Serves 6

This simple recipe highlights the special aroma and flavor of Basmati rice.

1 cup raw brown Basmati rice
½ cup raw wild rice
3 tablespoons unrefined peanut oil
3 scallions, minced
3 tablespoons minced fresh parsley
Juice of ½ lemon
Salt and freshly ground pepper to taste
½ cup toasted cashew pieces

Rinse the Basmati and wild rice and combine them in a heavy saucepan with 4 cups of water. Bring to a boil, then simmer, covered, until the water is absorbed, about 35 to 40 minutes.

Heat the oil in a large skillet. Add the cooked rice along with all the remaining ingredients except the cashews. Sauté over low heat for 10 minutes, stirring frequently. If the mixture seems dry, add a small amount of water. Stir in the cashews and serve at once.

"One grain fills not the sack, but helps his fellows."

—George Herbert
Jacula Prudentum (1640)

WILD RICE PILAF WITH SPINACH AND ALMONDS

Serves 6 to 8 as a side dish

This elegant grain dish is full of earthy textures and flavors.

⅔ cup raw wild rice
⅔ cup raw long-grain brown rice
3 tablespoons margarine
1 medium onion, finely chopped
1 small celery stalk, finely chopped
1 clove garlic, minced
6 ounces wild mushrooms, such as porcini, fresh shiitake, or other, thinly sliced
10-ounce package thawed frozen spinach
Juice of ½ lemon, or more or less to taste
2 tablespoons finely chopped fresh parsley
¼ teaspoon each dried thyme and ground cumin
½ cup slivered almonds
Salt and freshly ground pepper to taste

Rinse the wild and brown rice and combine them in a heavy saucepan with 3½ cups of water. Bring to a boil and simmer, covered, until the water is absorbed, about 35 to 40 minutes. Remove from the heat.

Heat 2 tablespoons of the margarine in a large skillet. Add the onion and sauté over moderately low heat until translucent. Add the celery and garlic and continue to sauté until the onion is lightly browned. Add the mushrooms and sauté until they have softened, about 5 minutes. Stir in the cooked wild and brown rice mixture along with the spinach, lemon juice, parsley, thyme, and cumin. Cook, stirring, for 5 minutes. Add the remaining tablespoon of margarine and the slivered almonds and cook for another 10 minutes over very low heat, stirring frequently. Season to taste with salt and pepper and serve at once.

BARLEY AND MUSHROOM PILAF

Serves 6

1 cup raw barley
2 tablespoons safflower or light olive oil
1 medium onion, chopped
2 medium celery stalks, chopped
2 cloves garlic, minced
2 cups coarsely chopped mushrooms
2 tablespoons chopped fresh parsley
2 tablespoons chopped fresh dill
1¼ cups cooked or canned navy or great northern beans (about ½ cup raw, cooked following the directions on page 215)
2 to 3 tablespoons soy sauce, to taste
1 tablespoon honey
Freshly ground pepper to taste

Cook the barley as directed in Cooking Grains (page 214).

Heat the oil in a large skillet. Add the onion, celery, and garlic. Sauté over moderate heat until the onion is translucent. Add the mushrooms and continue to sauté until the onion is golden. Add the cooked barley and all the remaining ingredients and cook over low heat, stirring frequently, for 10 minutes. Serve at once.

Barley is one of the most ancient of cultivated grains. Traditionally the symbol of abundance in India, barley was associated with birth and wedding rituals, and the god Indra was referred to as "he who ripens barley."

MILLET-STUFFED PEPPERS

Serves 4 generously

Millet is a tiny round yellow cereal grain that is a staple in other cultures, such as those in North Africa. It cooks to an almost mushy texture, tastes bland but pleasant, and makes a nice alternative to rice as a bed of grains or, as in this recipe, as a stuffing for vegetables. Millet is easy to find in natural food stores.

⅔ cup raw millet
4 large green bell peppers
2 tablespoons olive oil
1 large onion, chopped
1 clove garlic, minced
2 tablespoons wheat germ
¾ cup grated mild cheese of your choice, or ¾ cup soy cheese
⅓ cup fresh orange juice
1 teaspoon each dried oregano and ground cumin
Salt and freshly ground pepper to taste
Extra wheat germ for topping
Extra grated cheese or soy cheese for topping
Paprika for garnish

Cook the millet as directed in Cooking Grains (page 214). Preheat the oven to 350° F.

Cut each pepper in half and remove the seeds. Arrange the halves on a lightly oiled baking dish. Salt lightly if desired.

Heat the oil in a large skillet. Add the onion and garlic and sauté over moderate heat until the onion is golden. Add the millet, wheat germ, cheese, juice, and seasonings and stir together.

Stuff each pepper half generously with the millet mixture. Top with extra wheat germ and grated cheese, and sprinkle each with a little paprika for color. Cover loosely with foil and bake for 25 minutes. Uncover and bake for another 15 minutes or until the peppers are done to your liking. Serve at once.

MILLET AND MUNG BEAN STEW

Serves 6

This savory, Indian-inspired stew is easy and hearty.

1 cup raw millet
2 tablespoons safflower oil
1 large onion, chopped
2 large carrots, chopped
3 cloves garlic, minced
1½ to 2 cups cooked mung beans (about ⅔ cup raw, cooked following directions on page 215)
14-ounce can imported tomatoes, chopped, with liquid
1 teaspoon freshly grated ginger
2 to 3 tablespoons chopped fresh cilantro
1 teaspoon dry mustard
¼ teaspoon ground cloves
Salt to taste

Cook the millet as directed in Cooking Grains (page 214).

Heat the oil in a soup pot. Add the onion and carrots and sauté over moderate heat until the onion is translucent. Add the garlic and continue to sauté until the onion is golden and the carrots are crisp-tender. Add the remaining ingredients and simmer over low heat for 30 to 35 minutes, or until the carrots are tender and the flavors are well integrated. Adjust the salt to taste.

COUSCOUS-STUFFED EGGPLANT

Serves 4 generously

Couscous, which is presteamed, cracked semolina, is among the lightest and fluffiest of grains. It makes an excellent bed for bean and vegetable dishes and is also ideal as a stuffing, as it quickly absorbs all the flavors around it. Look for couscous in natural food stores.

1 cup raw couscous, regular or whole-grain
2 medium eggplants, about 1 pound each
3 tablespoons olive oil
3 or 4 cloves garlic, minced
4 scallions, chopped
3 medium ripe tomatoes, chopped
2 tablespoons lemon juice
¼ cup minced fresh parsley or basil
1 teaspoon each chili powder and ground coriander
½ teaspoon ground turmeric, optional
Salt and freshly ground pepper to taste
1 cup plain yogurt or pureed soft tofu

Prepare the couscous as directed in Cooking Grains (page 214). Preheat the oven to 375° F.

Cut the stem ends off the eggplants and cut each in half lengthwise. With a sharp knife, carefully cut away the eggplant pulp, leaving a shell about ½ inch thick all around. Chop the eggplant pulp that you have removed into small dice.

Heat the olive oil and 2 tablespoons of water in a large skillet. Add the diced eggplant and the garlic and cook, covered, over low heat until the eggplant is just tender. Stir occasionally. Add the scallions and tomatoes and cook until they have softened a bit. Add the remaining ingredients, including the couscous, stir together, and remove from the heat.

Arrange the eggplant shells in a lightly oiled shallow baking dish. Stuff with the couscous mixture and cover loosely with foil. Bake for 30 minutes, then uncover and bake for another 10 to 15 minutes, or until the eggplant shell can be easily pierced through with a fork but has not yet collapsed.

"Ceres, most bounteous lady, thy rich leas of Wheat, Rye, Barley, Vetches, Oats, and Pease."

—William Shakespeare
The Tempest (ca. 1611)

HERBED WHEAT BERRIES, BARLEY, AND BLACK-EYED PEAS

Serves 6

Wheat berries are simply whole wheat kernels—ground, they make whole wheat flour; cracked, they make bulgur. Combining their distinctive flavor and texture with those of barley and black-eyed peas makes for a very appealing pilaf.

½ cup raw wheat berries
⅓ cup raw barley
¼ cup olive oil
3 to 4 cloves garlic, minced
1 medium onion, finely chopped
1 medium carrot, thinly sliced
1½ cups cooked or canned black-eyed peas (about ⅔ cup raw, cooked following the directions on page 215)
Juice of ½ to 1 lemon, to taste
¼ teaspoon each dried dill, dried basil, and dried oregano
Salt and freshly ground pepper to taste
⅓ cup firmly packed chopped fresh parsley

Cook the wheat berries and barley separately (see Cooking Grains, page 214).

Heat half of the oil in a large skillet. Add the garlic, onion, and carrot and sauté over low heat until golden.

Add the remaining oil, the black-eyed peas, the cooked grains, and all the remaining ingredients except the parsley. Sauté over low heat for 10 minutes, stirring frequently. Add the parsley and sauté for 2 minutes or so longer.

GRITS WITH FRESH CORN AND TOMATOES

Serves 4 to 6

This is an inviting late-summer supper dish, with the flavors of the Southwest. Stone-ground grits are more flavorful than the grits available in supermarkets; they are available in natural food stores and through natural-foods mail-order outlets.

¾ cup uncooked yellow stone-ground hominy grits
2 tablespoons margarine
1 medium onion, chopped
1 small green bell pepper, diced
1 pound ripe tomatoes, chopped
2 mild or hot green chilies, chopped, optional
2 cups cooked fresh corn kernels (about 3 medium ears)
½ teaspoon each dried oregano and ground cumin
Salt and freshly ground pepper to taste
1 cup firmly packed grated cheddar cheese or cheddar-style soy cheese

Bring 3 cups of water to a boil in a heavy saucepan, preferably one with a nonstick surface. Sprinkle in the grits slowly to avoid lumping. Lower the heat and cook over very low heat until thick, about 25 to 30 minutes.

While the grits are cooking, heat the margarine in a large skillet. Add the onion and sauté until translucent. Add the green pepper and continue to sauté until the onion is golden. Add the tomatoes and chilies and sauté until the tomatoes have softened, about 5 to 7 minutes. Stir in the corn kernels and seasonings. When the grits are done, stir them into the skillet. Sprinkle in the cheddar cheese and cook until it melts. Serve at once.

Corn was probably first cultivated by the ancient Aztecs, Mayas, and other Indians of that period. To them, corn was the staff of life, just as rice has always been in the Orient, and was held in the same reverence. They developed many colorful varieties of corn (also known as maize), and with this cultivation grew elaborate ceremonies, rituals, and legends, along with various corn gods, goddesses, and spirits.

One South American legend tells of two brothers who took shelter on a mountaintop after a flood. There was no food anywhere. The brothers were nearly starved when suddenly two parrots appeared and offered them corn. Each day after that, the same parrots brought corn, with which the brothers fed themselves. One day, one of the men caught one of the parrots. The parrot turned into a lovely maiden, and she set about teaching the brothers how to cultivate corn.

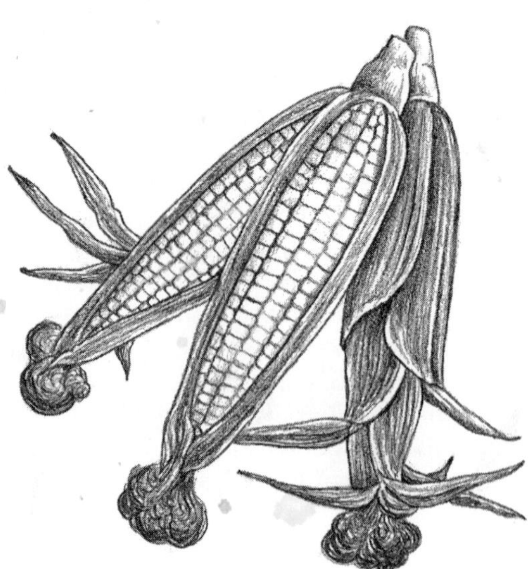

*WONDERFUL!

CORN ENCHILADAS

Serves 4

1 cup cooked or canned pinto beans (about ⅓ cup raw, cooked following the directions on page 215)
2 tablespoons olive oil
1 medium onion, chopped
2 cloves garlic, minced
1 cup canned crushed tomatoes
1½ cups cooked fresh or thawed frozen corn kernels
2 tablespoons minced mild green chilies, canned or fresh
1 teaspoon dried oregano
½ teaspoon each ground cumin and ground coriander
Salt and freshly ground pepper to taste
2 medium ripe tomatoes, finely diced
1 tablespoon minced cilantro or parsley
8 soft corn tortillas
1½ cups grated cheddar cheese, or cheddar-style soy cheese

Preheat the oven to 350° F.

Mash the beans well. Heat the oil in a large skillet. Add the onion and garlic and sauté over moderate heat until golden. Add the beans, crushed tomatoes, corn, chilies, and seasonings. Stir together and cook over moderately low heat for 10 minutes, stirring occasionally. Season with salt and pepper.

Combine the fresh tomatoes with the cilantro or parsley. Set aside.

Lightly oil one or two shallow baking dishes. Heat each tortilla on a dry skillet, just until it softens and becomes very flexible. Spoon a bit of the bean and corn mixture down the middle of each tortilla, fold one side over the other, and arrange on the baking dishes. Spoon the fresh tomato mixture over them evenly and top with the grated cheese. Bake for 20 minutes, or until the cheese is bubbly.

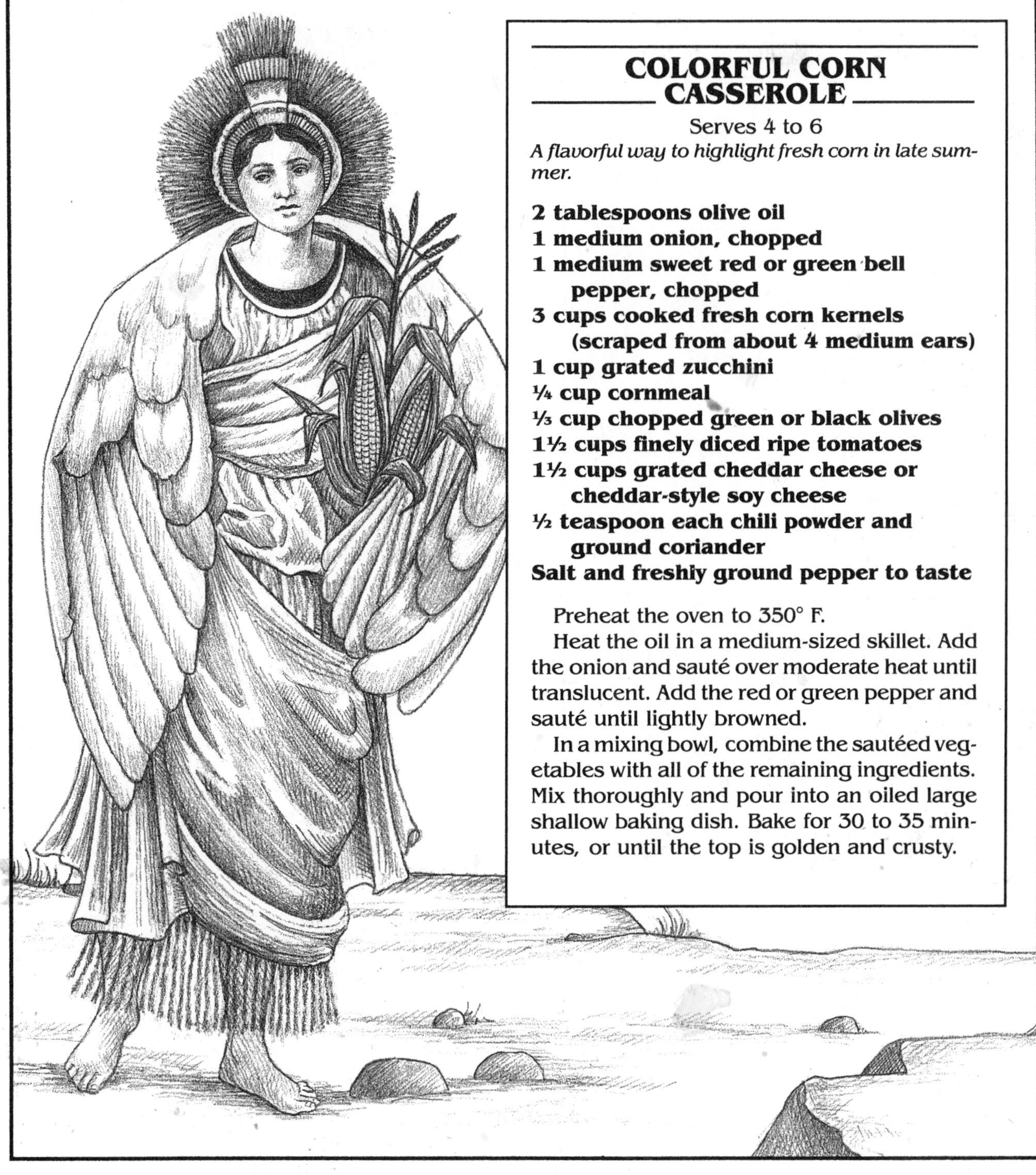

COLORFUL CORN CASSEROLE

Serves 4 to 6

A flavorful way to highlight fresh corn in late summer.

2 tablespoons olive oil
1 medium onion, chopped
1 medium sweet red or green bell pepper, chopped
3 cups cooked fresh corn kernels (scraped from about 4 medium ears)
1 cup grated zucchini
¼ cup cornmeal
⅓ cup chopped green or black olives
1½ cups finely diced ripe tomatoes
1½ cups grated cheddar cheese or cheddar-style soy cheese
½ teaspoon each chili powder and ground coriander
Salt and freshly ground pepper to taste

Preheat the oven to 350° F.

Heat the oil in a medium-sized skillet. Add the onion and sauté over moderate heat until translucent. Add the red or green pepper and sauté until lightly browned.

In a mixing bowl, combine the sautéed vegetables with all of the remaining ingredients. Mix thoroughly and pour into an oiled large shallow baking dish. Bake for 30 to 35 minutes, or until the top is golden and crusty.

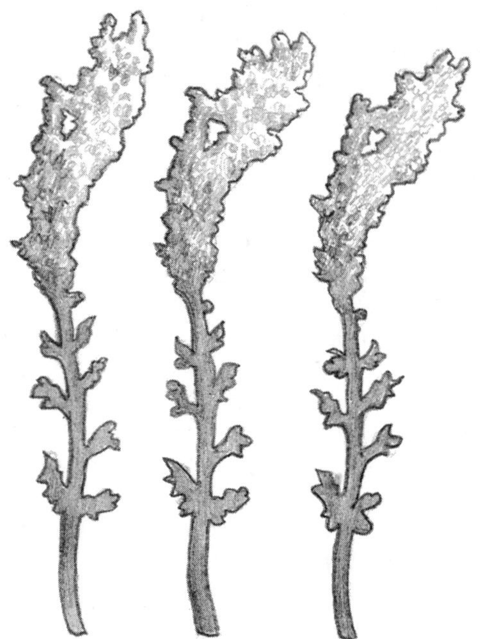

The grain quinoa was a staple in the ancient Andean and Incan cultures. So revered was it as a crop that Incan legend said it originated in the remains of a heavenly banquet. Quinoa fell into disuse after the sixteenth-century Spanish conquests of these cultures. Recently it has been revived and touted as a "supergrain," so superior are its nutritional qualities. Among grains, quinoa has one of the highest contents of high-quality protein, and it is rich in many other vital nutrients as well.

Quinoa is also a boon to the cook—it takes only 15 minutes to prepare and has an unusual, nutty flavor and a fluffy texture that make it highly versatile.

STIR-FRIED QUINOA AND BOK CHOY

Serves 4 to 6

1½ tablespoons safflower oil
1 cup raw quinoa
1 tablespoon sesame oil
1 large onion, quartered and thinly sliced
8 medium stalks bok choy, trimmed and sliced diagonally
1 large, crisp white turnip, peeled and diced
8 ounces fresh mung bean sprouts
2 tablespoons soy sauce, or more or less to taste
Freshly ground pepper to taste
Slivered almonds or toasted sunflower seeds for topping

Heat ½ tablespoon of the safflower oil in a medium-sized saucepan. Add the quinoa and toast it, stirring frequently, until it smells nutty. Pour in 2 cups of water, bring to a simmer, then cover and cook until the water is absorbed, about 15 minutes. Remove from the heat, fluff with a fork, and keep covered.

In the meantime, heat the sesame oil and the rest of the safflower oil in a wok. Add the onion and sauté over medium heat until translucent. Add the bok choy and turnip and turn the heat up to medium-high. Stir-fry until the vegetables are nearly crisp-tender, then add the sprouts and continue to stir-fry until they are slightly wilted. Flavor with soy sauce. Stir in the cooked quinoa, grind some pepper, then taste and add more soy sauce if desired, plus a bit of water if the mixture is dry. Cook, stirring, for another minute or so.

Top each serving with the almonds or sunflower seeds. Serve at once.

QUINOA AND SUMMER SQUASH SAUTÉ

Serves 4 to 6

1 teaspoon safflower oil
1 cup raw quinoa
2 cups Basic Vegetable Stock (page 30) or water
2 tablespoons olive oil
1 medium onion, chopped
2 cloves garlic, minced
2 medium zucchini, or 1 zucchini and one medium pattypan squash, sliced into bite-sized pieces
1 medium yellow summer squash, sliced into bite-sized pieces
6 large or 10 medium mushrooms, sliced
1 or 2 fresh green chili peppers, seeded and minced, or 1 4-ounce can mild green chilies
2 to 3 tablespoons chopped cilantro or fresh parsley
½ teaspoon each dried oregano and ground cumin
Salt and freshly ground pepper to taste

Heat the safflower oil in a large heavy skillet. Add the quinoa and toast it, stirring frequently, until it smells nutty, about 5 minutes. In the meantime, bring the water or stock to a boil in a heavy saucepan. Stir in the quinoa, bring to a simmer, then cover and cook until the liquid is absorbed, about 15 minutes. Remove from the heat, fluff with a fork, and keep covered.

Heat the olive oil in the same heavy skillet. Add the onion and garlic and sauté over moderate heat until translucent. Add the pattypan squash and zucchini, yellow squash, mushrooms, and chilies and stir-fry until the squashes are touched with golden spots. Stir in the cooked quinoa along with the herbs and seasonings. Cook over very low heat, stirring frequently, for 8 to 10 minutes. Serve at once.

It is no longer common knowledge that beans were formerly forbidden foods, held under the most solemn taboos. Among the ancient Egyptians, beans were sacred, and were actually worshipped. They were associated with the doctrines of immortality and transmigration, and eating them was forbidden due to the belief that they possessed a soul. In ancient Greece, eating beans was forbidden because they were objects not of worship but of scorn. They were considered evil, a negative influence on dreams, and were associated with lunacy. Oddly, beans were held in greatest contempt by Pythagoras, the father of Western vegetarianism. Pythagoras would be duly ashamed if he knew that he was depriving his considerable legion of followers of a protein-rich vegetarian staple.

KIDNEY BEAN AND VEGETABLE CHILI

Serves 6

This saucy chili is almost invariably a favorite among those just getting acquainted with entrees composed of beans and grains.

2 tablespoons olive oil
1 large onion, chopped
1 medium green bell pepper, chopped
1 small zucchini, thinly sliced
1 cup cooked fresh or thawed frozen corn kernels
14-ounce can imported plum tomatoes with liquid, chopped
1 cup canned crushed or pureed tomatoes
2 teaspoons chili powder, or more or less to taste
1 teaspoon ground cumin
½ teaspoon each ground coriander and dried oregano
4 cups cooked or canned pinto or red beans (about 1½ to 1⅔ cups raw, cooked following the directions on page 215)
Hot cooked rice, couscous, or bulgur
Tortilla chips

Heat the oil in a soup pot. Add the onion and sauté over moderate heat until translucent. Add the green pepper and sauté until it softens and the onion begins to turn golden. Add the remaining ingredients except the last 2 and cook over low heat for 25 minutes, stirring occasionally. Serve in bowls over hot grains, accompanied by crisp tortilla chips.

OPEN-FACED AVOCADO-BEAN ENCHILADAS

Serves 4 generously

4 cups cooked or canned pinto or black beans (about 1½ to 1⅔ cups raw, cooked following directions on page 215)
8 corn tortillas
2 tablespoons olive oil
1 medium green bell pepper, finely chopped
1 medium onion, finely chopped
2 cloves garlic, minced
4-ounce can mild or hot green chilies, chopped
1 teaspoon ground cumin
Salt to taste
2 cups canned crushed tomatoes
Shredded lettuce
1 large ripe avocado, finely diced
1 large ripe tomato, finely chopped
Grated cheddar cheese or cheddar-style soy cheese
Sour cream or plain yogurt, optional

Coarsely mash the cooked beans and set them aside.

Heat a medium-sized skillet. Toast each tortilla over moderate heat on both sides until crisp.

Heat the olive oil in a large skillet. Add the green pepper, onion, and garlic and sauté over moderate heat until all are tender but not browned. Add the beans, chilies, seasonings, and crushed tomatoes and stir well. Cook over low heat for 10 minutes, stirring occasionally.

Assemble the enchiladas as follows: Place a bit of shredded lettuce on each tortilla, followed by the bean mixture and some diced avocado and tomato. Top with a sprinkling of grated cheese, and, if desired, a small dollop of sour cream or yogurt. To eat, pick up the whole thing, break it in half and pick it up, or cut small pieces off with a knife and fork.

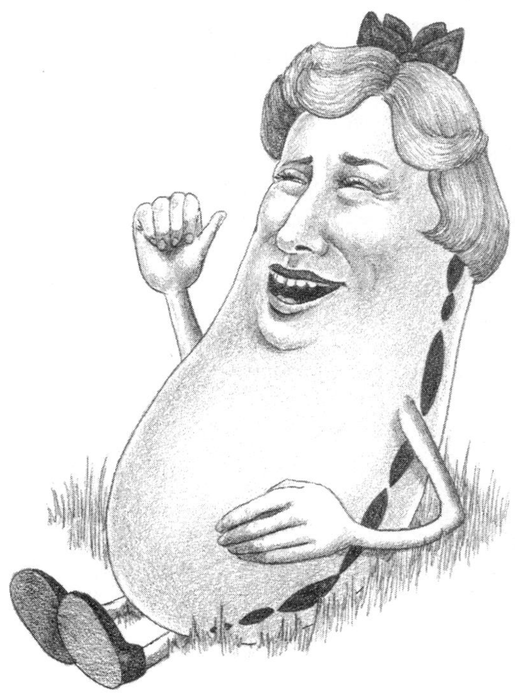

Did you ever wonder why beans have seams? In Grimm's Fairy Tales, a bean laughs so hard at the demise of her friends the Straw and the Coal that her sides split. A kind tailor passing by spots her and sews her sides back together. Ever since, beans have had seams.

NAVY BEAN AND VEGETABLE STEW WITH POTATO DUMPLINGS

Serves 6

Because stews are commonly based on meat, they often become a thing of the past for vegetarians. High-protein navy beans fill and satisfy in this stew, which is subtly scented with wine. The dumplings add a homey touch.

2 tablespoons safflower oil
1 heaping cup chopped onion
3 cloves garlic, minced
2 tablespoons unbleached white flour
2 cups cooked or canned navy beans (about ⅔ cup raw, cooked following the directions on page 215)
1½ cups diced butternut squash
2 medium carrots, sliced
¼ pound string beans, trimmed and halved
2 medium potatoes, peeled and diced
1 heaping cup shredded white cabbage

Sauce:
14-ounce can imported plum tomatoes with liquid, chopped
⅓ cup dry white wine
2 tablespoons honey
2 tablespoons soy sauce
1 tablespoon cider vinegar
1 teaspoon each dried thyme, dry mustard, and paprika

Preheat the oven to 325° F.

Heat the oil in a medium-sized skillet. Add the onion and sauté until translucent. Add the garlic and continue to sauté until the onion is lightly browned. Sprinkle in the flour and stir until it is absorbed. Transfer the mixture to a deep 2-quart casserole dish and add the beans and vegetables. Combine the sauce ingredients in a mixing bowl and stir until well blended. Pour over the vegetable mixture and stir to combine. Cover the casserole and bake for 1½ to 2 hours, or until the vegetables are tender. Serve hot, topping each serving with 3 dumplings.

POTATO DUMPLINGS

1¼ cups cold, cooked, well-mashed potatoes
¾ cup cornmeal
½ cup whole wheat pastry flour
1 teaspoon safflower oil
Salt to taste
Margarine for sautéing
Grated Parmesan cheese, optional

Combine the first 5 ingredients in a mixing bowl and work together until well blended. Form into 18 balls, each about 1 inch in diameter. Bring water to a rolling boil in a large pot. Gently drop in the dumplings, one at a time. Cook at a fairly brisk simmer for 15 minutes, then drain.

Heat just enough margarine to coat the bottom of a heavy skillet. Sauté the dumplings, in batches if necessary, over moderate heat, until golden brown on all sides. Sprinkle with Parmesan cheese if desired. Serve hot with the stew.

SIMPLE SEASONED BLACK BEANS

Serves 6

This quick and easy preparation is hearty and satisfying served over hot cooked grains. You can also serve it on a crisp tortilla, topped with chopped fresh tomatoes.

2 tablespoons olive oil
1 cup chopped onion
3 cloves garlic, minced
4 cups cooked or canned black beans (about 1½ to 1⅔ cups raw, cooked following the directions on page 215)
Juice of ½ lemon, or more to taste
1 teaspoon ground cumin
¼ cup chopped fresh parsley
Salt and freshly ground pepper to taste

Heat the oil in a large saucepan. Add the onion and sauté over moderate heat until translucent. Add the garlic and sauté until the onion is golden. Add the beans along with about ½ cup of liquid from the can or from cooking. Bring to a simmer. Mash some of the beans with the back of a wooden spoon, enough to thicken the liquid. Add the remaining ingredients and simmer over very low heat for 10 to 15 minutes, then serve.

"The Pythagoreans make a point of prohibiting the use of beans, as if thereby the soul and not the belly was filled with wind!"

—Cicero
De Divination (44 B.C.)

ADZUKI BEANS WITH SQUASH AND BULGUR

Serves 4 to 6

Adzuki beans, popular in Japan, are now readily available in natural food stores in this country. They are small and red, like kidney beans, but they cook quicker and are more digestible and tastier.

1 cup raw bulgur
2 cups cooked adzuki beans (about ¾ cup raw, cooked following the directions on page 215)
2 tablespoons safflower oil
1 teaspoon dark sesame oil
2 cloves garlic, minced
4 scallions, chopped
2 heaping cups peeled, diced butternut squash
2 to 3 tablespoons miso, to taste, dissolved in ½ cup warm water
2 tablespoons dry red wine
2 tablespoons honey
1 to 2 teaspoons freshly grated ginger, to taste

Cook the bulgur as directed in Cooking Grains (page 214).

Prepare the beans and have them ready.

Heat the safflower and sesame oils in a large skillet. Sauté the garlic and scallions until the garlic is lightly golden and the scallions are wilted. Stir in the beans and the bulgur.

Steam the squash dice in a deep saucepan with an inch or so of water until they are tender but still firm. Stir into the mixture in the skillet.

Combine the miso, wine, honey, and ginger in a small bowl and whisk together. Pour into the skillet. Cook over low heat, stirring frequently, for another 10 minutes, or until well heated through. Serve at once.

In the early Greek and Roman eras, beans were widely used as ballots. Casting a white bean signified an affirmative vote, whereas a dark bean was a negative vote. Previously, it was mentioned that beans have had to overcome their supernatural taboos, but by the Christian era, abstention from beans took on political overtones. Plutarch, circa 95 A.D., claimed that to "abstain from beans" meant that one should stay out of politics. Others after him also wrote of beans in this manner.

THREE BEANS AND TWO CHEESES

Serves 6

Since the three beans in this dish all have different cooking times, using good-quality canned beans expedites this hearty, savory bean casserole.

1 tablespoon safflower oil
1 medium onion, chopped
1 small green bell pepper, chopped
1½ cups canned kidney beans
1½ cups canned navy or great northern beans
2 cups canned chick-peas
14-ounce can imported plum tomatoes with liquid, chopped
3 tablespoons soy sauce
2 tablespoons honey
1 teaspoon chili powder, or more to taste
1 teaspoon each ground coriander, paprika, and dry mustard
1 cup grated sharp cheddar cheese or cheddar-style soy cheese
1 cup grated Monterey Jack cheese or mozzarella-style soy cheese
Hot cooked grains, such as couscous

Preheat the oven to 400° F.

Heat the oil in a small skillet. Add the onion and sauté until translucent. Add the green pepper and sauté until both are lightly browned, then combine with the beans in a mixing bowl along with the remaining ingredients, except the cheeses. Mix thoroughly. Lightly oil a large shallow baking casserole and pour the bean mixture into it. Top with the grated cheeses. Bake for 25 minutes or until the cheese is bubbly. Serve over grains; the lightness of couscous is a particularly nice complement to the heartiness of the beans.

BOSTON BAKED BEANS

Serves 6

Traditionally, the beans in this dish were oven-cooked for 5 to 8 hours. By precooking the beans, however, you can cut down the baking time considerably. Be sure to cook the beans to the texture you like, since the additional baking doesn't seem to soften them any further.

4 cups cooked or canned navy beans (about 1⅔ cups raw, cooked following the directions on page 215)
⅓ cup molasses
2 tablespoons brown sugar
1 teaspoon each dry mustard, ground ginger, and salt
1 tablespoon safflower oil
1 large onion, sliced into rings

Preheat the oven to 350° F.

Combine all the ingredients except the oil and onion in a 1½-quart baking dish, along with ¼ cup of water. Mix thoroughly. Cover and bake 30 minutes.

Heat the oil in a skillet. When it is hot, add the onion, stirring to separate the rings, and sauté until brown. After the beans have baked for 30 minutes, top with the onions and bake, uncovered, for another 10 minutes. Serve at once.

> ***"To absteine from beanes, that is not to meddle in civile affaires...for in the old times the election of magistrates was made by the pullyng of beanes."***
>
> —John Lyly
> *Euphues* (1579)

CHICK-PEA CROQUETTES

Makes about 12 croquettes

These nicely spiced croquettes can be served as a protein supplement to grains or vegetables. They are also good stuffed in warm pita bread, along with shredded lettuce, tomatoes, and Tofu "Mayonnaise" or one of its variations (page 58).

1 tablespoon olive oil
1 medium celery stalk, finely diced
1 clove garlic, minced
2 cups cooked or canned chick-peas (about ¾ cup raw, cooked following the directions on page 215)
2 eggs, beaten
¼ cup finely chopped black or green olives
¼ cup cornmeal
¼ cup wheat germ
1 teaspoon ground cumin
½ teaspoon each dried thyme and dried basil
¼ teaspoon each ground coriander and dry mustard
Salt and freshly ground pepper to taste
Oil for frying

Heat the olive oil in a small skillet. Add the celery and garlic and sauté over moderately low heat until the celery is tender but not browned.

In a large mixing bowl, mash the chick-peas well. Add the beaten eggs and all of the remaining ingredients except the oil and mix together thoroughly. Cover and refrigerate for 30 minutes to 1 hour.

Heat enough oil to coat the bottom of a large skillet. When it is very hot, turn the heat to moderate. Shape the chick-pea mixture into palm-sized croquettes and cook on both sides until nicely browned. Use more oil as needed. Drain the croquettes on paper towels.

CHICK-PEAS IN OLIVE-TAHINI SAUCE

Serves 6

The flavors of chick-peas and tahini (sesame paste) are exceptionally compatible. This is an off-beat way to combine them.

2 tablespoons olive oil
2 cloves garlic, minced
3 large celery stalks, chopped
1 medium sweet red or green bell pepper, finely chopped
1 recipe Olive-Tahini Sauce (page 57)
4 cups cooked or canned chick-peas (about 1⅓ cups raw, cooked following the directions on page 215)
2 to 3 scallions, finely chopped
¼ cup wheat germ
½ teaspoon each dried basil and ground coriander
Salt and freshly ground pepper to taste
Hot cooked grains

Heat the oil in a large skillet. Add the garlic and celery and sauté over moderate heat until the celery is golden. Add the bell pepper and sauté until all the vegetables are lightly browned. Pour the Olive-Tahini Sauce into the skillet and add the remaining ingredients except the cooked grains. Mix until well combined, then cook for 5 to 7 minutes. Serve at once over grains.

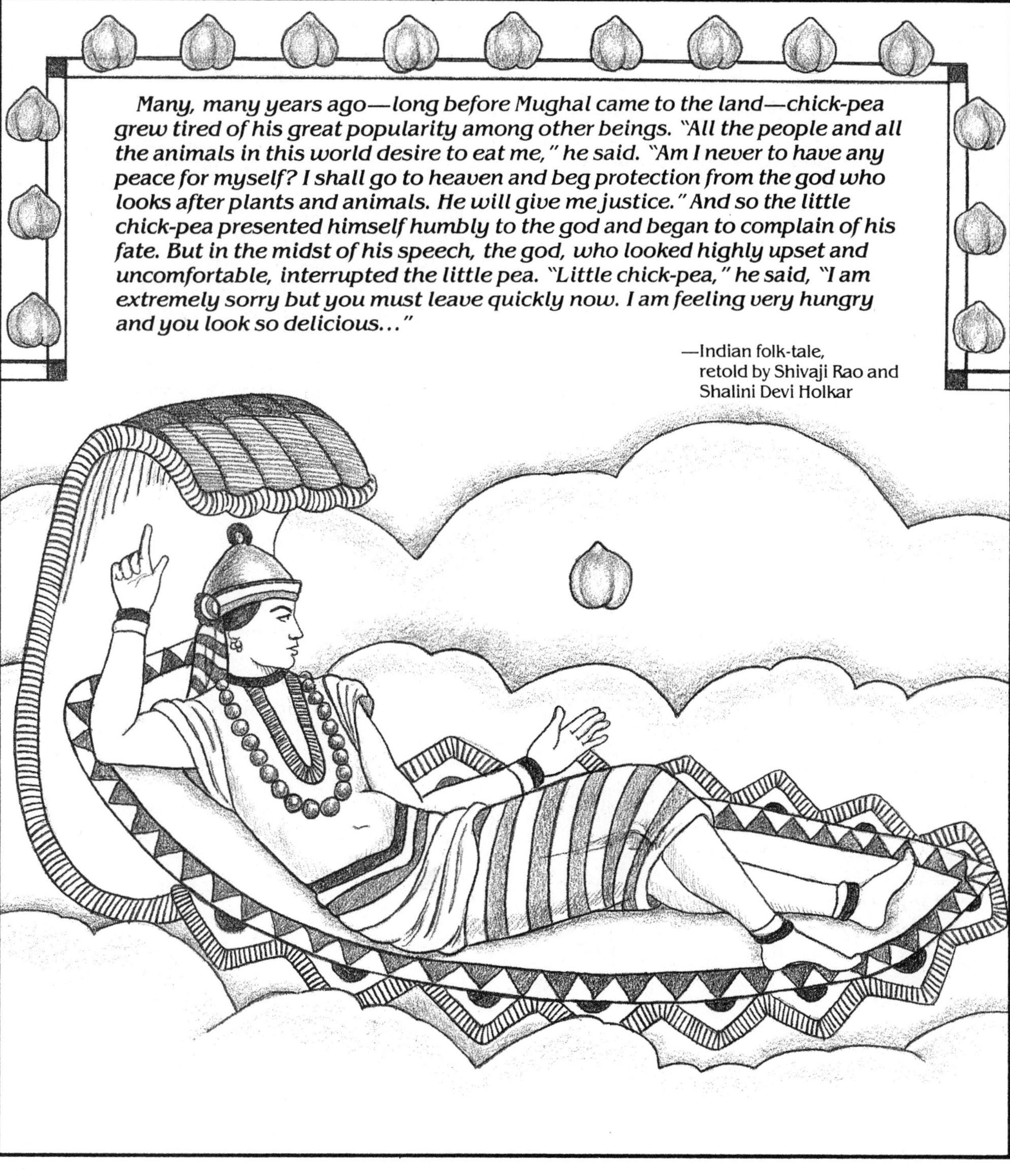
Many, many years ago—long before Mughal came to the land—chick-pea grew tired of his great popularity among other beings. "All the people and all the animals in this world desire to eat me," he said. "Am I never to have any peace for myself? I shall go to heaven and beg protection from the god who looks after plants and animals. He will give me justice." And so the little chick-pea presented himself humbly to the god and began to complain of his fate. But in the midst of his speech, the god, who looked highly upset and uncomfortable, interrupted the little pea. "Little chick-pea," he said, "I am extremely sorry but you must leave quickly now. I am feeling very hungry and you look so delicious..."
—Indian folk-tale,
retold by Shivaji Rao and
Shalini Devi Holkar

Lentils have been cultivated for thousands of years. They have always been an inexpensive item and have had to overcome a certain snobbery as a "poor man's" food. These little legumes are packed with protein and have become a vegetarian staple. Prepared carefully, they can be as enticing as a more exotic food.

Your Terrine de Lentils, Madame

CURRIED LENTILS WITH SPINACH

Serves 4 to 6

Lentils have a definite affinity with curry spices, which, when combined with the tomatoes here, form a fragrant, savory broth.

1 cup raw lentils
1 tablespoon safflower oil
2 cloves garlic, minced
½ pound fresh spinach leaves, stemmed, washed, and chopped
14-ounce can imported plum tomatoes with liquid, chopped
2 teaspoons good curry powder or Home-Mixed Curry (page 207), or more or less to taste
½ teaspoon freshly grated ginger
¼ teaspoon each cinnamon and ground nutmeg
Hot cooked grains or mashed potatoes

Wash and sort the lentils and cook them until they are tender but still keep their shape, following the directions in Cooking Beans (page 215).

Heat the oil in a large skillet. Add the garlic and sauté over moderately low heat for 1 minute or so. Add the spinach leaves, cover, and steam until they are wilted.

Add the lentils and the remaining ingredients, except the cooked grains or mashed potatoes, to the skillet. Cover and simmer over very low heat for 20 minutes. This dish is especially good over brown rice or couscous; for a delicious change of pace, you can also try it over mashed potatoes.

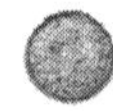    

SWEET AND SOUR LENTILS WITH FINE NOODLES

Serves 4 to 6

1 cup raw lentils
¼ cup (scant) soy sauce
¼ cup honey
⅓ cup rice vinegar or white wine vinegar
1 teaspoon freshly grated ginger, or more or less to taste
1 heaping cup raw fine egg noodles
2 tablespoons sesame oil
1 clove garlic, minced
1 large carrot, thinly sliced
½ medium green or red bell pepper, finely chopped
4 scallions, chopped

Wash and sort the lentils and cook them until they are tender but still keep their shape, following the directions in Cooking Beans (page 215).

In a small bowl, combine the soy sauce, honey, vinegar, and ginger, and mix well. Set aside.

Cook the egg noodles al dente, drain them, and set them aside. (Watch them carefully—they cook very quickly.)

Heat the sesame oil in a large skillet. Add the garlic and carrot and sauté over moderately low heat until the carrot is crisp-tender. Add the bell pepper, scallions, cooked lentils, and soy sauce and honey mixture. Simmer over low heat for 15 to 20 minutes, then add the noodles and simmer just until they are heated through.

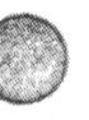

CHILI LENTIL AND RICE PILAF

Serves 6

This is a good everyday dish, substantial and high in protein, and one that keeps well for several days. A big green salad is enough to complete the meal.

1 cup raw lentils
1 cup raw brown rice
2 cloves garlic, minced
2 bay leaves
2 tablespoons soy sauce
2 tablespoons olive oil
1 large onion, chopped
1½ to 2 cups steamed string beans, cut into 1-inch pieces
14-ounce can imported plum tomatoes with liquid, chopped
6-ounce can tomato paste
2 tablespoons chili powder, or more or less to taste
1 teaspoon each ground cumin, dried oregano, and paprika
Dash of cayenne pepper
Extra soy sauce to taste

Wash the lentils and rice, then place them in a large pot along with the garlic, bay leaves, and soy sauce. Add 5 cups of water and bring to a boil. Cover and simmer over low heat. Check after about 25 minutes, stir, and continue to simmer, uncovered, until the lentils are tender but still hold their shape. Drain off any excess liquid.

Heat the oil in a large skillet. Add the onion and sauté over moderate heat until golden. Add the lentils and rice and all of the remaining ingredients, stir well, and simmer over low heat for 15 minutes.

"Green Peas, boiled carefully with onions, and powdered with cinnamon, ginger, and cardamoms, well pounded, create for the consumer considerable amorous passion and strength in coitus."

—Shaykh Nefzawi
The Perfumed Garden (ca. 1400)

LUSTY CURRIED PEAS

Serves 4 to 6

The combination of peas and sweet potato in a savory curry sauce is most enjoyable.

2 large sweet potatoes
2 tablespoons margarine
1 large onion, chopped
4 cups thawed frozen green peas
14-ounce can imported plum tomatoes with liquid, chopped
1 tablespoon honey
1 teaspoon cinnamon
1 teaspoon good curry powder or Home-Mixed Curry (page 207), or more to taste
½ teaspoon freshly grated ginger
Salt to taste
Dash each ground nutmeg and cayenne pepper
Plain yogurt for garnish

Cook, bake, or microwave the sweet potatoes until tender but still firm. When cool enough to handle, peel and dice them.

Heat the margarine in a large skillet. Add the onion and sauté until translucent. Stir in all the remaining ingredients except the yogurt and simmer over low heat for 15 minutes. Garnish each serving with a small scoop of yogurt.

RICE AND PEAS WITH CURRY CHEESE SAUCE

Serves 6

Perhaps this mild curry would have tempted Beau Brummell to give peas another try.

1⅓ cups raw brown rice
2 tablespoons soy sauce
2 tablespoons margarine
2 to 3 cloves garlic, minced
1 large celery stalk, finely chopped
1 recipe Curry Cheese Sauce (page 54)
2 cups thawed frozen green peas
1 teaspoon dried mint
¼ teaspoon each ground nutmeg, ground cumin, and ground turmeric
½ cup plain yogurt
Sesame seeds or chopped peanuts for garnish

Cook the rice as directed in Cooking Grains (page 214), adding the soy sauce to the cooking water. When done, transfer to a casserole dish and cover.

Heat the margarine in a large skillet. Add the garlic and celery and sauté over moderate heat until the celery is lightly browned. Pour in the Curry Cheese Sauce, then add the peas and seasonings. Cook over low heat until the peas are heated through and the sauce is bubbly. Pour the mixture over the rice in the casserole dish, add the yogurt, and mix thoroughly.

Garnish each serving with sesame seeds or chopped peanuts.

George Bryan Brummell (1778–1840), better known as Beau Brummel, was the undisputed fashion leader of early nineteenth-century England. He was also known as something of a wit. When asked if he ever ate vegetables, he replied,

"I once ate a pea."

SEITAN "REUBEN"

Makes 6 sandwiches

Seitan, as the Japanese call cooked wheat gluten, is one of the latest ancient Oriental foods to make its way into the Western natural foods market. Although seitan can be made at home with wheat flour and water via an easy but lengthy process, it is more convenient to buy it in natural food stores in ready-to-use form. Seitan is remarkably meatlike in texture and high in protein, making it a good analog in recipes that imitate beef dishes, such as the two given here.

1½ cups finely shredded white cabbage
2 tablespoons mayonnaise
Freshly ground pepper to taste
1 pound seitan, thinly sliced
Sweet and Savory Grilling Sauce (page 54)
12 slices hearty rye bread
6 slices Swiss cheese or mozzarella-style soy cheese
Half-sour dill pickles

Combine the cabbage and mayonnaise in a small mixing bowl and add a few grindings of pepper. Stir together and set aside.

Preheat the broiler. Line a large baking sheet with foil and oil lightly. Arrange the seitan slices on it in a single layer and brush each generously with the grilling sauce. Broil 5 to 7 minutes or until the edges start looking crisp. Turn the slices over and brush with more sauce. Broil another 5 minutes. Turn the oven down to 350° F.

Remove the foil lining from the baking sheet and discard it. Replace with fresh foil and arrange the sandwiches on it as follows: On each of 6 slices of rye bread, layer ⅙ of the cabbage mixture, followed by the seitan and 1 slice of the cheese. Place in the oven and bake just until the cheese melts. In the meantime, lightly toast or warm the remaining bread. Top the sandwiches and serve them with dill pickle slices alongside.

SWEET AND SOUR SEITAN "PEPPERSTEAK"

Serves 4 to 6

This stir-fry is rather elaborate to prepare, but it is offbeat and very satisfying.

2 tablespoons peanut oil
1 teaspoon sesame oil
1 medium onion, halved and sliced
2 cloves garlic, minced
2 medium green bell peppers (or 1 green pepper and 1 sweet red pepper), cut into 1-inch-square pieces
½ pound mushrooms, sliced
1 cup snow peas, trimmed
2 plum tomatoes, diced
16-ounce can unsweetened pineapple chunks with juice
1 teaspoon freshly grated ginger
2 to 3 tablespoons rice vinegar, to taste
2 tablespoons soy sauce
½ pound seitan, diced
1½ tablespoons cornstarch
Hot cooked rice
Sesame seeds for topping

Heat the oils in a wok. Add the onion and garlic and stir-fry over moderate heat until the onion is just beginning to turn golden. Add the peppers, mushrooms, and snow peas and stir-fry over moderately high heat for 3 to 4 minutes. Add the tomatoes, pineapple with liquid, ginger, vinegar, and soy sauce. Stir together and simmer over moderate heat until the snow peas are just crisp-tender. Stir in the seitan. Remove about ¼ cup of the liquid in the wok and transfer it to a cup. Dissolve the cornstarch in it and stir it back into the wok. Simmer for another 5 minutes. Serve at once over hot cooked rice, garnishing each serving with sesame seeds.

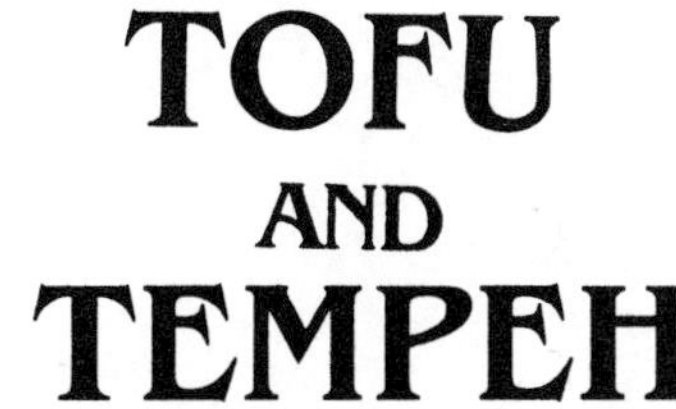

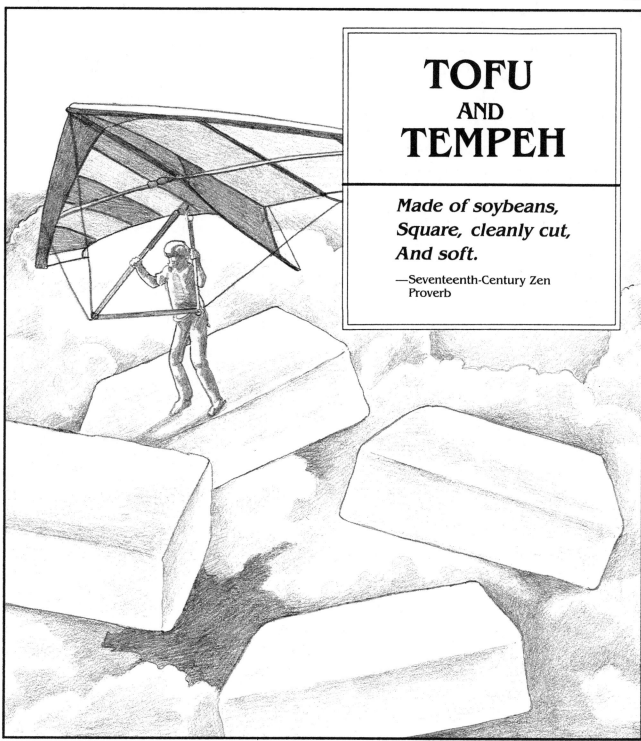

TOFU AND TEMPEH

Made of soybeans,
Square, cleanly cut,
And soft.

—Seventeenth-Century Zen
Proverb

Tofu is believed to have originated in China about two thousand years ago and to have reached Japan during the eighth century A.D., carried over by Buddhist monks who traveled widely in the region. Today, tofu (its Japanese name) is a staple food in both Japan and China, where it is more commonly referred to as bean curd.

In the West, tofu has gone from being a health-food oddity to being a supermarket staple. But many who have seen it and even tasted it are still not sure what it is! Think of tofu as being analogous to cheese—just as dairy cheese is coagulated from milk, so tofu is coagulated from soymilk.

To make tofu, soybeans are partially cooked, then pureed. Soymilk is extracted from the puree, then poured into shaping containers and solidified with one of two natural coagulants.

As a food, tofu is best known as an excellent source of protein as well as a good source of calcium. In the Far East, tofu comes in many textures. Here it is basically available in soft, medium, firm, and occasionally silken varieties.

TOFU WITH SIMMERED LEEKS AND TOMATOES

Serves 4 to 6

2 large or 3 medium leeks, white and palest green parts only, chopped
1 tablespoon safflower oil
1 pound firm tofu, diced
2 large or 3 medium ripe, juicy tomatoes, diced
2 to 3 tablespoons soy sauce, to taste
2 tablespoons dry wine or sherry
1 tablespoon white wine vinegar or rice vinegar
1 tablespoon honey
1 teaspoon dark sesame oil
Hot cooked grains or noodles

Rinse the chopped leeks well to remove any grit. Heat the oil with 3 tablespoons of water in a wok or large skillet. Add the leeks and "sweat" them over low heat, covered, for about 10 minutes or until they are crisp-tender. Add the remaining ingredients except the grains and simmer, covered, for 10 minutes. Lift the lid and stir occasionally. Uncover and simmer for another 5 minutes. Serve at once over hot cooked grains or noodles.

MUSHROOMS AND TOFU IN WINE

Serves 4 to 6

A friend devised this quick dish abounding in mushrooms. Grating the tofu allows it to soak up all the flavors of the aromatic sauce.

1 tablespoon safflower oil
2 cloves garlic, minced
1 large onion, chopped
1½ pounds mushrooms, sliced or coarsely chopped
½ medium green bell pepper, finely chopped
½ cup dry white wine
¼ cup soy sauce
½ teaspoon freshly grated ginger
2 teaspoons sesame oil
1½ tablespoons cornstarch
¾ pound firm tofu, coarsely grated
Hot cooked grains or noodles
Crushed almonds or crisp chow mein noodles for garnish

Heat the oil in a large skillet. Add the garlic and onion and sauté over moderate heat until the onion is translucent.

Add the mushrooms, green bell pepper, wine, soy sauce, ginger, and sesame oil to the skillet and stir together. Turn the heat down to low, cover, and simmer until the mushrooms are tender.

Dissolve the cornstarch in a small amount of water and add it to the skillet. Stir in the grated tofu, cover, and simmer for 5 minutes longer or until the liquid has thickened. Serve over grains or noodles and garnish with crushed almonds or crisp chow mein noodles.

Some turn up their noses at tofu because it is so bland, but it is precisely that blandness that makes it such an incredibly versatile food. Its porous texture makes it a sponge for flavorings, so a smart cook can make an endless variety of delicacies from it. I think of tofu as a very basic and simple food, and while it can be featured in some pretty fancy concoctions, I prefer to use it primarily in straightforward ways, as an analog for eggs (such as in Tofu Eggless "Egg Salad," page 121), or in dishes that traditionally contain meat or fish (such as Tofu Filets, page 123, with Tofu Tartar Sauce, page 58).

I can't imagine a well-rounded vegetarian diet without tofu. I hope the skeptical will try—and ultimately enjoy—these recipes.

TOFU RANCHEROS

Serves 6

A variation of a Southwestern classic, conventionally made with fried eggs.

Sauce:

1½ tablespoons olive oil
1 medium onion, chopped
1 clove garlic, minced
1 small green bell pepper, finely diced
14- or 16-ounce can crushed tomatoes
4-ounce can mild or hot chopped green chilies
½ teaspoon each dried oregano and ground cumin
Salt to taste

1 pound firm tofu
¼ cup cornmeal
Oil for frying
6 corn tortillas
1¼ cups grated Monterey Jack, cheddar cheese, or cheddar-style soy cheese
1 medium firm, ripe avocado, sliced

Tofu talk:
An old Chinese metaphor for petty fault-finding is "finding a bone in your tofu." Another Chinese saying holds that a hopeless situation is "as futile as trying to clamp two pieces of tofu together."

Heat the oil in a medium-sized skillet. Add the onion and garlic and sauté over moderate heat until the onion is translucent. Add the green bell pepper and continue to sauté until the onion is golden. Add the remaining sauce ingredients and simmer over low heat, covered, for about 15 minutes.

In the meantime, cut the tofu into ¼-inch-thick slices and pat between paper towels. Cut into ¼-inch dice. Combine in a plastic bag with the cornmeal and shake to coat the dice. Heat enough oil to coat the bottom of a medium-sized nonstick skillet. When the oil is hot, add the tofu dice and sauté over moderately high heat, stirring frequently, until golden. Remove from the heat.

To assemble, pass each tortilla briefly through the sauce with tongs to soften it, then place it on an individual plate. Divide the tofu among the tortillas, then top with more sauce and a sprinkling of grated cheese. Garnish with avocado slices.

TOFU EGGLESS "EGG SALAD"

Serves 6

This makes a delicious sandwich filling for lunch, served on whole wheat rolls or in pita bread.

1 pound firm tofu, crumbled
¼ to ⅓ cup mayonnaise, as needed
1 to 2 teaspoons prepared mustard, to taste
1 stalk celery or ½ medium green bell pepper, finely diced
1 tablespoon minced scallion
¼ teaspoon curry powder or Home-Mixed Curry (page 207)
Salt to taste

In a mixing bowl, combine the tofu with enough mayonnaise to moisten. Add the remaining ingredients and mix until well combined.

SCRAMBLED TOFU

Serves 4

This easy preparation will please the palate for breakfast, lunch, or dinner. Serve it with toast for a simple meal; add baked potatoes and a salad for a substantial meal.

1 pound soft or medium-firm tofu
2 tablespoons margarine
1 medium green bell pepper
1 cup sliced mushrooms
2 medium tomatoes, finely diced
2 scallions, minced
½ teaspoon good curry powder or Home-Mixed Curry (page 207)
2 tablespoons minced fresh herbs (parsley, dill, or basil, or a combination), optional
Dash turmeric for color, optional
Salt and freshly ground pepper to taste

Crumble the tofu coarsely with your hands and set aside.

Heat the margarine in a large skillet. Add the green bell pepper, mushrooms, tomatoes, and scallions and sauté over moderate heat, stirring frequently, until all are tender. Add the tofu and the remaining ingredients and stir together well. Sauté, stirring frequently, for 5 minutes. Serve at once.

"Go bump your head against the corner of a cake of tofu" is a Japanese expression meaning "Get lost!"

TOFU SHEPHERD'S PIE

Serves 4 to 6

This simple casserole will serve you well as a tasty, hearty everyday main dish. You may want to double up the recipe and make two casseroles, one to use at once and one for the next night's supper.

4 medium potatoes
¼ cup low-fat milk or soymilk
½ teaspoon salt
1 teaspoon plus 2 tablespoons safflower oil
2 large carrots, diced
1 heaping cup finely chopped fresh broccoli
1 cup thawed frozen peas
½ pound grated firm tofu
2 or 3 scallions, chopped
2 tablespoons chopped fresh parsley
2 tablespoons soy sauce
2 tablespoons dry red wine
1 teaspoon smoke-flavored yeast, optional

Cook or microwave the potatoes in their jackets until they can be easily pierced. When cool enough to handle, peel and mash well with the milk or soymilk, salt, and 1 teaspoon of the oil. Set aside.

Preheat the oven to 375° F.

Heat the rest of the oil in a large skillet. Add the carrots and broccoli and sauté until crisp-tender. Stir in the remaining ingredients and sauté for 5 minutes, stirring frequently. Pour the mixture into a lightly oiled 10-inch round casserole dish or a 1½-quart casserole dish. Top with the mashed potatoes, spreading them evenly.

Bake for 30 to 35 minutes or until the top of the potatoes begins to turn golden and crusty. Let stand for 5 minutes, then cut into wedges or squares to serve.

BROILED BARBECUE TOFU

Serves 4 to 6

Serve on whole-grain rolls and accompany with baked potatoes and a green salad for a simple but satisfying meal.

1½ pounds firm tofu
2 tablespoons safflower oil
1 large onion, quartered and thinly sliced
1 medium green or red bell pepper, diced
1 cup sliced mushrooms
Sweet and Savory Grilling Sauce (page 54)

Slice the tofu ¼ inch thick and pat briefly between paper towels to drain off excess water.

Heat the oil in a medium-sized skillet. Add the onion and sauté until translucent. Add the bell pepper and sauté until the onion is golden. Add the mushrooms and continue to sauté until they are wilted and the bell pepper begins to turn golden. Remove from the heat.

Preheat the broiler. In a shallow baking pan lined with foil, layer as follows: first a thin layer of the grilling sauce, then a single layer of the tofu slices, then another layer of the sauce, this time generous. Top it all with the sautéed vegetables. Broil for 5 to 7 minutes or until the vegetables are just beginning to get touched with charred spots. Serve at once.

TOFU MOCK "TUNA SALAD"

Serves 6

When I gave up meat, I never missed it, but when I gave up fish, I missed the taste of tuna salad. I can't claim that this tofu salad could pass for tuna, but with the flavor of celery and mayonnaise and the salty tang of soy sauce, it makes a very tasty substitute.

1 pound firm tofu
1 large celery stalk
1 scallion, minced
½ cup mayonnaise
2 tablespoons soy sauce
1 teaspoon kelp powder, optional (see note)

Freeze the tofu for at least 24 hours, then thaw thoroughly. This gives the tofu an interesting spongy and chewy texture.

Crumble the tofu finely and place in a mixing bowl. Add the celery and scallions.

In a small bowl, mix the mayonnaise with the soy sauce and optional kelp powder. Add to the tofu mixture and mix until completely combined. Serve on bread or rolls or in pita bread.

NOTE: Kelp powder, which is derived from a dried sea vegetable, lends a slightly "fishy" flavor to this salad. It is available in natural food stores.

TOFU "FILETS"

Serves 4

You can serve these tasty cutlets on their own, with the Tofu Tartar Sauce topping, or use them in a sandwich, dressed with the sauce and some lettuce.

1 pound firm tofu
1 egg or 2 egg whites, beaten
2 tablespoons soy sauce
¼ cup wheat germ
¼ cup cornmeal
¼ teaspoon each paprika and dried basil
Dash dried thyme
Oil for frying
Tofu Tartar Sauce (page 58)

Slice the tofu ¼ inch thick. Place the slices on several layers of paper towel, cover with a few more layers, and pat to remove some of the moisture.

Beat the egg or egg whites together with the soy sauce in a small bowl. Combine the wheat germ with the cornmeal and seasonings on a plate.

Heat enough oil to coat the bottom of a large nonstick skillet. Dip each slice of tofu into the egg mixture, then dredge both sides in the wheat-germ mixture. Fry the slices until golden on both sides. Drain briefly on paper towels and serve at once with the sauce.

TOFU AND EGGS IN PEANUT SAUCE

Serves 4 to 6

This peanut-flavored egg and tofu combination is excellent served as a protein-packed accompaniment to vegetable stir-fries and Oriental noodle dishes. You can also simply serve it over hot cooked rice.

1 recipe Peanut Sauce (page 63)
Safflower oil for frying
4 eggs, well beaten
1 pound tofu
1 tablespoon sesame oil
3 scallions, chopped
16-ounce can Chinese straw mushrooms, drained (save the liquid for another use, or for making the Peanut Sauce)
Soy sauce to taste, optional
3 tablespoons toasted sunflower seeds

Prepare the Peanut Sauce according to the recipe and set aside until needed.

Heat just enough oil to coat the bottom of a 9- or 10-inch nonstick skillet. When the skillet is hot enough to make a drop of water sizzle, pour in the beaten eggs. Tip the skillet to distribute them, then keep tipping, lifting the edges of the egg with a spatula to allow the loose egg to run underneath. When the bottom is lightly browned and the top is fairly set, flip with a wide spatula and cook for just a minute or so. Remove to a plate. Cut the eggs into ½-by-2-inch strips. Slice the tofu so that it resembles the eggs.

Heat the sesame oil in the same skillet. When it is hot, add the scallions and sauté them over moderately low heat until wilted. Stir in the eggs, tofu, Peanut Sauce, and mushrooms. Flavor with a bit of soy sauce if desired. Sauté, stirring gently, until just heated through. Transfer to a serving dish and top with the sunflower seeds. Serve at once.

TEMPEH BURGERS

Makes 10 to 12 patties

Serve these high-protein patties with Mushroom Gravy (page 55) or in pita sandwiches with tomatoes, sprouts or shredded lettuce, and your favorite dressing.

10 or 12 ounces tempeh
2 eggs, beaten, optional (see note below)
½ cup (scant) tomato sauce
¼ cup wheat germ
1 scallion, minced
1½ tablespoons soy sauce
½ teaspoon each chili powder, garlic powder, and ground cumin
¼ teaspoon dried basil, optional
Safflower oil for frying

Dice the tempeh and place in a saucepan with 1 inch of water. Cover and steam over medium-low heat for 10 minutes. Drain and place in a mixing bowl. Mash well, add the remaining ingredients except the oil, and stir until well blended.

Heat just enough oil to coat a wide nonstick skillet. Shape the mixture into flat, palm-sized patties. Fry over medium heat on both sides, flipping carefully, until golden brown.

Serve in one of the ways suggested above.

NOTE: Using eggs in this mixture helps to hold the burgers together and yields a less crumbly result. However, the recipe also works without eggs. Let the burgers brown slowly and thoroughly on the first side, and flip carefully.

TEMPEH "SLOPPY JOES"

Serves 4 to 6

Serve this easy and quick dinner offering on whole-grain rolls or in pita pockets.

2 tablespoons safflower oil
1 medium onion, finely chopped
½ medium green bell pepper, finely chopped
10 ounces tempeh, finely crumbled
1¼ cups tomato sauce
1 to 2 teaspoons chili powder, to taste
½ teaspoon each ground cumin, dried oregano, and garlic powder
1 tablespoon soy sauce, or more or less to taste
1 teaspoon honey

Heat the oil in a skillet. Add the onion and sauté until golden. Stir in the green pepper and tempeh and sauté over medium heat, stirring frequently, until the tempeh is lightly browned. Add the remaining ingredients, stir together well, and simmer over low heat for 8 to 10 minutes.

TEMPEH TACOS

Serve in crisp taco shells with shredded lettuce and, if desired, shredded cheese or soy cheese.

A staple soy food of Indonesia, tempeh (pronounced tem-PAY) is slowly gaining in popularity in the West, much as tofu did before it. But whereas tofu is soft and bland, tempeh has a chewy texture and an unusual flavor that is somewhat nutty and slightly fermented. It is an even more concentrated source of protein than tofu and is a bit more exotic, if somewhat less versatile.

To make tempeh, cooked soybeans are spread on trays and inoculated with beneficial mold cultures. As the mold multiplies and ferments, the soybeans bind together into firm cakes.

Tempeh cakes are readily available in the refrigerator sections of natural food stores, where they come in 10- or 12-ounce packages. Tempeh is a ready-to-use food and lends itself to many quick and easy preparations. Like tofu, it is commonly used as a meat substitute and analog, in preparations such as Tempeh "Sloppy Joes." If you like the unusual flavor and texture of tempeh, you will find it a useful staple food.

TEMPEH WITH JAPANESE NOODLES

Serves 6

10 to 12 ounces tempeh
Oil for frying
3 tablespoons soy sauce, or more or less to taste
2 tablespoons safflower oil
1 teaspoon dark sesame oil
2 tablespoons sherry or dry wine
1 large onion, halved or sliced
1 cup shredded cabbage
1 cup snow peas, trimmed and halved crosswise
1 cup mung bean sprouts
½ pound Japanese noodles, cooked (udon, jinenjo, or soba)
Freshly ground pepper to taste

Cut the cake of tempeh in half crosswise, slice through each half so that it is only half as thick, and then cut into ½-inch dice. Heat just enough oil to coat the bottom of a wok and add 1 tablespoon of the soy sauce. Over moderately high heat, stir-fry the tempeh dice until golden and slightly crisp. Remove from the heat, transfer to a container, and set aside.

Heat the oils and sherry in the wok. Add the onions and cabbage and stir-fry until the onion is golden. Add the snow peas and bean sprouts and stir-fry until the vegetables are crisp-tender. Stir in the cooked noodles and the tempeh. Season with the rest of the soy sauce and black pepper. Stir-fry for another 5 minutes, then serve at once.

TEMPEH, CAULIFLOWER, AND CASHEW CURRY

Serves 6

2 medium potatoes
2 tablespoons margarine
1 large onion, chopped
2 cloves garlic, minced
2 heaping cups small cauliflower florets
14-ounce can imported plum tomatoes
1 cup diced zucchini
1 teaspoon each freshly grated ginger, ground cumin, ground coriander, and ground turmeric
½ teaspoon cinnamon
2 green chilies, chopped, or 1 4-ounce can chopped mild chilies, optional
1 tablespoon safflower oil
10 ounces tempeh, cut in half through its thickness, then cut into ½-inch dice
Salt to taste
½ cup cashews

Cook or microwave the potatoes in their skins. When they are cool, peel and dice them, then set aside.

Heat the margarine in a large skillet. Add the onion and garlic and sauté until the onion is golden. Add the cauliflower and sauté for another 5 minutes. Add the tomatoes, zucchini, spices, and optional chilies. Stir together, then cover and simmer over low heat for 15 minutes.

In the meantime, heat the safflower oil in a smaller skillet. Add the diced tempeh and sauté over moderate heat until golden on all sides. Add the tempeh to the first skillet along with salt to taste and simmer for another 10 to 15 minutes over low heat. Stir in the cashews and serve.

PASTA

A romantic legend tells of how spaghetti first arrived in Italy. In the thirteenth century, Marco Polo voyaged to China, and during his stay, he became enamored of a lovely Chinese maiden. One sunny day, he and his beloved became engrossed with one another while she was preparing her daily batch of bread dough. The maiden neglected to see that the dough was overflowing, dripping in long, thin strings. Soon, the hot sun dried it up. To hide his sweetheart's mistake, Marco Polo gathered up the dough strings and took them back to his ship, where the cook boiled them in a broth that night. The dish was an immediate hit with the crew, and upon the ship's return to Italy, the sailors spread the word of this new delicacy, where it soon became a favorite. Take this charming legend as you might eat your spaghetti—with a grain of salt.

Pasta, in various forms called macaroni or noodles, has had its origins traced as far back as China of 5000 B.C. A versatile, nutritious vehicle for tasty sauces and vegetables in numerous combinations, it is one of those foods that nearly everyone loves.

Until fairly recently, pasta was more often referred to as macaroni, which is most commonly taken to mean the tubular variety, and that is the name under which it entered England in the eighteenth century. More on that later in this chapter. There are two interesting versions as to how macaroni got its name. In one legend, a thirteenth-century king who was something of an epicure was served this new type of dish consisting of delicious tubes covered with a rich sauce. Upon tasting it, he exclaimed, "Ma Caroni!" which means something like "how very dear," that is, dear as in darling. The other version has it that German bakers made dough figures in the shape of men, shells, stars, etc. These were taken to Italy by German merchants. The Italians were reluctant to buy them due to their large size and high price and protested "Ma Caroni!"—again "how very dear," but this time interpreted as "how very expensive." The German bakers reduced the size and price of the dough shapes but they were from then on called "macaroni."

BAKED PASTA WITH EGGPLANT

Serves 4 to 6

2 tablespoons olive oil
1 large eggplant, peeled and diced
1 clove garlic, minced
½ pound medium-sized shaped pasta, such as rotelle, ziti, or shells
1 large green bell pepper, cut into julienne strips
½ cup sliced or chopped black olives
¼ cup chopped fresh parsley
1 recipe Quick Tomato-Herb Pasta Sauce (page 135)
½ pound part-skim ricotta cheese
⅓ cup grated Parmesan cheese
Salt and freshly ground pepper to taste
1 to 1½ cups grated mozzarella cheese

Preheat the oven to 325° F.

Heat 1 tablespoon of the olive oil and ¼ cup of water in a large skillet. Add the eggplant and garlic and cook, covered, over moderately low heat, stirring occasionally, until eggplant is tender. At the same time, begin cooking the pasta. When it is cooked al dente, remove from the heat and drain immediately.

Heat the remaining oil in a small skillet. Add the green pepper and sauté over moderate heat just until it has lost its raw quality. Remove from the heat and stir in the olives and parsley.

In a mixing bowl, combine the sauce, eggplant, pasta, ricotta, Parmesan, and salt and pepper. Mix thoroughly.

Oil a large shallow baking dish and layer it as follows: first, all of the pasta and eggplant mixture, then the green pepper mixture, then the grated mozzarella. Bake for 30 to 35 minutes.

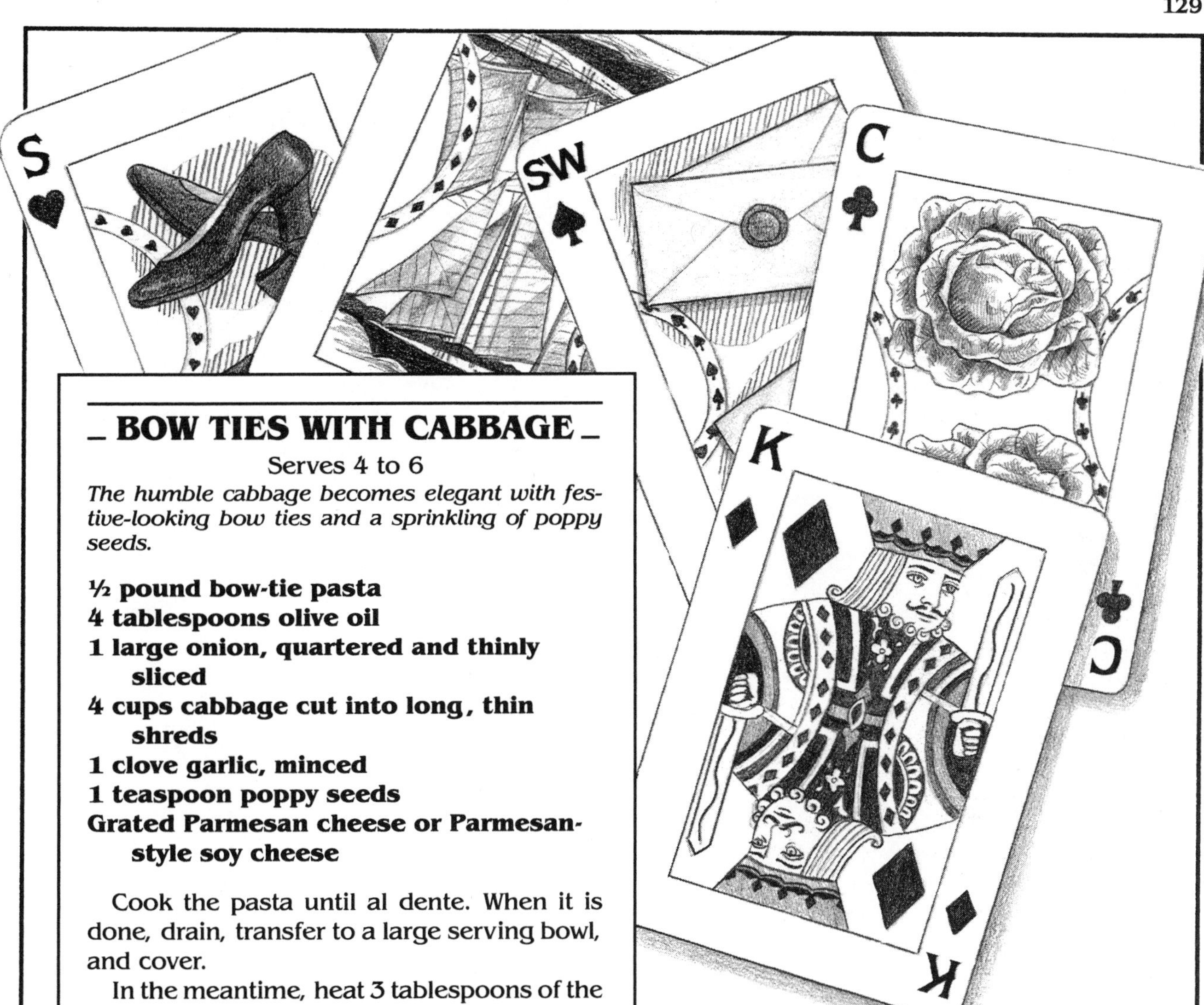

BOW TIES WITH CABBAGE

Serves 4 to 6

The humble cabbage becomes elegant with festive-looking bow ties and a sprinkling of poppy seeds.

½ pound bow-tie pasta
4 tablespoons olive oil
1 large onion, quartered and thinly sliced
4 cups cabbage cut into long, thin shreds
1 clove garlic, minced
1 teaspoon poppy seeds
Grated Parmesan cheese or Parmesan-style soy cheese

Cook the pasta until al dente. When it is done, drain, transfer to a large serving bowl, and cover.

In the meantime, heat 3 tablespoons of the olive oil in a large skillet with 2 tablespoons of water. Add the onion, cabbage, and garlic. Sauté, covered, over moderate heat, until the cabbage is tender and everything is lightly browned, about 20 minutes. Combine the cooked pasta with the cabbage mixture and the remaining olive oil in the serving bowl and toss together. Sprinkle in the poppy seeds and toss again. Serve at once, and pass around the Parmesan cheese.

"The time has come," the Walrus said,
"to talk of many things,
Of shoes—and ships—and
sealing wax—
Of Cabbages and Kings . . ."

—Lewis Carroll
Through the Looking-Glass (1871)

Yankee Doodle came to town
Riding on a pony
Stuck a feather in his cap
And called it "Macaroni."

These lyrics are familiar to so many English-speaking children, yet who has ever wondered why that feather was called "macaroni"? It's not as nonsensical as it might seem.

SHELLS WITH BEANS AND BROCCOLI

Serves 6

Broccoli is a vegetable of Italian origin, long known to have a wonderful affinity with pasta. The addition of beans makes this a very substantial dish.

½ pound small shell pasta
2 tablespoons olive oil
2 cups broccoli florets, steamed
2 cloves garlic, minced
1 small green or red bell pepper, cut into julienne strips
2 cups cooked or canned navy beans (about ¾ cup raw, cooked following the directions on page 215)
½ cup chopped or sliced black olives
2 tablespoons chopped fresh basil or ½ teaspoon dried basil
½ teaspoon dried oregano
Salt and freshly ground pepper to taste
Grated Parmesan cheese or Parmesan-style soy cheese for topping, optional

Cook the pasta al dente. When it is done, drain and transfer to a covered casserole dish.

In the meantime, heat the olive oil plus 2 tablespoons of water in a large skillet. Add the broccoli, garlic, and bell pepper and sauté over moderate heat until the broccoli and pepper are crisp-tender. Add all of the remaining ingredients except the last 2 and sauté for another 5 minutes or until well heated through, stirring frequently. Combine the skillet mixture with the pasta in the casserole dish and toss well. Add salt and pepper to taste, and top each serving with grated Parmesan cheese.

PASTA WITH CAULIFLOWER, CURRANTS, AND NUTS

Serves 6

Cauliflower, like broccoli, goes beautifully with pasta. The currants give this rich dish an unexpected flavor twist without making it sweet.

1½ cups part-skim ricotta cheese
3 tablespoons grated Parmesan cheese
½ cup low-fat milk
Dash nutmeg
½ pound medium-sized shaped pasta, such as rotelle or ziti
2 tablespoons olive oil
1 small head cauliflower, cut into bite-sized pieces and florets
⅓ cup toasted pine nuts or ½ cup chopped walnuts
⅓ cup currants (raisins may be substituted)
Salt and freshly ground pepper to taste

Combine the first 4 ingredients in a small bowl, mix well, and set aside.

Cook the pasta al dente. When it is done, drain, transfer to a large serving bowl, and cover.

In the meantime, heat the olive oil in a large skillet. Sauté the cauliflower pieces over moderate heat until crisp-tender and just starting to brown lightly. Add a small amount of water if the skillet starts to get dry. Remove from the heat.

In the large bowl, combine the cooked pasta and cauliflower with the remaining ingredients and toss well. Serve at once.

During the 1700s, when an English soldier wrote the lyrics of "Yankee Doodle Dandy," macaroni was new to England and quickly became a very popular, and indeed, quite a fashionable food. As a result, anything elegant or stylish, whether it was clothing, food, music, manners, or a feather in one's cap, was called "macaroni," so positive was the connotation of the word.

Your hat is so simple, yet so smart, and so very, very Macaroni!

LINGUINI AGLIO OLIO WITH ZUCCHINI

Serves 6 generously

A friend who grew up with traditional Italian cookery contributed this recipe for Aglio Olio (which means garlic and oil), a simple but delicious and fragrant Italian classic.

1 pound linguini, broken in half
½ cup extra-virgin olive oil
8 cloves garlic, minced
3 medium zucchini, quartered lengthwise and sliced
¼ cup chopped fresh parsley
1 teaspoon dried oregano
Salt and freshly ground pepper to taste
½ cup grated Parmesan cheese

Cook the linguini al dente. When it is done, drain, transfer to a large, deep serving bowl, and cover.

While the pasta is cooking, heat half the olive oil in a large skillet. Add the garlic and sauté over low heat for 2 minutes, stirring frequently. Add the zucchini and sauté over low heat, stirring frequently. Just before the zucchini is tender, add the parsley and sauté until it is slightly wilted and the zucchini is tender but not browned. Remove from the heat and combine with the linguini in the serving bowl. Add the remaining olive oil, oregano, and salt and pepper, and toss well. Add the Parmesan cheese and toss again.

"Garlicke ingendreth naughty and sharp blood."

—John Gerarde
The Herball (1636)

CURRIED ZITI WITH BROCCOLI AND CHICK-PEAS

Serves 6

Adding a curry flavor to pasta is not the usual thing to do, but this blend of Italian and Indian flavors has a nice synergy.

½ pound ziti
2 tablespoons margarine
1 medium onion, chopped
1 or 2 cloves garlic, minced
1 pound very ripe tomatoes, chopped, or 14-ounce can imported plum tomatoes with liquid, chopped
2 tablespoons minced fresh parsley or cilantro
1 recipe Curry Cheese Sauce (page 54)
3 heaping cups broccoli, cut into bite-sized pieces and steamed
1½ cups cooked or canned chick-peas (about ⅔ cup raw, cooked following the directions on page 215)
Salt and freshly ground pepper to taste

Cook the pasta al dente. When it is done, drain and transfer to a large covered casserole dish.

In the meantime, heat the margarine in a large skillet. Add the onion and garlic and sauté over moderate heat until golden. If using fresh tomatoes, add them and cook until they have softened, then stir in the parsley or cilantro; if using canned tomatoes, simply add them to the skillet along with the parsley or cilantro. Add the remaining ingredients and simmer for 10 to 15 minutes. Add more curry powder or Home-Mixed Curry if desired.

Pour over the pasta, toss together, and serve at once.

DOUBLE SPINACH NOODLES

Serves 4 to 6

½ pound spinach noodles or spinach fettucine
2 tablespoons margarine
2 cloves garlic, minced
1½ cups sliced mushrooms
1 pound fresh spinach, stemmed, well washed, and chopped
1 cup reduced-fat sour cream
¼ cup grated Parmesan cheese
2 tablespoons minced fresh basil or 1½ teaspoons dried basil leaves
½ teaspoon dried oregano
Dash nutmeg
Salt and freshly ground pepper to taste

Cook the spinach noodles al dente. When they are done, drain and transfer to a covered container.

In the meantime, melt the margarine in a large skillet. Add the garlic and mushrooms and sauté over low heat until the mushrooms are about half done. Add the spinach, cover, and cook over low heat until it has wilted. Add the cooked noodles and the remaining ingredients and simmer over low heat for about 10 minutes.

A frog he would a-wooing go,
Whether his mother would let him
or no.
With a rowley, powley, gammon
and spinach,
Heigh ho! says Anthony Rowley.

—Old English Nursery Rhyme

"Music is like spaghetti. If you like spaghetti, you do not eat it morning, noon, and night. You only have it once in a while. It should be kept distant so that you have a real hunger for it."

—Dimitri Mitropoulos,
quoted by Giuseppe Prezzolini in
Spaghetti Dinner (1955)

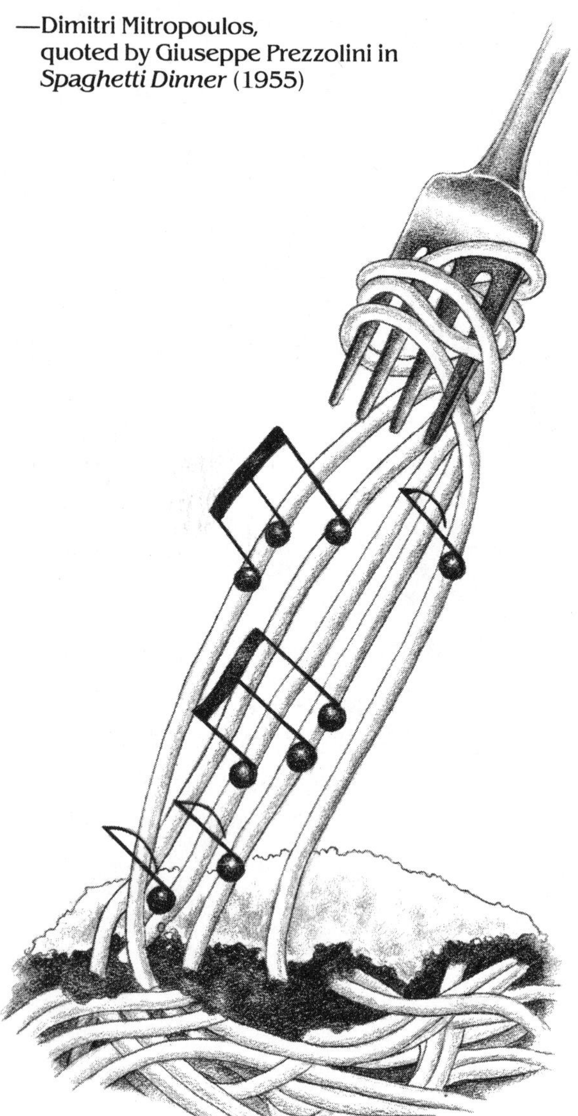

VERMICELLI PRIMAVERA

Serves 4 to 6

Primavera *means spring in Italian, and it is also the name of a light dish that combines pasta with fresh vegetables. You may substitute other spring vegetables if you like.*

2½ tablespoons olive oil
3 or 4 cloves garlic, minced
2 cups chopped or sliced mushrooms
1½ cups string beans or asparagus, cut into 1-inch pieces and steamed
1½ cups finely chopped broccoli or fresh green peas, steamed
2 cups finely chopped cauliflower, steamed
14-ounce can imported plum tomatoes with liquid, chopped
½ teaspoon dried oregano
¼ teaspoon dried thyme
Dash dried rosemary
Fresh parsley and/or basil leaves to taste
½ pound vermicelli (extra-thin spaghetti)
Salt and freshly ground pepper to taste
Grated Parmesan cheese or Parmesan-style soy cheese for topping

Heat the olive oil in a large skillet. Add the garlic and sauté over low heat until golden. Add the mushrooms and cook until they are slightly wilted, then add the remaining ingredients except the last 3. Cover and simmer over very low heat for 8 to 10 minutes.

In the meantime, cook the vermicelli al dente. When it is done, drain and combine in a large bowl with the vegetable mixture. Toss together. Season with salt and pepper and toss again. Top each serving with grated Parmesan cheese.

QUICK TOMATO-HERB PASTA SAUCE

Serves 4 to 6 with pasta

For those of us who don't have the time to make long-simmering pasta sauces, this quick version is quite satisfactory.

2 tablespoons olive oil
2 or 3 cloves garlic, minced
14-ounce can imported plum tomatoes with liquid, chopped
14-ounce can crushed or pureed tomatoes
3 tablespoons minced fresh parsley
1 tablespoon minced fresh basil, optional
2 teaspoons Italian herb seasoning mix
Salt and freshly ground pepper to taste

Heat the olive oil in a large, heavy saucepan. Add the garlic and sauté over low heat until golden. Add all the remaining ingredients, stir together, and cover. Simmer over low heat for 15 minutes, stirring occasionally and leaving the cover on slightly ajar so that the steam can escape.

Variations:
Add approximately 2 cups of sautéed vegetables, such as eggplant, zucchini, mushrooms, or a combination; or 2 cups of steamed, chopped broccoli; or ½ cup of chopped black olives.

"Don't be intimidated by foreign cookery. Tomatoes and oregano make it Italian. Wine and tarragon make it French. Sour cream makes it Russian. Lemon and cinnamon make it Greek. Soy sauce makes it Chinese. Garlic makes it good. Now you are an International Cook."

—Alice May Brock
Alice's Restaurant Cookbook (1969)

Basil was once an emblem of love in Italy. A young man wishing to marry his sweetheart might approach her with a sprig of basil in his hair or hat.

FETTUCINE ALFREDO WITH MUSHROOMS AND BASIL

Serves 4 to 6

Fresh basil's wonderful affinity with pasta is highlighted in this recipe and the next, this one with a lightened version of classic Alfredo sauce. Though still somewhat rich, it at least does away with the requisite heavy cream and egg yolks. Look for fresh basil in late summer and early autumn, when it is sold in large, fragrant bunches in produce stores and at farmers' markets.

¾ pound white or green fettucine
2 tablespoons olive oil
½ pound coarsely chopped mushrooms
⅔ cup chopped fresh basil leaves
1½ cups whole milk
2 tablespoons margarine
3 tablespoons unbleached white flour
⅓ cup grated Parmesan cheese
Salt and freshly ground pepper to taste

Cook the fettucine al dente. When it is done, drain, transfer to a large casserole dish, and cover.

In the meantime, heat the olive oil in a skillet. Add the mushrooms and sauté over moderately low heat until tender. Stir in the basil leaves, remove from the heat, and cover.

Heat the milk and margarine in a heavy saucepan. Meanwhile, dissolve the flour in just enough water to make it smooth and pourable. When the milk is just under the boiling point, pour in the dissolved flour slowly, stirring constantly with a whisk. Turn to moderately low heat and whisk almost continuously until the mixture thickens. Then add the grated Parmesan cheese, and the mushrooms and basil. Pour over the fettucine, toss, and add salt and freshly ground pepper to taste.

ROTELLE WITH TOMATOES, ARTICHOKES, AND BASIL

Serves 4 to 6

Rotelle, a corkscrew-shaped pasta, is an excellent receptacle for this light, zesty sauce made of fresh tomatoes, basil, and marinated artichokes. This summer pasta dish is a favorite of mine, and I think anyone who loves fresh basil will also enjoy it.

½ pound rotelle
1 tablespoon olive oil
1 or 2 cloves garlic, minced
1 medium sweet red bell pepper, cut into julienne strips
1 pound very ripe tomatoes, diced
½ cup firmly packed chopped fresh basil leaves, or more or less to taste
¾ pound marinated artichoke hearts, either from jars or bought by weight
1 tablespoon red wine vinegar
1 teaspoon dried oregano
Salt and freshly ground pepper to taste
1½ cups diced mozzarella or Gruyère cheese, optional

Cook the pasta al dente. When it is done, drain and transfer to a covered casserole dish.

In the meantime, heat the olive oil in a large skillet. Add the garlic and red pepper and sauté until the pepper is softened but not browned. Add the tomatoes and sauté just until they have lost their raw quality; do not let them soften. Add the remaining ingredients, except for the cheese, and cook until just heated through.

Combine the pasta with the vegetable mixture in the casserole dish and toss together. This dish is best served warm or even at room temperature, not hot. Once the mixture has cooled down, add the diced cheese and toss again.

In ancient Greece, it was believed that unless the sowing of basil was accompanied by cursing or railing, it would not flourish.

VEGETABLE LO MEIN

Serves 4 to 6

Since noodles most likely originated in the Orient, some of the most delectable ways to prepare them come from that part of the world. Several possibilities are presented on the next pages.

½ pound spaghetti or linguini, broken in half
2 tablespoons sesame oil
3 heaping cups broccoli, cut into bite-sized pieces and florets
1 medium onion, chopped
2 medium celery stalks, sliced diagonally
1 cup firmly packed fresh bean sprouts
6- or 8-ounce can bamboo shoots
1¼ cups thawed frozen green peas
1 recipe Basic Chinese Sauce (page 52)
Soy sauce to taste, optional

Cook the noodles al dente and drain. In the meantime, heat the sesame oil and 3 tablespoons of water in a wok. Add the broccoli and onion and stir-fry over moderately high heat for 2 to 3 minutes, then add the celery and stir-fry until it is nearly crisp-tender. Add the bean sprouts and stir-fry just until they are wilted. Add the bamboo shoots and peas, stir-fry until they are heated through, then remove from the heat. Pour the Basic Chinese Sauce over the vegetables and return to moderate heat just until everything is heated through. Combine the vegetables and noodles in a serving bowl and toss well. Add soy sauce to taste if desired.

SWEET-AND-SOUR BUCKWHEAT NOODLES WITH ASPARAGUS

Serves 4 to 6

1 tablespoon safflower or peanut oil
1 tablespoon sesame oil
1 medium onion, chopped
2 cloves garlic, minced
1½ pounds asparagus, trimmed and cut into 1-inch lengths
14-ounce can imported plum tomatoes with liquid, chopped
¼ cup dry white wine
3 tablespoons rice vinegar
3 tablespoons honey
3 tablespoons soy sauce
1½ tablespoons cornstarch
½ pound buckwheat noodles (soba), broken in half
Freshly ground black pepper

Heat the oils in a large skillet or wok. Add the onion and garlic and sauté until the onion is translucent. Add the asparagus and stir-fry over moderately high heat until it is crisp-tender, about 5 to 7 minutes. Add the tomatoes, wine, vinegar, honey, and soy sauce. Dissolve the cornstarch in a small amount of water and stir into the mixture. Lower the heat and simmer.

Cook the buckwheat noodles al dente. When they are done, drain and rinse briefly under cool running water. Stir them into the skillet or wok and season to taste with freshly ground black pepper. Cook, stirring, for another minute, then serve at once.

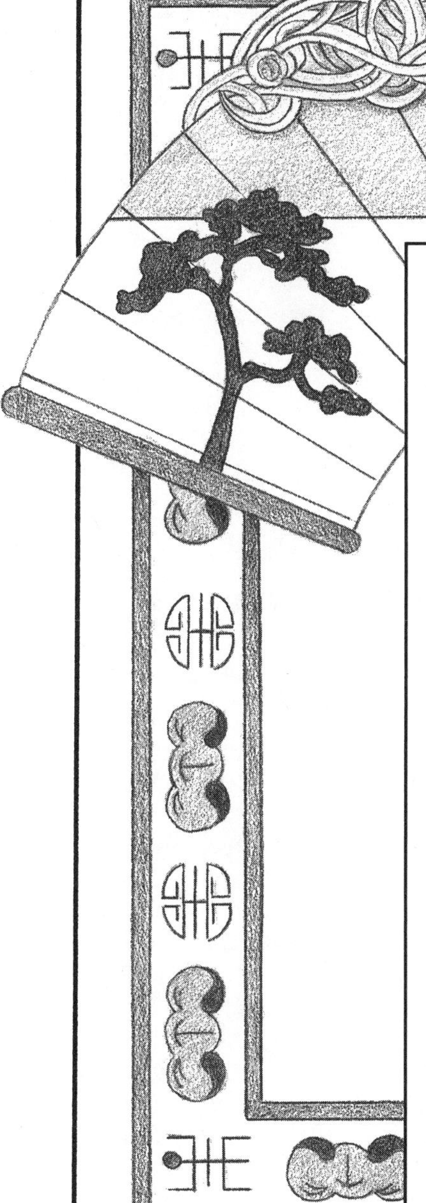

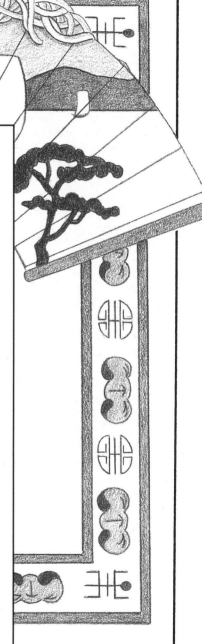

BUCKWHEAT NOODLES WITH SNOW PEAS

Serves 4 to 6

Buckwheat is used more extensively in the Far East than in the West; in Japan, it is used to make buckwheat noodles, or soba, which have a hearty, slightly nutty flavor. For Japanese families, these noodles symbolize friendship, festivity, and wealth, and so it is traditional to eat them on New Year's Eve as a harbinger of prosperity for the upcoming year. Look for buckwheat noodles in Oriental food stores.

2 tablespoons sesame oil
1 large onion, cut in half and sliced
1 large carrot, thinly sliced
1½ to 2 cups snow peas
½ pound buckwheat noodles (soba)
1 recipe Basic Chinese Sauce (page 52)
Soy sauce to taste

Heat the sesame oil in a large skillet or wok. Stir-fry the onion and carrot over moderately high heat until crisp-tender. Add the snow peas and stir-fry just until they have lost their raw quality but are still quite crisp.

Break the noodles in half and cook them al dente. Watch them carefully, as they cook rather quickly. Drain and add to the vegetable mixture along with the Basic Chinese Sauce. Toss together. Cook just until everything is thoroughly heated through. Serve with extra soy sauce.

COLD SESAME NOODLES

Serves 4 to 6

Sesame noodles are a vegetarian favorite. Some recipes call for peanut butter, but this version is rich with the flavor of tahini.

1 large celery stalk
1 medium turnip, peeled
1 large carrot
1 tablespoon sesame oil
2 cloves garlic, minced
¾ pound udon noodles or linguini

Sauce:
⅓ cup tahini (sesame paste)
2 tablespoons miso (see page 29)
2 teaspoons sesame oil
1 tablespoon honey
2 tablespoons dry sherry
1 tablespoon rice vinegar or white wine vinegar
1 teaspoon freshly grated ginger
Cayenne pepper to taste
2 tablespoons sesame seeds

Cut the celery, turnip, and carrot into 1½- to 2-inch-long matchstick-shaped pieces. Heat the sesame oil and 2 tablespoons of water in a skillet. Add the garlic and matchstick-cut vegetables. Stir-fry just until crisp-tender.

In the meantime, cook the noodles al dente. When they are done, drain and rinse under cool water until they are just warm.

Combine all the sauce ingredients in a small bowl with ½ cup warm water and whisk together until well blended. Use your own judgment with the ginger and cayenne; this dish can be mildly spicy to very fiery, depending on how much of each you use.

Combine the vegetables with the noodles and sauce in a serving bowl and toss together until the noodles are evenly coated with the sauce. Serve at once.

UDON WITH SPINACH-MISO PESTO

Serves 4 to 6

Miso adds a rich, hearty flavor to this pesto, making a bold substitute for Parmesan cheese.

Pesto sauce:
¾ pound spinach, washed and stemmed
½ cup firmly packed fresh basil
¼ cup walnuts
¼ cup olive oil
2 tablespoons miso, or more or less to taste
2 tablespoons chopped fresh parsley

½ pound udon noodles
1 tablespoon olive oil
2 cloves garlic, crushed or minced
1 Italian frying pepper, seeded and minced
14-ounce can imported plum tomatoes with liquid, chopped
¼ cup sliced black olives
Freshly ground pepper to taste

Steam the spinach just until it is wilted. Squeeze out as much moisture as possible, then place the spinach in the container of a food processor along with the rest of the pesto ingredients. Process until the mixture is a coarse puree.

Cook the udon noodles al dente. Drain and transfer to a serving container. Toss with the pesto and cover.

Heat the olive oil in a medium-sized skillet. Add the garlic and frying pepper and sauté over low heat until the garlic is golden. Add the tomatoes, olives, and black pepper and simmer over low heat for 5 minutes. Stir this mixture into the noodles and serve at once, or let cool and serve at room temperature.

RICE STICKS WITH EXOTIC MUSHROOMS

Serves 4 to 6

Look for the mushrooms and the delicate-tasting rice-stick noodles in natural food stores or Oriental groceries.

½ ounce dried cloud-ear mushrooms
2 tablespoons unrefined peanut oil
1 teaspoon sesame oil
1 medium onion, halved and sliced
2 cloves garlic, minced
2 cups firmly packed thinly sliced white or savoy cabbage
15-ounce can oyster (shimeji) or straw mushrooms
2 tablespoons soy sauce
8-ounce bundle rice sticks
1½ cups liquid from canned and dried mushrooms
1½ tablespoons cornstarch

If using cloud-ears, cover them with boiling water in a covered ovenproof dish and soak for about 45 minutes. Cut them into thin strips about 2 inches long. Reserve the liquid.

Heat the oils in a large heavy skillet or wok. Add the onion and stir-fry until translucent. Add the garlic and cabbage and stir-fry until the cabbage is crisp-tender. Add the mushrooms and soy sauce and stir-fry for another minute or so.

Bring water to a boil in a medium-sized saucepan. Immerse the bundle of rice sticks and simmer for 3 to 5 minutes, until they are done. Drain, place on a cutting board, and chop in several places to shorten.

Use a bit of the mushroom liquid to dissolve the cornstarch. Pour the remaining liquid into the skillet or wok and stir in the dissolved cornstarch. Add the cooked rice sticks and toss the mixture together throughly but gently. Serve at once.

FRIED EGG NOODLES

Serves 4 to 6

This recipe was inspired by traditional dishes of Malaysia and Singapore. Use Oriental egg noodles or substitute standard egg noodles.

6 to 8 dried shiitake mushrooms
½ pound narrow ribbon egg noodles
3 tablespoons peanut oil
3 large celery stalks, sliced diagonally
2 to 3 cloves garlic, minced
10-ounce package frozen French-cut string beans, thawed
2 to 3 tablespoons soy sauce, to taste
1 tablespoon dry sherry, optional
1 teaspoon freshly grated ginger
1 tablespoon safflower oil
2 eggs, beaten
Minced scallions for garnish

Soak the mushrooms for 15 minutes in hot water. Drain and reserve the liquid for another use; trim and discard the tough stems and slice the caps into strips.

Cook the egg noodles al dente. When they are done, drain.

In the meantime, heat the peanut oil in a large skillet or wok. Add the celery and garlic and stir-fry over moderately high heat until the celery is crisp-tender. Add the noodles, mushrooms, string beans, soy sauce, optional sherry, and ginger and stir-fry for 10 minutes. Lower the heat and continue to fry, stirring occasionally, until the noodles begin to brown lightly.

Heat the safflower oil in a small skillet. When it is hot enough to make a drop of water sizzle, pour in the beaten eggs. Fry until set on top, then flip and fry briefly on the other side. Remove from the skillet and cut into narrow strips.

Remove the noodle mixture from the heat. Serve at once, garnishing each serving with strips of egg and some minced scallion.

CORN PASTA WITH PESTO AND FRESH CORN

Serves 4 to 6

Abounding with fresh corn, basil, and tomatoes, this aromatic dish is perfect for a quick summer supper. Corn pasta is a tasty alternative to wheat pasta, and a boon to those who are allergic to wheat.

Pesto:
1 cup fresh basil leaves
½ cup fresh parsley leaves
½ cup pine nuts or walnuts
1 or 2 cloves garlic
⅓ cup freshly grated Parmesan cheese
⅓ cup olive oil
Freshly ground black pepper to taste

½ pound corn pasta, preferably shells or elbows
2 medium ears fresh, cooked sweet corn
2 large ripe tomatoes, finely diced
1 tablespoon lemon juice

Place all the ingredients for the pesto in the container of a food processor and process to a coarse puree.

Cook the pasta al dente. When it is done, drain and transfer to a serving bowl. Toss gently with the pesto.

Scrape the corn kernels off the cob with a sharp knife. Add them, along with the tomatoes and lemon juice, to the pasta mixture. Toss gently but thoroughly and serve at once.

WHOLE WHEAT PASTA WITH RED PEPPER SAUCE

Serves 4 to 6

4 large sweet red bell peppers
½ pound whole wheat pasta, preferably small shapes such as shells or twists
3 tablespoons extra-virgin olive oil
2 cloves garlic, minced
2 medium ripe, juicy tomatoes
2 tablespoons unbleached white flour
1 cup low-fat milk or soymilk
2 to 3 tablespoons fresh chopped basil
½ teaspoon dried oregano
1 tablespoon red wine vinegar
Salt and freshly ground pepper to taste
Grated Parmesan cheese or Parmesan-style soy cheese for topping

Place the red peppers under a broiler and broil on all sides until the skin is charred. Let them cool in a paper bag.

Meanwhile, cook the pasta al dente. When it is done, drain and transfer to a covered serving dish.

When the peppers are cool enough to handle, slip the skins off, remove the seeds and stems, and cut them into approximately 1-inch dice. Set aside.

Heat the oil in a heavy saucepan. Add the garlic and sauté over moderate heat for 1 minute. Add the tomatoes and cook until they have softened a bit, about 5 minutes. Sprinkle in the flour and continue to stir until it dissolves. Reduce the heat and slowly stir in the milk or soymilk. Add the red peppers, basil, and oregano and cook, stirring, until the sauce thickens, about 5 to 8 minutes. Remove from the heat and stir in the vinegar. Pour over the pasta and toss together well. Season to taste with salt and pepper and serve at once, topping each serving with Parmesan cheese, if desired.

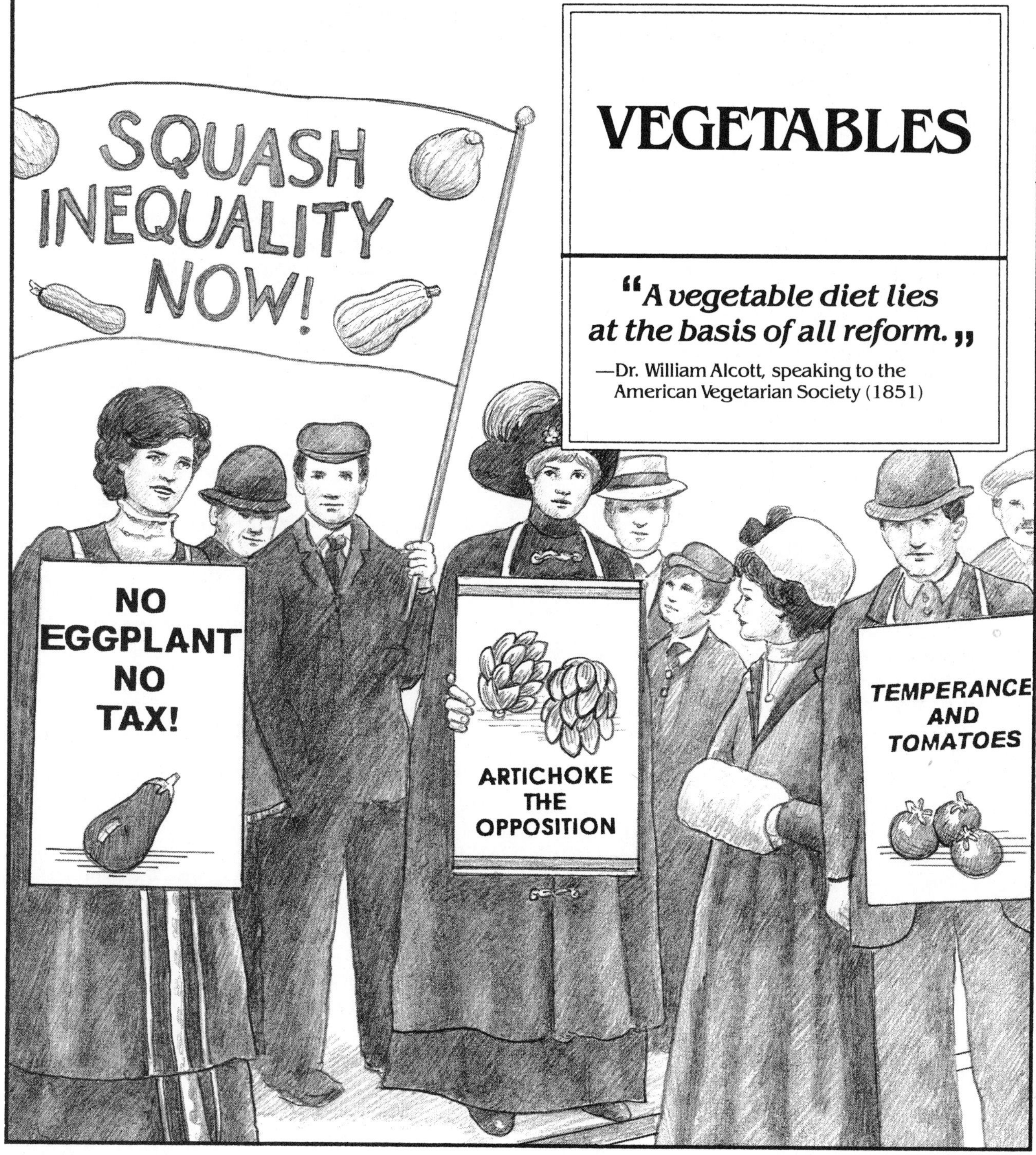

VEGETABLES

“A vegetable diet lies at the basis of all reform.”

—Dr. William Alcott, speaking to the American Vegetarian Society (1851)

The word "vegetable" is one of the vaguest in the culinary vocabulary. The Merriam-Webster dictionary defines a vegetable as a "usually herbaceous plant grown for an edible part that is usually eaten with the principal course of a meal."

When Dr. William Alcott declared that "a vegetable diet lies at the basis of all reform," it is safe to assume that he was speaking of anything edible in the plant kingdom, including grains, legumes, and nuts, yet these are not defined as vegetables, although they may in some way fit the dictionary definition. To add to the confusion, some vegetables are actually fruits botanically, including tomatoes, cucumbers, and the squash family, the latter being closely related to the melon family. Just as some vegetables are the fruits of a plant, others derive from differing parts of plants—cauliflower and broccoli are flowers, cabbage and the lettuces are leaves, asparagus is a stalk, carrots and turnips are roots.

So, while we do have a pretty clear idea of what we consider to be vegetables, it is more difficult to actually define what one is. A battle over this question once went all the way to the U.S. Supreme Court—more on that later in this chapter. You will find recipes in this chapter that concentrate on a select group of vegetables, garnished with some of their fascinating histories.

HERBED VEGETABLE BREAD LOAF

Serves 4 to 6

Nothing enhances the flavor of vegetables like herbs, as the recipes on these two pages will attest.

3 tablespoons margarine
1 medium carrot, cut into quarters lengthwise and sliced
2 cloves garlic, minced
1 medium sweet red or green bell pepper, finely chopped
1 medium zucchini, finely diced
4 eggs, beaten
2 tablespoons low-fat milk
1 cup cooked fresh or thawed frozen corn kernels
1 cup thawed frozen green peas
4 average slices whole-grain bread, cut into ½-inch-square pieces
2 tablespoons minced fresh parsley
1 tablespoon minced chives or scallions
½ teaspoon each dried thyme, dried oregano, and dried summer savory
¼ teaspoon each ground cumin and dry mustard
Wheat germ or sunflower seeds for topping

Preheat over to 350° F.

Heat the margarine in a medium-sized skillet. Add the carrot and garlic and sauté over moderately low heat until both are golden. Add the red or green pepper and zucchini and sauté until they are just tender.

In a mixing bowl, beat the eggs well with the milk. Add all the remaining ingredients except the topping and mix thoroughly. Pour into an oiled 9-by-5-inch loaf pan, sprinkle with wheat germ, and bake for 50 minutes or until nicely browned. Let stand for 10 minutes before serving. Cut into slices to serve.

KUKU SABZI (Persian Spinach and Fresh Herbs Pie)

Serves 4 to 6

Persian kukus are very much like frittatas. Some time is required for preparation, with all the stemming and chopping, but this is an unusual treat for anyone who loves the strong flavor of fresh herbs.

1 pound fresh spinach, stemmed, well washed, and chopped
¾ cup chopped fresh parsley or ½ cup chopped fresh parsley and ¼ cup chopped fresh basil leaves
¼ cup chopped fresh dill
3 scallions, chopped
3 eggs
½ cup fine bread crumbs
1 teaspoon good curry powder or Home-Mixed Curry (page 207)
Salt and freshly ground pepper to taste

In a large skillet, steam the spinach over moderate heat, covered, until wilted but still bright green (you may have to do half at a time). Transfer the steamed spinach to a colander and squeeze out as much liquid as possible.

Place the spinach in a mixing bowl and add all the fresh herbs, including the scallions. Break the eggs right into the mixture, then add all the remaining ingredients and mix thoroughly. To cook, follow the instructions on page 216, How to Fry and Flip a Skillet Pie or Frittata. Cut into wedges to serve.

"Much virtue in herbs, little in men."

—Benjamin Franklin
Poor Richard's Almanack (1734)

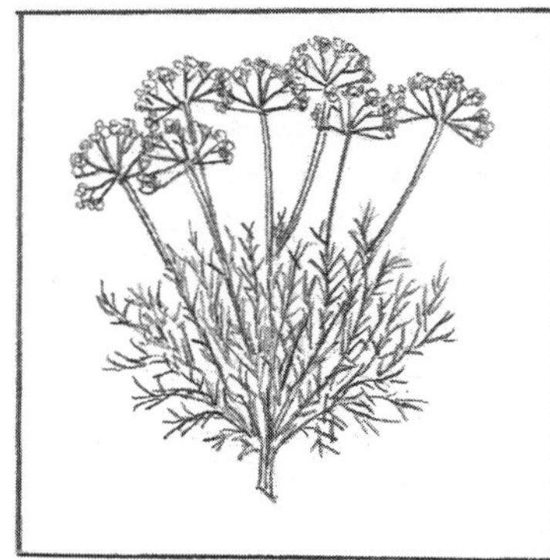

Dill Anethum graveolens, L

Virtues: An herb of savor and beauty, it soothes the stomach, cures hiccoughs, and works against witchcraft. For cookery, there are few herbs more welcome than dill.

Boris Clary Homo Sapiens

Virtues: Rarely smokes and tells lies infrequently.

STIR-FRIED ALMOND BROCCOLI AND CAULIFLOWER

Serves 4 to 6

Broccoli and cauliflower are both members of the cabbage family, and they not only complement each other's flavor, they look very appetizing together.

2 tablespoons sesame oil
2 cloves garlic, minced
4 tablespoons dry sherry or dry white wine
2 tablespoons soy sauce
3 heaping cups broccoli, cut into bite-sized pieces and florets
3 heaping cups cauliflower, cut into bite-sized pieces and florets
½ cup sliced or slivered almonds

Heat the sesame oil in a wok. Add the garlic and sauté over low heat for 1 minute or so. Add the sherry, soy sauce, and 2 tablespoons of water. Turn the heat to moderately high and add the broccoli and cauliflower. Stir quickly to coat the vegetables with the liquid and continue to stir-fry until they are just crisp-tender. Add the almonds and stir-fry just until they are well distributed. Serve at once.

"Opinyuns are jist like any other kind ov vegetable—worth jist what they will fetch."

—Josh Billings
Josh Billings' Farmer's Alminax (ca. 1870)

BROCCOLI BREAD PUDDING

Serves 4 to 6

This simple but delicious way to highlight broccoli has become a standard offering for my family, and guests enjoy it, too.

2 tablespoons margarine
1 large onion, chopped
1 clove garlic, minced
4 cups finely chopped broccoli
1 teaspoon each dried basil and dried dill
Salt and freshly ground pepper to taste
4 eggs, beaten
¼ cup low-fat milk
1 cup cottage cheese
½ cup reduced-fat sour cream
4 average slices whole-grain bread, torn into small pieces
Wheat germ and sesame seeds for topping

Preheat the oven to 350° F.

Heat the margarine in a large skillet. Add the onion and sauté over moderate heat until translucent. Add the garlic, broccoli, and seasonings and continue to sauté until the onion is nicely browned and the broccoli is tender but still bright green.

In the meantime, beat the eggs and milk together. Stir in the cottage cheese, sour cream, and bread. Stir in the broccoli mixture and mix thoroughly.

Pour the mixture into an oiled 2-quart baking dish and sprinkle first with wheat germ and then with sesame seeds. Bake for 35 to 40 minutes or until the top is nicely browned.

CAULIFLOWER-AVOCADO BAKE

Serves 4 to 6

1 large head cauliflower
Salt and freshly ground pepper to taste
1 medium ripe avocado, peeled and cut into small dice
2 tablespoons safflower oil
1 medium sweet red or green bell pepper, cut into julienne strips
2 to 3 scallions, chopped
3 tablespoons finely chopped fresh parsley
1 cup firmly packed grated mild cheese or soy cheese
Sesame seeds for topping

Preheat the oven to 350° F.

Cut the cauliflower into bite-sized pieces and florets and steam or stir-fry them until crisp-tender. Season with a bit of salt and pepper. Oil a large shallow baking dish and arrange the cauliflower pieces in it. Sprinkle the diced avocado over the cauliflower.

Heat the oil in a small skillet. Add the red or green pepper and sauté over moderate heat until it softens a bit, then add the scallions and parsley and sauté until they are wilted. Spread this mixture evenly over the cauliflower and avocado and top with the grated cheese. Sprinkle the sesame seeds generously over the top. Bake for 20 minutes.

"Training is everything. The peach was once a bitter almond; cauliflower is nothing but cabbage with a college education."

—Mark Twain
Pudd'nhead Wilson (1896)

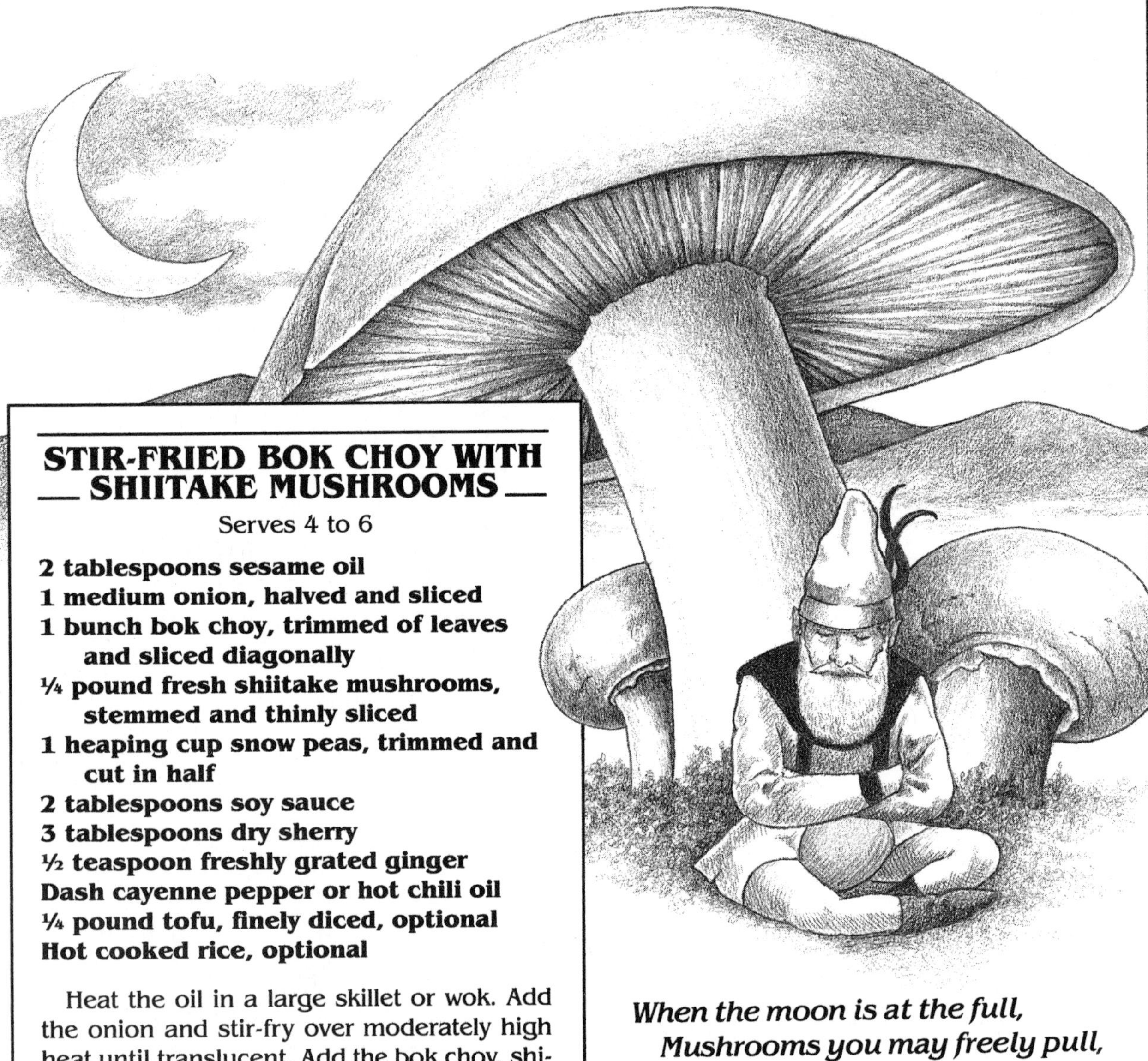

STIR-FRIED BOK CHOY WITH SHIITAKE MUSHROOMS

Serves 4 to 6

2 tablespoons sesame oil
1 medium onion, halved and sliced
1 bunch bok choy, trimmed of leaves and sliced diagonally
¼ pound fresh shiitake mushrooms, stemmed and thinly sliced
1 heaping cup snow peas, trimmed and cut in half
2 tablespoons soy sauce
3 tablespoons dry sherry
½ teaspoon freshly grated ginger
Dash cayenne pepper or hot chili oil
¼ pound tofu, finely diced, optional
Hot cooked rice, optional

Heat the oil in a large skillet or wok. Add the onion and stir-fry over moderately high heat until translucent. Add the bok choy, shiitakes, snow peas, soy sauce, and sherry. Stir-fry until the vegetables are crisp-tender. Add the ginger, cayenne, and optional tofu. Season with additional soy sauce if desired and serve at once over hot cooked rice or on its own as a side dish.

When the moon is at the full,
Mushrooms you may freely pull,
But when the moon is on the wane,
Wait ere you think to pluck again.

—Old English Rhyme

MUSHROOM BREAD PUDDING

Serves 4 to 6

1 tablespoon margarine
1 pound mushrooms, sliced
3 eggs
1 cup reduced-fat sour cream
⅓ cup grated Parmesan cheese
½ teaspoon dried basil
¼ teaspoon each dried thyme and dried summer savory
Salt and freshly ground pepper to taste
Fresh French or Italian bread, as needed, cut into ½-inch-thick slices

Preheat the oven to 325° F.

Heat the margarine in a large skillet. Add the mushrooms and sauté over moderate heat until just tender. Remove from the heat and drain off excess liquid.

In a mixing bowl, beat the eggs until bubbly, then stir in the sour cream. Add the mushrooms and all of the remaining ingredients except the bread and mix thoroughly.

Oil a deep 9-by-9-inch casserole dish and line the bottom completely with a single layer of the sliced bread. Pour half of the mushroom mixture evenly over it. Add another layer of bread and the rest of the mushroom mixture. Bake for 25 minutes.

Mushrooms, which today are considered almost a delicacy, had to overcome a bad reputation of long standing. They were once considered a wicked food, as these two seventeenth-century writers will attest:

"Many have eaten and do eat mushrooms more for wantonnesse than for neede . . ."

—John Gerarde
The Herball (1636)

"I have the same opinion of dances that physicians have of mushrooms: the best of them are good for nothing."

—Saint Francis de Sales
Introduction to the
Devout Life (1609)

Fairies and other sprites had a strong affinity with mushrooms, having often been seen dancing, cavorting, or just resting around them. Perhaps this association with the impish creatures fueled the notion that mushrooms meant mischief.

Few people I know dislike eggplant, yet as with mushrooms, it has had a very turbulent history, as evidenced by the variety of strange names it has had. In Italian, it is called "melanzana," a corruption of the ancient Latin "mala insana," which translated into English as Raging Apple or Mad Apple. John Gerarde in his Herball *(1636) concluded that "... doubtless these Apples have a mischievous qualitie, the use whereof is utterly to be forsaken."*

In the Bible, the Apple of Sodom was a large purple eggplant. Its outward beauty was deceptive, for its fruit would turn to ash on the lips of anyone who tried to partake of it—and thereby was a symbol of sin.

EGGPLANT-RICOTTA "SANDWICHES"

Serves 4

Eggplant slices filled with ricotta cheese make a nice change of pace from Eggplant Parmigiana.

1 pound part-skim ricotta cheese
¼ cup grated Parmesan cheese
2 medium eggplants, more round than long
1 recipe Quick Tomato-Herb Pasta Sauce (page 135)
1½ cups grated mozzarella cheese

Combine the cheeses in a mixing bowl, mix well, and set aside.

Peel each eggplant and slice crosswise into 8 slices. Broil several slices at a time, brushed with a little oil, in the broiler of your oven, until both sides are lightly browned and tender but firm. Turn the oven to 350° F.

Oil one or two shallow baking dishes, as needed, and pour in just enough pasta sauce to coat the bottom. Make "sandwiches" by spreading the ricotta mixture on one eggplant slice and covering it with another slice of the same size. Arrange in the baking dishes, top with more sauce, and sprinkle with the grated mozzarella.

Bake for 25 to 30 minutes. Serve at once.

EGGPLANT MOUSSAKA

Serves 6 to 8

Moussaka, a hearty layered Greek casserole, is often quite rich and complicated. This version is neither. The eggplant slices are oven-steamed with water rather than fried or grilled with oil, and the usual eggy custard topping is replaced with a deceivingly rich-tasting topping of cottage cheese and tofu.

2 medium eggplants, about 1 pound each
2 tablespoons olive oil
1 cup finely chopped onion
14-ounce can pureed or crushed tomatoes
¼ teaspoon each dried oregano and dried thyme
Salt and freshly ground pepper to taste

"Custard" topping:
1 cup low-fat cottage cheese
10 ounces silken or soft tofu
¼ cup grated Parmesan cheese
1 cup fine whole-grain bread crumbs
1 cup grated mild white cheese, such as mozzarella

Preheat the oven to 425° F.

Wash the eggplants, trim the stems, and slice crosswise into ¼-inch-thick slices. Line a baking sheet or two, as needed, with foil. Oil lightly and sprinkle with water. Arrange the eggplant slices on the sheets so that they are slightly overlapping, and cover with foil. Bake until easily pierced with a fork but not mushy, 10 to 15 minutes. Remove from the oven and uncover. Turn the oven down to 350° F.

Heat the oil in a heavy saucepan. Add the onion and sauté over moderate heat until golden. Remove from the heat. Stir in the tomato puree and herbs, and season with a bit of salt and pepper.

Combine the cottage cheese, tofu, and Parmesan cheese in the container of a food processor. Process until completely smooth.

Oil a wide 2-quart casserole dish. Layer the casserole as follows: first, half of the bread crumbs, then half of the tomato mixture, then the eggplant slices in one or two overlapping layers, then the remaining tomato mixture, then the remaining crumbs. Finally, spread the "custard" over the top, evenly and gently, using a cake spatula, and finish with the grated cheese. Bake for 30 to 35 minutes, or until the top is touched with light-brown spots. Let stand 10 minutes, then cut into squares to serve.

There are few things more useful in vegetable cookery than tomatoes. Cultivated by the Indians of the Americas, tomatoes reached Europe via the Spanish after their sixteenth-century conquest of Mexico. From there the tomato traveled all over Europe under many interesting names. In Italy, it was first called "pomo dei mori," apple of the Moors, then "pomo d'oro," golden apple. In France and Germany it was considered an aphrodisiac and thus was called, respectively, "pomme d'amour" and "liebesapfel," both meaning apple of love. From England the tomato traveled back to the American colonies, where until the early nineteenth century it was considered poisonous, being related to the deadly nightshade. As late as 1860, the apprehension lingered, as evidenced by a recipe in Godey's Lady's Book *which recommended cooking tomatoes for at least three hours before eating.*

TOMATOES STUFFED WITH CURRIED EGGPLANT

Serves 6

One of the most delightful ways to highlight the tomato is to stuff it with tasty mixtures. Here are two possibilities.

6 large, firm, ripe tomatoes
1 medium eggplant
2 tablespoons safflower oil
2 cloves garlic, minced
¼ cup wheat germ or bread crumbs
2 tablespoons chopped fresh parsley
1½ to 2 teaspoons good curry powder or Home-Mixed Curry (page 207)
Salt and freshly ground pepper to taste

Preheat the oven to 350° F.

Cut each tomato in half, carefully scooping out the pulp with the aid of a knife and spoon. Chop the pulp and reserve it in a bowl. Arrange the tomato halves in an oiled large shallow baking dish.

Peel the eggplant and cut it into small dice. Heat the oil and ¼ cup of water in a large skillet. Add the eggplant and garlic, cover, and cook until the eggplant is tender, stirring occasionally and adding enough water to keep it from sticking to the bottom of the pan. Remove from the heat. Add the tomato pulp and all the remaining ingredients and mix thoroughly. Stuff each tomato half with the mixture.

Bake for 30 to 35 minutes or until the tomatoes are done to your liking.

TOMATOES STUFFED WITH ORZO AND PEAS

Serves 6

What goes better with tomatoes than pasta? The tiny size and pleasant texture of orzo suits these stuffed tomatoes perfectly.

6 large, firm, ripe tomatoes
⅔ cup raw orzo (rice-shaped pasta)
2 tablespoons margarine
2 tablespoons minced fresh parsley
2 tablespoons minced fresh chives
⅔ cup steamed fresh or thawed frozen green peas
2 tablespoons grated Parmesan cheese or soy Parmesan, optional
1 teaspoon paprika
½ teaspoon each dried summer savory and dried basil
Salt and freshly ground pepper to taste
Wheat germ for topping

Preheat the oven to 350° F. Prepare the tomatoes as directed in the previous recipe.

Cook the orzo al dente and drain immediately. Splash with cool water.

In the meantime, heat the margarine in a large skillet. Add the reserved tomato pulp, parsley, and chives and sauté over low heat until the tomatoes are softened but have not yet been reduced to a liquid. Add the peas, optional Parmesan cheese, seasonings, and the orzo. Stir together until thoroughly mixed and remove from the heat.

Stuff each tomato half and sprinkle with wheat germ. Bake for 30 to 35 minutes or until the tomatoes are done to your liking.

The argument over whether the tomato is a fruit or a vegetable once went all the way to the U.S. Supreme Court. According to the Tarriff Act of 1883, fruits could be imported duty free but vegetables could not. In 1886, one importer argued that since tomatoes were botanically fruits, he should be able to bring them in duty free. The Supreme Court handed down its decision in 1893, judging that although tomatoes are a fruit of the vine, as are squashes, beans, and the like, they as "all those vegetables... are usually served at dinner... and not, like fruits generally, as a dessert." Thus, tomatoes were pronounced vegetables by law.

After "Jurisprudence" by Daniel Chester French

"Oh, I must try some, if it is an Indian dish," said Miss Rebecca. "I am sure everything must be good that comes from there."

"Give Miss Sharp some curry, my dear," said Mr. Sedley, laughing.

Rebecca had never tasted the dish before.

"Do you find it as good as everything else from India?" said Mr. Sedley.

"Oh, excellent!" said Rebecca, who was suffering tortures with cayenne pepper.

"Try a chili with it, Miss Sharp," said Joseph, really interested.

"A chili," said Rebecca, gasping. "Oh, yes!" She thought a chili was something cool, as its name imported, and was served with some. "How fresh and green they look," she said, and put one into her mouth. It was hotter than the curry; flesh and blood could bear it no longer. She laid down her fork. "Water, for Heaven's Sake, water!"

—William Makepeace Thackeray
Vanity Fair (1848)

Menu for an Indian-Style Curry Feast:

CURRIED MIXED VEGETABLES
SAMOSAS (page 175)
INSTANT TOMATO AND APPLE CHUTNEY (page 155)
CUCUMBER RAITA (page 42)
BANANA RAITA (page 199)

CURRIED MIXED VEGETABLES

Serves 6

You may not want to buy your spices whole and then roast and grind them as Indian cooks do, but you can give your curries a wonderfully complex flavor by mixing ground curry spices rather than using dull commercial curry powder. Begin with Home-Mixed Curry as a spice base and embellish it with additional seasonings plus fresh ginger and garlic. The amounts given here will produce a moderately spicy result and are intended to be used only as a guideline; the degree of spiciness in a curry is very much a matter of personal taste.

2 tablespoons margarine
1 large onion, chopped
1 large carrot, thinly sliced
1 medium eggplant, peeled and diced
2 cloves garlic, minced
2 cups cauliflower florets, steamed
¾ cup string beans, cut into 1-inch pieces and steamed
¾ cup thawed frozen green peas
14-ounce can imported plum tomatoes with liquid, chopped
1 teaspoon freshly grated ginger
2½ to 3 teaspoons Home-Mixed Curry (page 207), or more or less to taste
Salt to taste
Hot cooked rice, millet, or couscous

Heat the margarine in a 12-inch skillet or wok. Add the onion, carrot, eggplant, garlic, and ¼ cup of water. Cover and cook over low heat, stirring occasionally, until the vegetables are nearly tender. Add all of the remaining vegetables and seasonings and mix well. Simmer over very low heat for 20 minutes. The vegetables should be more tender than they would be for a stir-fry, but not overdone. Adjust the seasoning. Use more of whichever individual spices you like the flavor of—for example, add a dash more of cinnamon or coriander. Serve over grains.

INSTANT TOMATO AND APPLE CHUTNEY

Serves 6 or more as a relish

A chutney is a spicy relish served with Indian curries. Many chutneys are actually pickles that must be stored in sterilized jars for weeks before they can be eaten. Some, though, can be made and eaten immediately, such as this easy sweet and spicy version.

1 tablespoon safflower oil
1 medium onion, chopped
2 medium sweet apples, peeled, cored, and diced
1 tablespoon honey
1 pound very ripe red tomatoes, chopped, or 14-ounce can imported plum tomatoes, lightly drained and chopped
1 teaspoon freshly grated ginger, or more or less to taste
1 teaspoon ground cumin
½ teaspoon cinnamon
¼ teaspoon cayenne pepper or crushed red pepper, or more or less to taste

Heat the oil in a large skillet. Add the onion and sauté until translucent. Add the apples, honey, and tomatoes if using fresh ones. Cover and cook on low heat for 10 minutes, stirring once or twice. If using canned tomatoes, add them at this point, along with the remaining ingredients. The ginger and cayenne or crushed red pepper will determine the degree of spiciness; be conservative at first and add a little at a time as desired. Once everything is in the skillet, simmer, uncovered, over very low heat for about 20 minutes or until the tomatoes have been reduced to a loose sauce. Taste and adjust the seasonings.

The sixth-century philosopher Lao-Tzu liked to experiment with plant foods and taught his followers that overcooking vegetables destroyed their nutrients. The Taoists based their diets on raw or partially cooked vegetables and it was this tradition that may have led to the art of stir-frying. Stir-fried vegetables, just barely done, are at the height of their color and look as appealing as they taste. Prepared in complementary combinations, each vegetable retains its unique flavor and character in the texture that has come to be known as "tender-crisp."

Menu for a Chinese-Style Banquet:

"BUDDHA'S DELIGHT" or SWEET AND SOUR VEGETABLES
with rice, couscous, or noodles
TOFU AND EGGS IN PEANUT SAUCE (page 124)
SUNFLOWER COLESLAW (page 35)
PINEAPPLE AND ORANGES IN YOGURT (page 200)
Almond Cookies

"BUDDHA'S DELIGHT" (Stir-Fried Mixed Vegetables)

Serves 4 to 6

This was inspired by the dish of the same name commonly found on menus in Chinese restaurants, often one of the few things that a vegetarian can order. It's never exactly the same at any two places, but it's almost always delicious. Putting together a colorful stir-fry at home is relatively easy and quick. If you are making this dish for guests, have the vegetables cut but don't start frying until about 25 minutes before you want to serve this course, as it is best when the vegetables are at their brightest and crispest. The trickiest part is that everything has to be ready all at once, so the last 5 to 10 minutes of preparation can be a bit hectic.

First, think about what you'd like to serve the vegetables on. Here are some possibilities:

Brown rice: *Have it ready before starting, then heat through as needed before serving. See Cooking Grains, page 214.*

Fine Chinese noodles, buckwheat noodles, or vermicelli: *Start cooking these as you prepare the sauce.*

Couscous: *An offbeat, tasty alternative to rice; start preparing it right before you begin stir-frying. See Cooking Grains, page 214.*

You will need up to 3 heaping cups of cut raw vegetables per serving, that being a general guideline for healthy appetites. Choose from the following vegetables, using anywhere from 6 to 9 different ones, and try to select at least 2 per category for a variety of textures. Always use fresh vegetables, except for those specified as canned, which generally are not available otherwise.

Hard vegetables:

Broccoli, cut into bite-sized pieces
Carrot, sliced
Cauliflower, cut into bite-sized pieces
Celery, sliced diagonally
Onion, chopped or cut into rings

Medium-hard vegetables:
Bok choy, sliced diagonally
Cabbage, shredded
Sweet red or green peppers, diced
Turnips, cut into matchsticks

Soft vegetables:
Canned baby corn
Canned bamboo shoots
Canned water chestnuts, sliced
Mung bean sprouts
Mushrooms
Scallions, chopped
Snow peas, stemmed

Before beginning to stir-fry, assemble and set aside all the ingredients for:

1 recipe Basic Chinese Sauce (page 52)

To begin stir-frying, place the following in a wok:

1 tablespoon sesame oil
2 tablespoons safflower oil

Heat the oils together over moderately high heat. When they are really hot, add your hard vegetables and 2 tablespoons of water and stir-fry, stirring continuously. Add the medium-hard vegetables when the first batch is about halfway to crisp-tender. The ones in the "soft" category have to be just wilted or heated through at the end. After doing this once you will have a good feeling for when the vegetables should be added in relation to each other. Stir continuously until all the vegetables are crisp-tender.

When the vegetables are done, turn off the heat and leave the wok uncovered while you prepare the Basic Chinese Sauce according to the recipe. When it is done, pour it over the vegetables and just heat through over moderately high heat. Serve immediately.

"...We [the Chinese] eat food for its texture, the elastic or crisp effect it has on our teeth, as well for fragrance, flavor, and color... The idea of texture is seldom understood, but a great part of the popularity of bamboo shoots is due to the fine resistance the young shoots give to our teeth."

—Lin Yu tang
My Country and My People (1938)

THE LOGICAL VEGETARIAN

G. K. Chesterton (1874–1936) was a prominent English essayist of the late nineteenth and early twentieth century. He was a foe of our vegetarian friend George Bernard Shaw and the two engaged in public and written debate on vegetarianism and other subjects. Chesterton could be quite cantankerous in his anti-vegetarian essays, but in this tongue-in-cheek poem, he was a bit more charming.

You will find me drinking rum,
Like a sailor in a slum,
You will find me drinking beer like a
Bavarian.
You will find me drinking gin
In the lowest kind of inn,
Because I am a rigid Vegetarian.

So I cleared the inn of wine,
And I tried to climb the sign,
And I tried to hail the constable as
'Marion'.
But he said I couldn't speak,
And he bowled me to the Beak
Because I was a Happy Vegetarian.

Oh, I knew a Doctor Gluck,
And his nose it had a hook,
And his attitudes were anything but
Aryan;
So I gave him all the pork
That I had, upon a fork
Because I am myself a Vegetarian.

I am silent in the Club,
I am silent in the pub,
I am silent on a bally peak in Darien;
For I stuff away for life
Shoving peas in with a knife,
Because I am at heart a Vegetarian.

No more the milk of cows
Shall pollute my private house
Than the milk of the wild mares of the
Barbarian;
I will stick to port and sherry,
For they are so very, very,
So very, very, very Vegetarian.

STIR-FRIED VEGETABLES WITH TOFU

Serves 4

This stir-fry is less elaborate than the previous recipe. It's superquick to make and has the zip of an extra measure of sherry, since Chesterton has assured us that it is so very vegetarian.

2 tablespoons sesame oil
2 medium green bell peppers, diced
1 large celery stalk, sliced diagonally
2 cloves garlic, minced
1½ cups fresh mung bean sprouts
2 or 3 scallions, chopped
¼ cup toasted sunflower seeds
¼ cup dry sherry
2 to 3 tablespons soy sauce, to taste
½ teaspoon freshly grated ginger
1 pound tofu, diced
Crisp chow mein noodles for garnish, optional

Heat the sesame oil in a large skillet or wok. Add the green peppers, celery, and garlic and stir-fry over moderately high heat until the peppers and celery are about half done; add the bean sprouts, scallions, and sunflower seeds and continue to stir-fry just until the sprouts are wilted and the rest of the vegetables are crisp-tender.

Add the remaining ingredients and lower the heat. Cook for another 2 or 3 minutes or until everything is nicely heated through. Serve the stir-fry on its own or over grains or noodles.

LEEK PIE WITH POTATO CRUST

Serves 4 to 6

2 medium potatoes, peeled and grated
2 large leeks, white and palest green parts only
2 tablespoons margarine
1½ cups sliced mushrooms
3 tablespoons dry white wine
1 tablespoon safflower oil
¼ cup bread crumbs
½ cup part-skim ricotta cheese or ½ cup finely crumbled tofu
1 teaspoon dried dill
½ teaspoon dried oregano
¼ teaspoon dry mustard
¼ cup grated Parmesan cheese or Parmesan-style soy cheese
Salt and freshly ground pepper to taste

Preheat the oven to 375° F.

Place the grated potatoes in a colander. Let drain for 10 minutes, then squeeze out some of the moisture.

Chop the leeks and wash carefully in a colander, removing all the grit.

Heat the margarine in a skillet until it begins to foam. Add the leeks and sauté over moderately low heat for 5 minutes, stirring frequently. Add the mushrooms and the wine and sauté until the mushrooms are just tender. Transfer to a mixing bowl.

In the same skillet, heat the oil and 2 tablespoons of water and cook the grated potato over moderate heat until nearly tender; do not brown. Add water as needed to keep it from sticking.

In the meantime, combine the leeks and mushrooms with the bread crumbs, ricotta cheese or tofu, and seasonings. When the potatos are ready, stir the Parmesan cheese into them and add a little salt and pepper.

Oil a 9-inch round or square baking dish and pat half the potato mixture into the bottom. Pour the entire leek mixture over it, smooth it over, and top with the remaining potatoes. Bake for 35 to 40 minutes or until the potatoes are golden-brown and crusty. Let stand for 5 to 10 minutes, then cut into wedges or squares and serve.

The leek has long been a national emblem of Wales and has decorated the Welsh military uniform. A Welsh soldier of long ago wrote this verse in praise of the leek:

I like the leeke above all herbs and floures;
When first we wore the same the field was ours.
The leeke is white and green, whereby is ment
That Britaines are both stout and eminent.
Next to the lion and the unicorne,
The leeke's the fairest emblym that is worne.

SOY AND HONEY-GLAZED SQUASH

Serves 4 to 6

A simple and savory side dish.

1 large butternut squash
¼ cup honey
¼ cup apple juice
2 tablespoons soy sauce
1 teaspoon dark sesame oil
1 teaspoon dried tarragon

Slice the squash in half crosswise through the widest part. Scoop out the seeds and fibers and discard. Slice the squash crosswise into ½-inch-thick rounds, then peel and dice. Combine the remaining ingredients in a small bowl and stir together. Heat the liquid mixture gently in a large, heavy saucepan and stir in the diced squash. Cover and cook over moderate heat until the squash is just tender, about 15 minutes. Continue to cook over low heat, uncovered, until the liquid is reduced and glazes the squash, about another 15 minutes. Serve at once.

Squash is truly a food of the Americas. Its name is possibly a corruption of "askoot-asquash," meaning "the fruit that is yellow" in an Indian dialect. Squash in its numerous varieties originated with the pre-Incan Indians thousands of years ago. Along with pumpkin, it was so abundant when the European settlers reached North America that it could sometimes drive pioneer wives like this to despair. By itself, squash may perhaps be monotonous, but with a little imagination, it is a most interesting, versatile vegetable.

> *"O dear! How can I tell it. Squash again for breakfast."*
>
> —Diary of a Pioneer Woman

SPAGHETTI SQUASH WITH BROCCOLI-ASPARAGUS PESTO

Serves 4 to 6

If you like pesto with pasta, you'll enjoy this off-beat version on spaghetti squash. And if you like this pesto, there's no reason not to use it on pasta.

1 large spaghetti squash

Pesto:
3 tablespoons olive oil
2 cloves garlic, minced
1 cup walnuts
½ cup grated Parmesan cheese or Parmesan-style soy cheese
2 cups chopped steamed broccoli
1½ cups chopped steamed asparagus
1 teaspoon dried oregano
Fresh basil leaves, optional

Salt and freshly ground pepper to taste

Preheat the oven to 350° F.

Cut the squash in half and remove the seeds and pulp. Place the squash halves, cut side up, in a shallow, foil-lined baking dish. Cover with more foil and bake for 40 to 45 minutes or until the squash can be easily pierced with a knife. When it is cool enough to handle, pull the spaghetti-like strands off the squash with a fork, using long up-and-down motions. Place in a serving bowl and cover.

Heat the olive oil in a small skillet. Add the garlic and sauté over low heat until golden. Place the walnuts in the container of a food processor and process until finely ground. Add the garlic along with the remaining pesto ingredients and process to a thick coarse puree. Combine with the spaghetti squash and toss well. Season with salt and pepper and toss again. Just before serving, warm in the microwave or in the oven.

SUMMER HARVEST SQUASH SAUTÉ

Serves 6

At the end of the summer and throughout most of the autumn, a variety of enticing squashes is available. Green, yellow, and orange squashes look very appealing together in this quick sauté with greens.

1 small butternut squash
2 tablespoons olive oil
1 large yellow summer squash, peeled, halved lengthwise, and sliced
1 large zucchini, halved lengthwise and sliced
2 tablespoons dry white or red wine
2 tablespoons soy sauce
3 cups chopped greens, such as spinach or Swiss chard
3 to 4 tablespoons minced fresh herbs of your choice
Freshly ground pepper to taste

To prepare the butternut squash, halve it lengthwise and remove the seeds and pulp. Then cut it crosswise into slices about 1 inch wide. Peel the slices, then cut into ¾-inch dice.

Heat the oil with 2 tablespoons of water in a large skillet. Add the diced butternut squash, cover, and steam over low heat, stirring occasionally, for 10 minutes or until the squash is about half done. Add the summer squash and the zucchini, adding a little more water if necessary, and cook over moderately low heat, stirring frequently, until the squashes are done to your liking.

Add the wine and soy sauce and stir together. Stir in the greens and fresh herbs, cover the skillet, and cook until they are wilted. Season to taste with pepper and additional soy sauce and serve.

GINGERED-RICE-AND-APPLE-STUFFED SQUASH

Serves 4

2 medium acorn or butternut squashes
¾ cup raw brown rice
2 tablespoons soy sauce
2 tablespoons margarine or fragrant nut oil
1 small onion, chopped
2 medium apples, peeled, cored, and sliced
⅓ cup chopped walnuts, almonds, or pecans
½ cup apple juice
¼ cup dry red wine
2 tablespoons honey
2 teaspoons freshly grated ginger, or more or less to taste
1 teaspoon good curry powder or Home-Mixed Curry (page 207)

Preheat the oven to 400° F.

Cut the squashes in half, place them cut side up in shallow baking dishes, and cover them with aluminum foil. Bake for 35 to 45 minutes or until they can be easily pierced with a fork but are still firm.

In the meantime, cook the rice with the soy sauce added to the cooking water, following the directions in Cooking Grains (page 214).

When the squashes are cool enough to handle, scoop out the pulp, leaving about a ½-inch-thick shell all around. Chop the scooped-out pulp and set aside.

Heat the margarine or nut oil in a large skillet. Add the onion and sauté over moderate heat until translucent. Add the apple and sauté until it softens, then add the chopped squash pulp, the cooked rice, and all of the remaining ingredients. Stir together and remove from the heat.

Stuff the squash halves with the rice mixture, arrange in lightly oiled baking dishes, and bake for 20 minutes. Serve at once; each squash half is one generous serving.

> *"Ginger sharpneth the sight, and provoketh slothful husbands."*
>
> —William Vaughn
> *Directions for Health* (1600)

WALNUT-CARROT CROQUETTES

Makes about 12 croquettes

These rich-tasting croquettes are excellent in pita sandwiches with shredded lettuce and a yogurt-based dressing.

1 tablespoon safflower oil
1 medium onion, chopped
¾ cup walnut halves
1½ cups finely grated carrot
¼ cup wheat germ
2 eggs, beaten
2 tablespoons soy sauce
½ teaspoon each paprika, ground cumin, and dry mustard
¼ teaspoon each dried basil and oregano
Dash garlic powder
Freshly ground pepper to taste
Oil for frying

Heat the oil in a small skillet. Add the onion and sauté over moderate heat until golden. Combine the onion with the walnut halves in the container of a food processor and process until the walnuts are very finely ground and the mixture is a coarse paste. Combine in a mixing bowl with the remaining ingredients and stir together until thoroughly mixed. Heat just enough oil to coat the bottom of a heavy skillet. Shape the walnut-carrot mixture into palm-size croquettes and fry on both sides until golden brown. Drain on paper towels.

CARROTS WITH MISSION FIGS

Serves 6

This makes a nice side dish when served with grain dishes or curried vegetables. Mission figs are also called black figs; they are available in natural food stores as well as in supermarkets.

2 tablespoons margarine
1 medium onion, quartered and sliced
1 pound carrots, thinly sliced
⅔ cup mission figs, trimmed and sliced
1 teaspoon honey
½ teaspoon freshly grated ginger
¼ teaspoon each salt and cinnamon

Heat the margarine in a large skillet. Add the onion and sauté over moderate heat until the rings separate. Add the carrots and sauté for 5 minutes. Add the remaining ingredients and sauté for another 7 to 10 minutes, stirring frequently, until the carrots are crisp-tender and lightly golden. Add drops of water if the skillet gets dry as the carrots cook. Serve at once.

"The carrot serveth for love matters; and Orpheus, as Pliny writeth, said that the use therof winneth love..."

—John Gerarde
The Herball (1636)

ZUCCHINI PANCAKES PARMESAN

Makes about 20 palm-size or 8 to 10 crepe-size pancakes

Zucchini is one of the few squashes that is not native to the Americas. It was developed in Italy.

4 cups firmly packed coarsely grated zucchini
3 eggs
½ cup matzo meal or bread crumbs
½ teaspoon each dried dill and marjoram
¼ teaspoon dried thyme
Salt and freshly ground pepper to taste
½ cup grated Parmesan cheese
Oil for frying

Place the grated zucchini in a colander for several minutes to drain, then squeeze out the moisture.

Beat the eggs well in a mixing bowl, add the zucchini and all of the remaining ingredients except the oil, and mix thoroughly.

You can fry the batter in either of two ways, as palm-size croquettes in a large skillet or as crepe-size pancakes in a small skillet, about 7 inches or so across. In either case, heat just enough oil to coat the bottom of the skillet; when it is hot enough to make a drop of batter sizzle, proceed to fry in whatever manner you've chosen until both sides are nicely browned and crisp-looking. Drain on paper towels.

WHEAT GERM–ZUCCHINI PIE

6 servings

¾ cup toasted wheat germ
¼ cup toasted sunflower seeds
⅓ cup grated Parmesan cheese or Parmesan-style soy cheese
2½ tablespoons margarine
1 medium onion, halved and sliced
2 medium zucchini (about 1 pound), sliced
1 teaspoon each dried oregano and dried dill
Salt and freshly ground pepper to taste
1 cup firmly packed grated mild white cheese or mozzarella-style soy cheese
2 large tomatoes, thinly sliced

Preheat the oven to 350° F.

In a mixing bowl, combine the wheat germ, sunflower seeds, and Parmesan cheese. Melt 1 tablespoon of the margarine and mix well with the wheat-germ mixture. Heat the remaining margarine in a large skillet. Add the onion and sauté until golden. Add the zucchini, cover, and sauté until crisp-tender, stirring occasionally. Sprinkle with the oregano and dill and season to taste with salt and pepper.

In an oiled 1½-quart round casserole dish, layer as follows: first, a fine layer of the wheat-germ mixture, then half of the zucchini mixture, then half of the mozzarella, then half of the tomato slices, then half of the wheat germ. Repeat. Bake for 30 to 35 minutes. Let cool 10 minutes, then cut into wedges to serve.

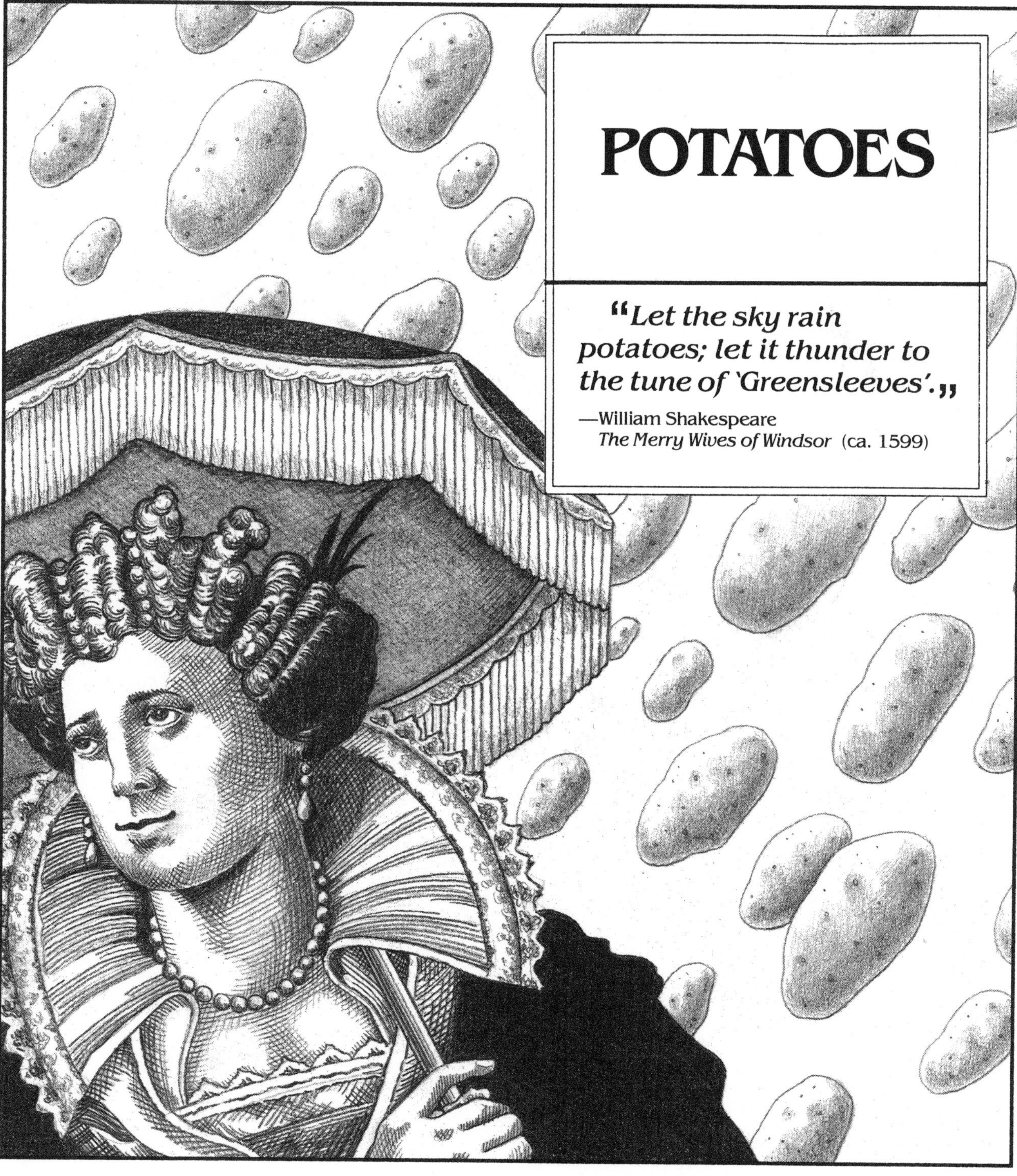

POTATOES

"*Let the sky rain potatoes; let it thunder to the tune of 'Greensleeves'.*"

—William Shakespeare
The Merry Wives of Windsor (ca. 1599)

The humble potato was originally cultivated by the Indians of Peru. It was carried back to Europe by the Spanish, and like other fruits and vegetables, found its way back to the Americas in the sixteenth century via the British. Sweet potatoes took a similar journey, though it is curious to note that botanically, sweet and white potatoes are unrelated—the white potato is a tuber of the nightshade family, and the sweet potato is a tuber of the morning glory family. The word "potato" is actually a corruption of "batata," the West Indian word for sweet potato.

As we know, the Irish took a particular liking to the potato (although there is really no "Irish" potato), and in days past had various medicinal uses for it. It was believed that a stone boiled with potatoes had the power to heal, and that the water they were boiled in alleviated sprains and aches. Other cultures adopted potato folk-medicine of their own, such as tying a potato to the neck in a stocking to ward off a sore throat, carrying a potato in the pocket to ward off rheumatism, rubbing a potato on the skin to soothe a burn, and much more.

Why an entire chapter on potatoes? Like pasta, they are one of those foods that almost everyone loves; they are quite versatile and are a good vehicle for many types of vegetarian dishes, whether main or side portions. Besides, so much lovely lore and wit exist on the subject to serve up with the recipes, that potatoes simply couldn't be shunted off to a corner of the Vegetables chapter.

WINTER POTATO AND STRING BEAN STEW

Serves 6

Potatoes combined with string beans in an herbed tomato sauce make an exceptionally warming winter stew.

5 large potatoes, well scrubbed
2 tablespoons olive oil
1 large onion, chopped
3 cloves garlic, minced
1/3 cup chopped fresh parsley
14-ounce can imported plum tomatoes with liquid, chopped
1 cup canned crushed or pureed tomatoes
1 tablespoon minced fresh dill or 1 teaspoon dry dill
1 teaspoon paprika
1/2 teaspoon dried marjoram
1/4 teaspoon each dried thyme and dried rosemary
1 pound thawed frozen string beans
Salt and freshly ground pepper to taste

Cook or microwave the potatoes in their skins until tender. When cool enough to handle, dice but don't peel them.

Heat the olive oil in a soup pot or Dutch oven. Add the onion and garlic and sauté over moderate heat until the onion is golden. Add the parsley, tomatoes, and seasonings and simmer over low heat for 5 minutes.

Stir in the potatoes and string beans. Add salt and pepper to taste. Cover and simmer over low heat for 35 to 40 minutes.

POTATO AND ZUCCHINI SKILLET PIE

Serves 6 to 8

Many potato dishes need little seasoning to be delicious. This crisp skillet pie, a variation on the traditional Jewish kugel, is one such example.

2 large potatoes, peeled and grated
1 medium zucchini, grated
1 small onion, grated
3 eggs, lightly beaten
¼ cup matzo meal or bread crumbs
Salt and freshly ground pepper to taste
Oil for frying

Combine the grated vegetables in a bowl. Pour in the lightly beaten eggs, the matzo meal or bread crumbs, and salt and pepper. Mix thoroughly.

Heat enough oil to coat the bottom of a 9- or 10-inch nonstick skillet. Pour in half of the potato-zucchini mixture. Follow the directions on page 216, How to Fry and Flip a Skillet Pie or Frittata, letting the pie get nice and brown. Repeat with the remaining mixture. Slice into wedges to serve.

"What I say is that, if a man really likes potatoes, he must be a pretty decent sort of fellow."

—A.A. Milne
Not That It Matters (1920)

According to Sir James Frazer, who wrote The Golden Bough, *it was customary for Lithuanian peasants to pull each other's hair at the table before eating the newly harvested potatoes. The meaning of this custom, however, escaped him.*

POTATOES AND EGGPLANT IN FRESH HERB SAUCE

Serves 4 to 6

Serve this with Tabouleh (page 48) for a simple, hearty meal.

5 medium potatoes, well scrubbed
2 tablespoons light olive oil
1 medium eggplant, peeled and diced
2 cloves garlic, minced
Wheat germ
Fresh Herb Sauce (page 64)
½ cup sliced or chopped black olives

Cook or microwave the potatoes in their skins until tender but still firm. When they are cool enough to handle, cut them in half lengthwise and slice them ¼ inch thick.

Heat the oil in a large skillet with ¼ cup of water, then add the diced eggplant and garlic. Cover and cook over moderate heat, stirring occasionally, until the eggplant is tender but not mushy. Sprinkle in enough wheat germ to coat the pieces evenly. Cover and remove from the heat.

Combine the potatoes, eggplant, Fresh Herb Sauce, and olives in a large casserole dish and toss together. Serve just warm, or warm the dish in the oven before serving.

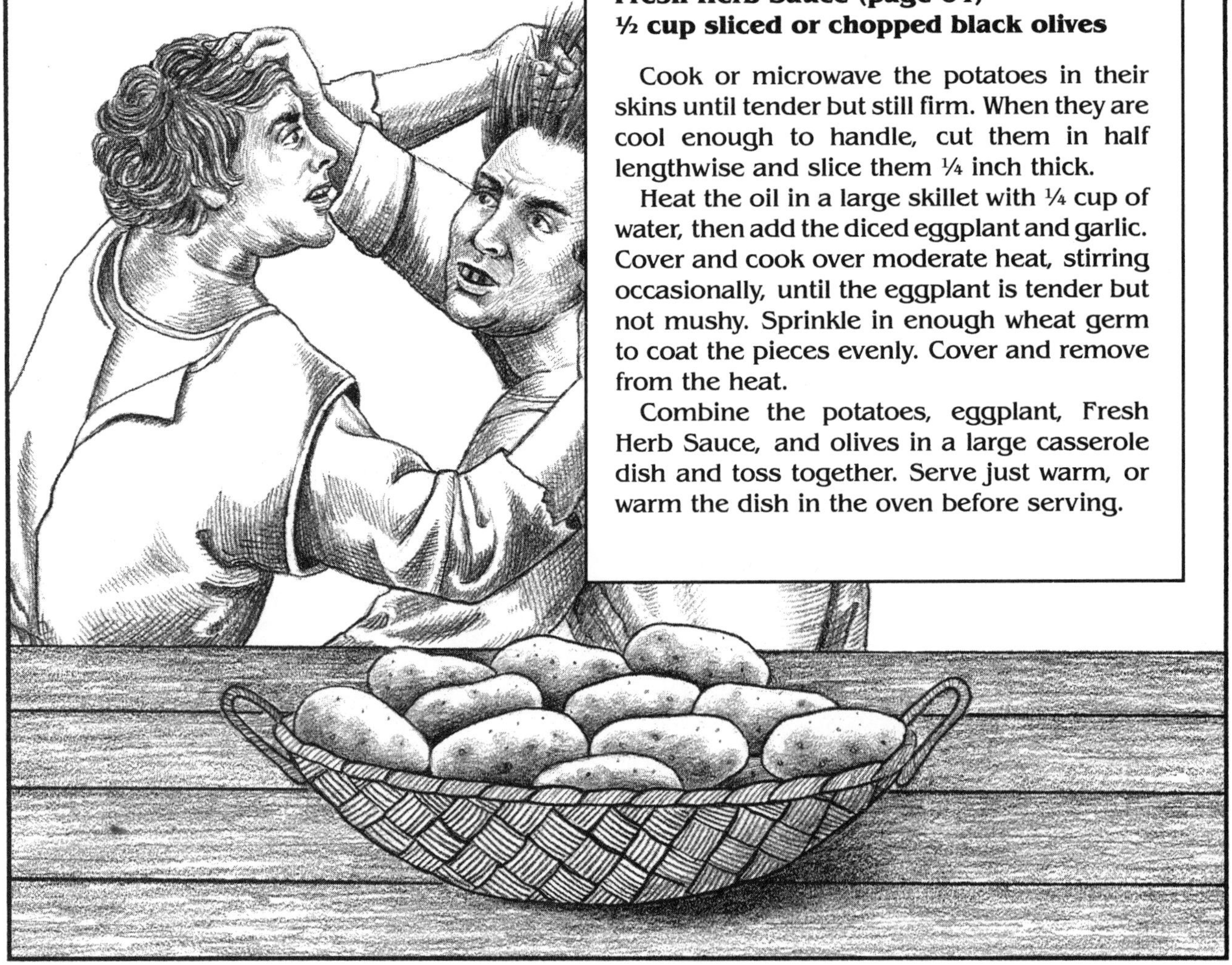

MOZZARELLA MASHED POTATO PIE

Serves 6

Mashed potatoes become surprisingly elegant in this simple casserole that is invariably a hit with guests.

5 to 6 medium potatoes
2 tablespoons margarine, cut into small pieces
⅔ cup low-fat milk or soymilk
Salt and freshly ground pepper to taste
⅓ cup bread crumbs, or a mixture of wheat germ and bread crumbs
½ pound part-skim mozzarella cheese or mozzarella-style soy cheese, grated
Paprika for topping

Cook or microwave the potatoes in their skins until tender. When they are done, preheat the oven to 350° F.

When the potatoes are cool enough to handle, peel them and place them in a large mixing bowl. Add the margarine and mash until the potatoes are smooth and fluffy. Stir in the milk or soymilk and season with salt and pepper.

Generously oil a 9-inch casserole dish (preferably round, though a square one will do). Line the bottom and sides of the dish with half of the bread crumbs. Pour in half of the mashed potatoes, smooth down, and top with half of the grated cheese. Repeat with the remaining potatoes and cheese. Sprinkle the remaining bread crumbs over the top and follow with a generous sprinkling of paprika.

Bake for 35 to 40 minutes or until the top is nicely browned. Allow to stand for 10 minutes, then cut into wedges or squares and serve.

POTATO AND LENTIL STEW

Serves 6

The flavors of potatoes and lentils complement each other nicely in this stew. It is hearty enough to serve as a main dish.

4 to 5 medium potatoes, well scrubbed
¾ cup raw lentils
2 tablespoons olive oil
1 large onion, chopped
1 medium celery stalk, chopped
2 cloves garlic, minced
⅓ cup chopped fresh parsley

Dressing:
1½ cups plain yogurt
1 to 1½ tablespoons Dijon mustard, to taste
1 tablespoon soy sauce or tamari
1 tablespoon red wine vinegar
1 teaspoon each dill seed or caraway seed, paprika, ground coriander, and ground cumin

Salt and freshly ground pepper to taste

Cook or microwave the potatoes in their skins until tender but still firm. When they are cool enough to handle, dice them, leaving the skins on. Cook the lentils, following the instructions in Cooking Beans (page 215), until they are tender but still hold their shape.

Heat the olive oil in a small skillet. Add the onion, celery, and garlic and sauté over moderate heat until the onion is golden. Stir in the parsley, then remove from the heat and cover.

Combine the potato dice, lentils, and skillet mixture in a serving container. Combine the ingredients for the dressing in a small bowl and whisk together. Pour over the potato-lentil mixture and toss well. Season with salt and pepper and toss again. Serve warm.

Potatoes on the table
To eat with other things,
Potatoes with their jackets off
May do for dukes and kings.

But if you wish to taste them
As nature meant you should,
Be sure to keep their jackets on
And eat them in a wood.

A little salt and pepper,
A deal of open air,
And never was a banquet
That offered nobler fare.

—Edward Verall Lucas (1868–1938)

POTATO BREAD KUGEL

Serves 6 or more

Potato kugel is a traditional Jewish specialty that is sometimes fried and sometimes baked; either way, the result should be brown and crisp outside and soft and moist inside. In this baked version, bread soaked in milk adds substance to the soft inner texture.

6 medium potatoes, peeled and grated (see note below)
4 average slices whole-grain bread
¾ cup milk or soymilk
1 large onion, grated
2 eggs, beaten
3 tablespoons safflower or vegetable oil
Salt and freshly ground pepper to taste

Preheat the oven to 375° F.

Place the grated potatoes in a colander. Let drain for 10 minutes, then squeeze out the moisture.

In the meantime, tear the bread into small pieces and put them in a large mixing bowl. Cover with the milk and allow to soak until the potatoes are ready. Add the grated potatoes, onion, and the remaining ingredients. Mix thoroughly, then pour into an oiled deep 1½-quart casserole dish and bake for 50 to 60 minutes, or until the outside is well browned and the potatoes inside are tender.

NOTE: If grating the potatoes in a food processor, run them through the grating blade twice, or they will be too coarse for the optimal baking time.

TZIMMES

Serves 6 to 8

Tzimmes, like kugel, is a traditional Jewish specialty. A rich sweet-potato casserole, it symbolizes the good things in life at Jewish holiday dinners.

4 large sweet potatoes, well scrubbed and thinly sliced
2 large carrots, sliced
2 medium sweet apples, peeled, cored, and diced
⅓ cup raisins or chopped prunes
⅓ cup chopped walnuts or pecans
3 tablespoons margarine, melted
¼ cup honey, or more or less to taste
¾ cup orange juice
½ teaspoon each cinnamon and salt
Dash each ground cloves and ground nutmeg

Preheat the oven to 350° F.

Combine the first 5 ingredients in a large casserole dish. Combine the remaining ingredients in a small bowl, mixing well, and toss with the sweet potato mixture. Bake, covered, for 30 minutes, then stir well and bake for another 15 to 20 minutes or until the vegetables are tender and the top of the casserole begins to get glazed and crusty.

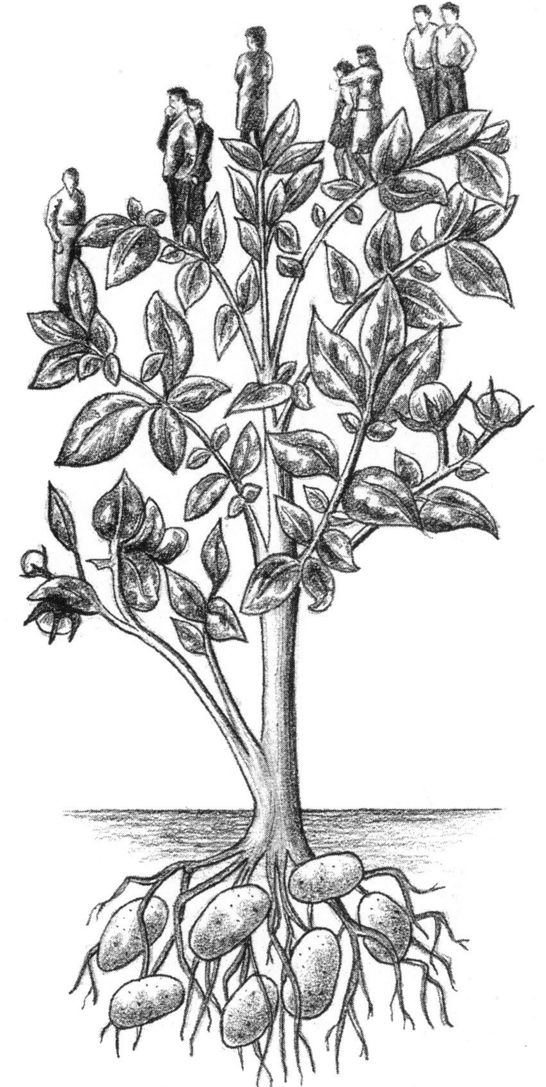

"Human nature will not flourish, any more than a potato, if it be planted and replanted, for too long a series of generations, in the same worn out soil."

—Nathaniel Hawthorne
The Scarlet Letter (1850)

LES TROIS POMMES

Serves 6

A seventeenth-century writer said of potatoes, "Eating of these roots doth excite Venus and increaseth lust." It stands to reason, then, that this rich combination of white and sweet potatoes, subtly sweetened with apple, should be perfectly suited to a romantic dinner.

4 medium potatoes, well scrubbed
2 large sweet potatoes, well scrubbed
2 tablespoons margarine
1 large onion, chopped
1 large sweet apple, peeled, cored, and thinly sliced
¾ cup reduced-fat sour cream
1½ cups grated mild white cheese
¾ cup low-fat milk
Dash nutmeg
Salt to taste

Cook or microwave the white and sweet potatoes in their skins until tender but still firm. When they are cool enough to handle, peel and slice them ¼ inch thick and put them in a mixing bowl.

Preheat the oven to 350° F.

Heat the margarine in a small skillet. Add the onion and sauté over moderate heat until lightly browned. Add the sautéed onion and the remaining ingredients to the potato mixture and mix thoroughly. Pour into an oiled large shallow baking dish for 35 minutes.

GOLDEN POTATO-CHEESE SQUARES

Serves 6 to 8

For a colorful meal, serve this with Tomatoes Stuffed with Curried Eggplant (page 152) and Marinated Cauliflower and Broccoli (page 40).

5 to 6 medium potatoes, well scrubbed
2 tablespoons margarine, cut into bits
1 cup low-fat milk
2 cups firmly packed grated cheddar, Colby, Edam, or Gouda cheese
2 teaspoons Dijon mustard
1 teaspoon paprika
Salt and freshly ground pepper to taste
½ teaspoon ground turmeric, optional

Cook or microwave the potatoes in their skins until tender. Once they are done, preheat the oven to 350° F.

When the potatoes are cool enough to handle, peel them and put them in a large mixing bowl with the margarine and a little of the milk. Mash until smooth. Add the remaining milk and the rest of the ingredients and mix thoroughly.

Pour the mixture into an oiled large shallow baking casserole and pat smooth. Bake for 30 minutes. Allow to stand for 5 to 10 minutes, then cut into squares and serve.

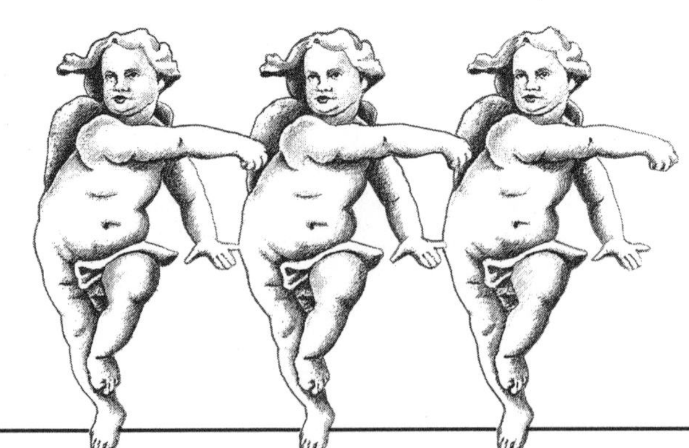

"*The greatest cure for a batting slump ever invented.*"

—Babe Ruth (1895–1948)
on scallions

SCALLIONED POTATO BAKE

Serves 4 to 6

If you've been having a batting slump lately, try the Babe's remedy.

5 to 6 medium potatoes, well scrubbed
2 tablespoons margarine
1 medium zucchini, sliced
5 to 6 scallions, chopped
3 tablespoons chopped fresh parsley
1 tablespoon minced fresh dill or 1 teaspoon dried dill
1 cup buttermilk
1 cup grated mild white cheese
Salt and freshly ground pepper to taste
Toasted sunflower seeds for topping

Cook or microwave the potatoes in their skins until tender. When they are cool enough to handle, peel and slice them.

Preheat the oven to 325° F.

Heat the margarine in a medium-sized skillet. Add the zucchini and scallions and sauté over moderate heat just until they have lost their raw quality. Do not brown. Add the parsley and continue to sauté just until it has wilted.

Combine the potatoes and sauteed vegetables with all of the remaining ingredients, except the sunflower seeds, in a large mixing bowl and mix together. Pour into an oiled large shallow baking dish. Sprinkle with the toasted sunflower seeds and bake for 30 to 35 minutes or until the top is lightly browned.

In European folk belief, it was said that potatoes should be planted on a starry night so that they'd have many eyes.

POTATOES WITH TOFU AND GREEN CHILI

Serves 4 to 6

4 or 5 medium potatoes
2 tablespoons safflower oil
2 tablespoons soy sauce
1 pound tofu, diced
1 tablespoon olive oil
1 large onion, quartered and thinly sliced
1 or 2 cloves garlic, minced
4-ounce can green chilies, chopped
½ teaspoon each dried oregano and ground cumin
1 tablespoon unbleached white flour
⅔ cup low-fat milk or soymilk
1½ cups grated Monterey Jack cheese or cheddar-style soy cheese

Preheat the oven to 375° F.

Cook or microwave the potatoes in their skins. When they are cool enough to handle, peel and dice them, then transfer to a large mixing bowl and set aside.

Heat the oil and soy sauce in a large skillet. Add the diced tofu and cook over moderately high heat, stirring frequently, until the pieces are lightly golden on most sides. Transfer to the mixing bowl. In the same skillet, heat the olive oil. Add the onion and garlic and sauté until the onion is lightly browned. Stir in the chilies and seasonings. Sprinkle in the flour and stir until it dissolves. Pour in the milk or soymilk and stir together. Simmer until the milk thickens. In the large mixing bowl, combine the skillet mixture with the potatoes and tofu. Pour into a lightly oiled large shallow baking dish. Sprinkle with the grated cheese.

Bake for 15 to 20 minutes, or until the cheese is bubbly.

SAMOSAS

Makes about 12

A crisp pastry filled with mildly curried potatoes, samosas are Indian in origin. Though they are a bit of a project to make, they turn a curried dinner into a feast. Very little oil is absorbed by them as they fry.

Pastry:
¾ cup unbleached white flour
¾ cup whole wheat flour
½ teaspoon salt
⅓ cup water
3 tablespoons margarine, melted

Combine the flours with the salt in a mixing bowl. Add the water and melted margarine and work into a stiff dough. Knead for 3 to 4 minutes, then cover with a towel and let rest while you prepare the filling.

Filling:
2 cups diced cooked and peeled potato (about 2 medium)
1 tablespoon margarine
¼ cup low-fat milk or soymilk
½ cup steamed fresh or thawed frozen green peas
1½ teaspoons good curry powder or Home-Mixed Curry (page 207), or more or less to taste
Salt to taste
Safflower oil for frying

Before starting, have the 6 potatoes ready.

For the dough, mash 2 of the potatoes well in a mixing bowl. Add the beaten egg, oil, and 2 tablespoons of water and mix well. In a separate bowl, combine the flours, baking powder, and salt. Work this mixture into the potato mixture to form a sticky dough. Turn it out onto a well-floured board and knead for a minute or two, adding flour until the dough loses its stickiness. Shape into a ball and cover with a towel.

Preheat the oven to 350° F.

Peel the 4 remaining potatoes and mash well. Add the melted margarine, milk, and salt and pepper. Mix until smooth.

To assemble the knishes, divide the dough into 4 parts. Roll each part out into a thin sheet and, with a sharp knife, cut as many 5-inch squares as possible, reusing any dough that has been cut away. Place a bit of the potato mixture in the center of each square (as much as it will hold comfortably) and fold each corner toward the center, overlapping the corners just a little. Pinch the seams shut. Arrange the knishes on an oiled and floured baking sheet. Bake for 35 minutes or until the dough is lightly browned.

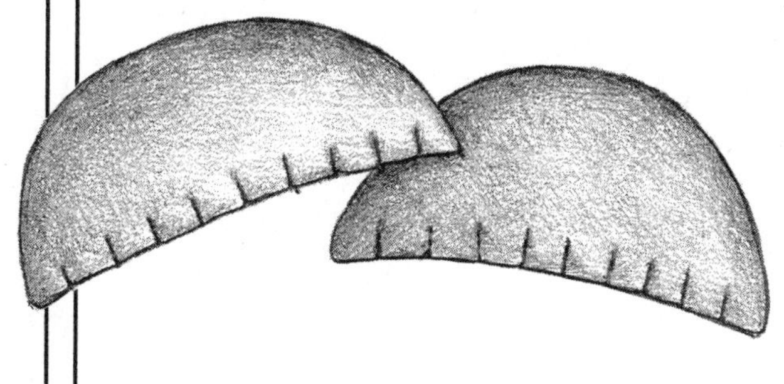

POTATO AND SPINACH STRUDEL

Serves 6

Inspired by the Greek favorites boreka and spanakopita, I devised this recipe to include certain elements of both. In most dishes that use strudel leaves, or filo, an enormous amount of buttering is required; however, I find that buttering only every third leaf is plenty, and the result is just as crisp and delectable.

5 medium potatoes, well scrubbed
10-ounce package frozen chopped spinach, thawed and well drained
1¼ cups buttermilk
¼ teaspoon each dried basil and dried thyme
Dash nutmeg
Salt and freshly ground pepper to taste
9 sheets frozen filo (strudel leaves), thawed
¼ cup (½ stick) butter or margarine
¼ pound feta cheese, finely crumbled

Cook or microwave the potatoes in their skins until tender. When they are cool enough to handle, peel and mash well in a bowl. Add the spinach to the mashed potatoes along with the buttermilk and seasonings. Mix thoroughly.

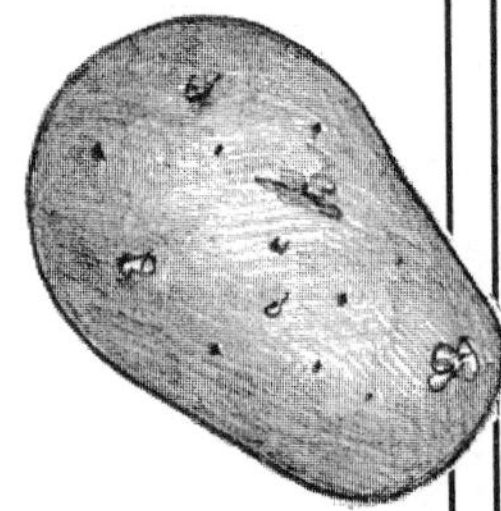

Preheat the oven to 375° F.

Cut the filo in half so that you have 18 leaves, each 8½ by 12 inches. You will need to use a shallow baking dish of approximately this size; if necessary, trim the filo to fit. Butter the baking dish well. Melt the remaining butter. Place 3 filo leaves in the baking dish. Use a pastry brush to spread the top one lightly but evenly with butter. Place 3 more leaves in the dish and butter again. Pour in half of the potato mixture, spread evenly, and sprinkle with half of the feta cheese. Repeat the placing and buttering process with the next 6 leaves, then spread the remaining potato mixture over them, followed by the remaining feta cheese. Top with the rest of the leaves, placing and buttering them in the same way, and pour whatever butter remains over the top, brushing it on evenly. Cut into 12 squares and bake for about 45 minutes, or until the top layer of filo looks brown and crisp.

POTATO KNISHES

Makes about 10 knishes

Potato knishes are in the Jewish tradition and rely primarily on the good basic flavor of potatoes.

Potato dough:

2 medium potatoes, cooked and peeled
1 egg, beaten
1 tablespoon safflower oil
¾ cup whole wheat flour
¾ cup unbleached white flour
2 teaspoons baking powder
1 teaspoon salt

Filling:

4 medium potatoes, cooked and peeled
2 tablespoons margarine, melted
1 cup low-fat milk or soymilk
Salt and freshly ground pepper to taste

Be eating one potato, peeling a second, have a third in your fist, and your eye on a fourth.

—Old Irish Proverb

Place the diced potato in a mixing bowl. Add the margarine and mash well. Add the remaining ingredients except the oil and mix thoroughly.

Turn the pastry dough out onto a floured board and divide it into 12 balls, each about 1 inch in diameter. Flatten each ball and roll it out so that it is as thin and as rounded as possible. Place a small amount of filling on one half of the circle, about ¼ inch from the edge. You'll discover how much each round can hold after doing one. Fold the other half over and press the edges closed with the tines of a fork. Turn the samosa over and press the edges on the other side as well.

Heat ½ inch of oil in a heavy skillet. When the oil is hot enough to make a drop of water sizzle, carefully drop in a few of the samosas at a time, and fry on both sides until the pastry is golden-brown. Remove with a slotted spoon and drain on paper towels.

SOUTHEAST ASIAN SPICY MASHED POTATOES

Serves 4 to 6

Here's a simple and very tasty idea based on a Southeast Asian recipe.

5 large potatoes
1 cup plain yogurt
2 tablespoons safflower oil
1 large onion, chopped
4-ounce can mild or hot chopped green chilies
½ teaspoon freshly grated ginger
Salt to taste

Cook or microwave the potatoes in their skins until tender. When they are cool enough to handle, peel and coarsely mash in a large bowl. Stir in the yogurt and cover.

Heat the oil in a small skillet. Add the onion and sauté over moderate heat until nicely browned. Stir into the mashed potatoes along with the remaining ingredients. Serve at once.

PECAN CANDIED YAMS

Serves 4 to 6

4 large sweet potatoes
2 tablespoons margarine
Juice of 2 oranges (about ¾ cup to 1 cup)
⅓ cup maple syrup
¼ teaspoon each cinnamon, ground nutmeg, and salt
⅔ cup coarsely chopped pecans

Cook or microwave the sweet potatoes in their skins until they are tender but still firm. When they are cool enough to handle, peel them, then cut them into quarters and slice them.

In a large skillet, heat the margarine until it melts. Add the orange juice, maple syrup, and seasonings. Stir in the potatoes and cook, uncovered, over moderate heat, stirring frequently, for 25 to 30 minutes or until glazed and lightly browned. Stir in the pecans and serve at once.

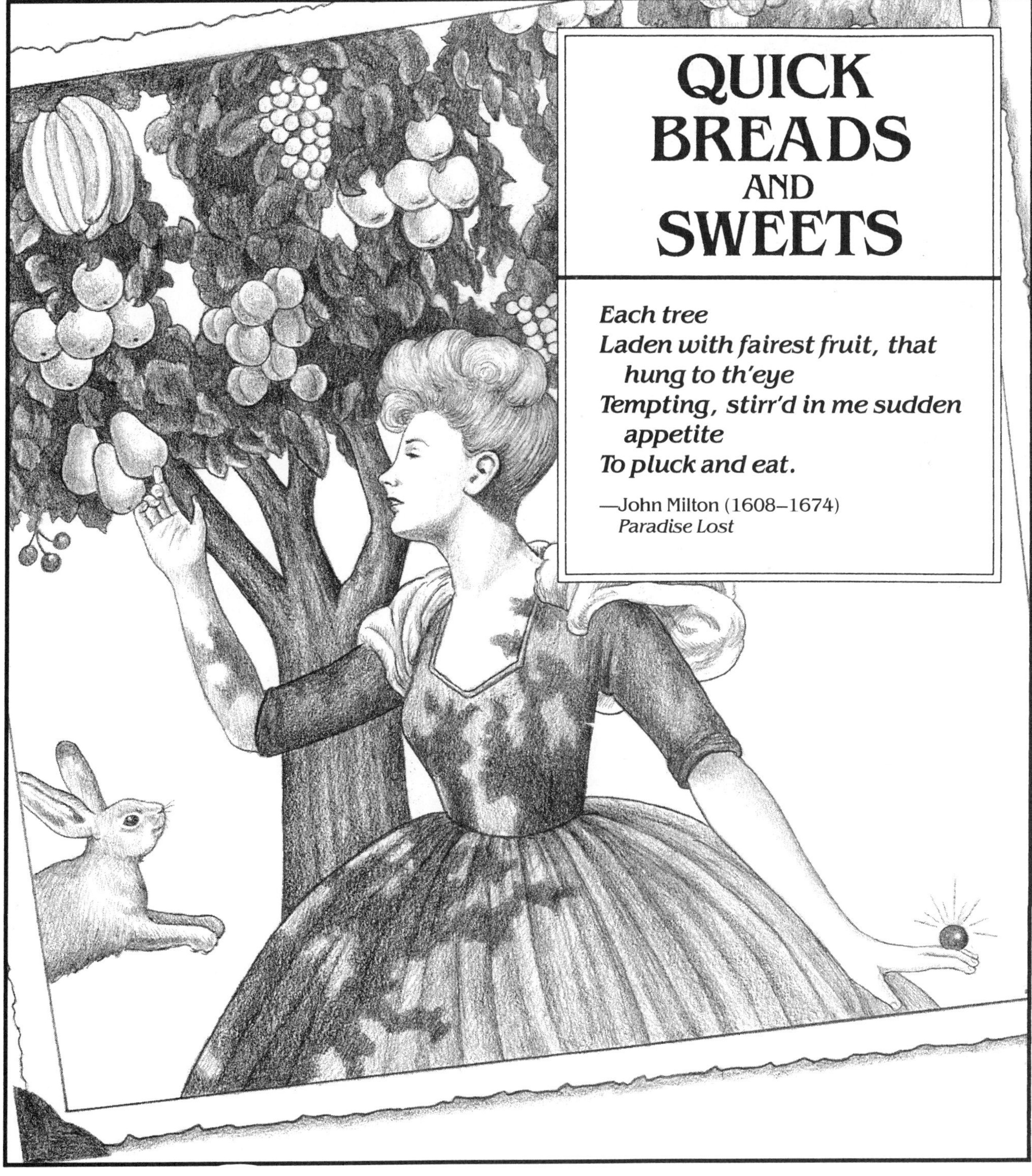

QUICK BREADS AND SWEETS

Each tree
Laden with fairest fruit, that
hung to th'eye
Tempting, stirr'd in me sudden
appetite
To pluck and eat.

—John Milton (1608–1674)
Paradise Lost

Bread, the most basic of foods for many cultures, is in all its simplicity the symbol of plenty. Sacred to many, bread is the object of rituals of the harvest and of religion.

Bread is also associated with home, hearth, and family, and few things evoke such a strong sense of comfort and nostalgia as the scent of freshly baked bread. Unfortunately, most people now have neither the time nor the inclination to bake their own bread, and my busy life, as much as I love home cooking, rarely allows me the hours it takes to prepare yeasted bread doughs for baking. As an alternative, I am offering here several quick bread recipes which can be popped in and out of the oven in a relatively short time. These can at least approximate the pleasure of freshly baked loaves.

Bread is better than the song of birds.

—Danish Proverb

CHEESE-HERB BREAD

Makes 1 loaf

2¼ cups whole wheat pastry flour
2½ teaspoons baking powder
½ teaspoon salt
½ teaspoon each dried basil and dried dill
¼ teaspoon each dried marjoram and dried thyme
2 eggs, beaten
2 tablespoons honey
½ cup low-fat milk or soymilk
¼ cup safflower or vegetable oil
1 cup grated mild cheddar or Monterey Jack cheese or cheddar-style soy cheese

Preheat the oven to 350° F.

Combine the flour, baking powder, salt, and herbs in a large mixing bowl. Stir together until well mixed.

In a separate bowl, combine the beaten eggs with the honey, milk, and oil. Add the wet ingredients to the dry, a little at a time. Stir briskly until thoroughly blended. Add the cheese and stir until it is evenly distributed within the dough.

Oil and flour a 9-by-5-by-3-inch loaf pan and transfer the dough into it. Bake for 50 minutes, or until the top is golden brown and a knife inserted in the center comes out clean.

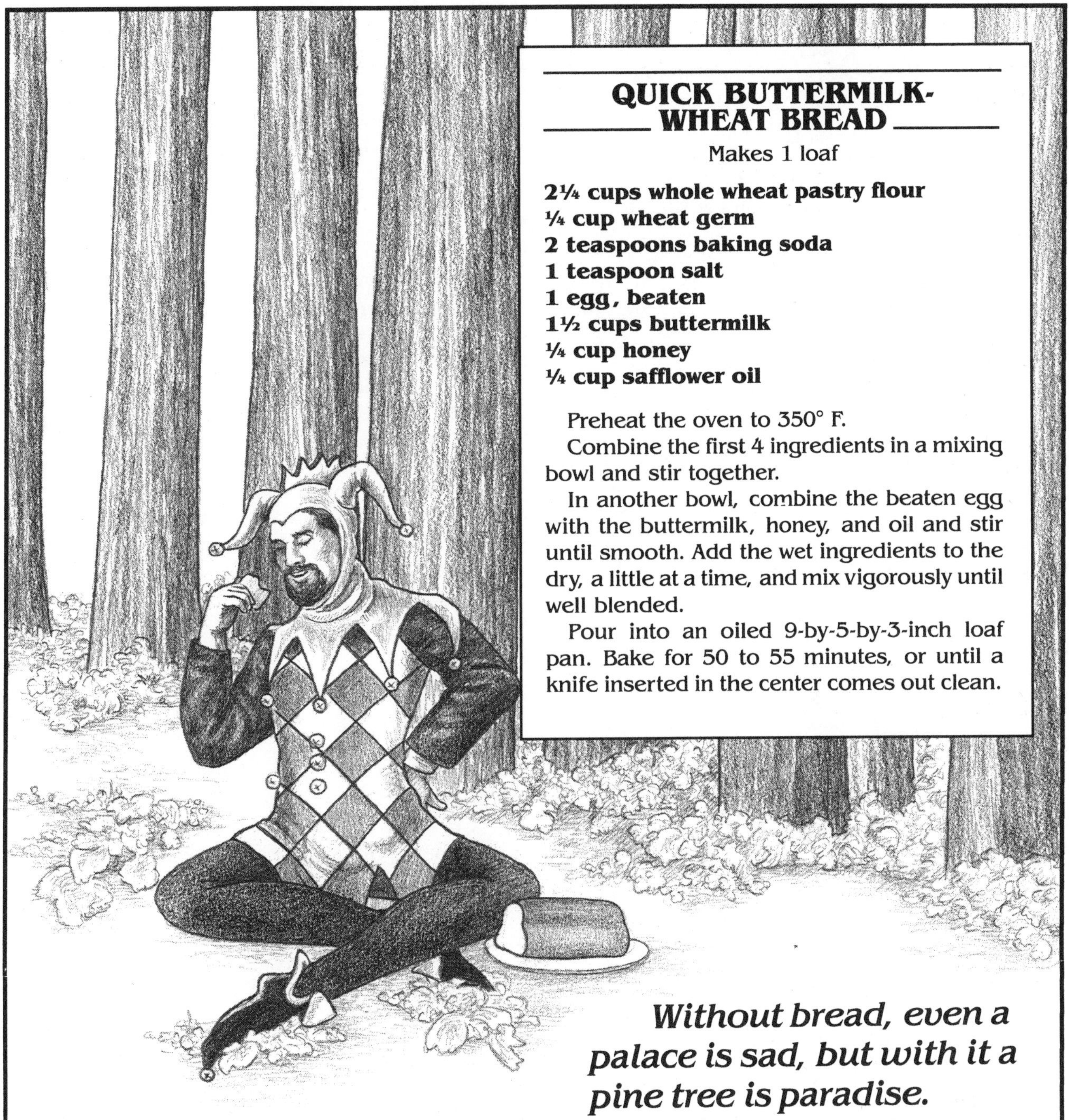

QUICK BUTTERMILK-WHEAT BREAD

Makes 1 loaf

2¼ cups whole wheat pastry flour
¼ cup wheat germ
2 teaspoons baking soda
1 teaspoon salt
1 egg, beaten
1½ cups buttermilk
¼ cup honey
¼ cup safflower oil

Preheat the oven to 350° F.

Combine the first 4 ingredients in a mixing bowl and stir together.

In another bowl, combine the beaten egg with the buttermilk, honey, and oil and stir until smooth. Add the wet ingredients to the dry, a little at a time, and mix vigorously until well blended.

Pour into an oiled 9-by-5-by-3-inch loaf pan. Bake for 50 to 55 minutes, or until a knife inserted in the center comes out clean.

Without bread, even a palace is sad, but with it a pine tree is paradise.

—Slavic Proverb

Long ago, it was believed that if cumin was fed to lovers, it would inspire them to remain faithful. It was customary for young ladies in Europe to present their soldier sweethearts with loaves of bread baked with cumin in order to insure their loyalty until their return.

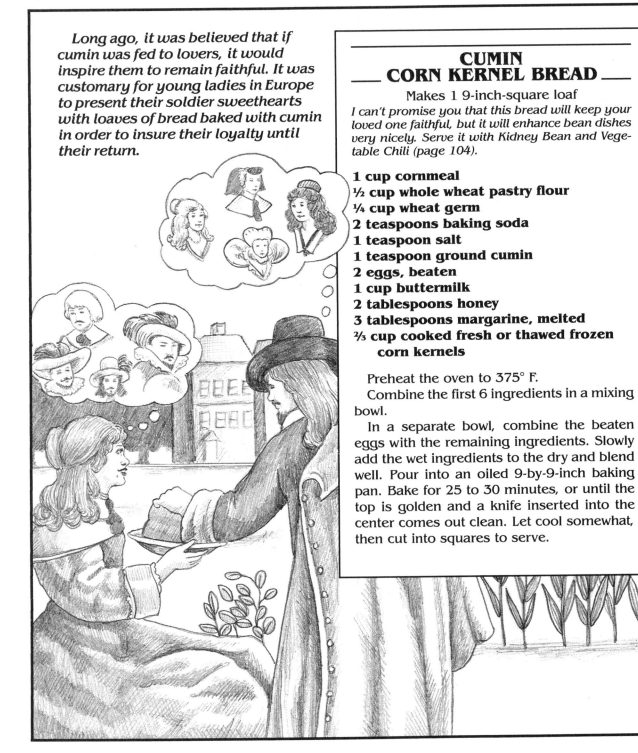

CUMIN CORN KERNEL BREAD

Makes 1 9-inch-square loaf

I can't promise you that this bread will keep your loved one faithful, but it will enhance bean dishes very nicely. Serve it with Kidney Bean and Vegetable Chili (page 104).

1 cup cornmeal
½ cup whole wheat pastry flour
¼ cup wheat germ
2 teaspoons baking soda
1 teaspoon salt
1 teaspoon ground cumin
2 eggs, beaten
1 cup buttermilk
2 tablespoons honey
3 tablespoons margarine, melted
⅔ cup cooked fresh or thawed frozen corn kernels

Preheat the oven to 375° F.

Combine the first 6 ingredients in a mixing bowl.

In a separate bowl, combine the beaten eggs with the remaining ingredients. Slowly add the wet ingredients to the dry and blend well. Pour into an oiled 9-by-9-inch baking pan. Bake for 25 to 30 minutes, or until the top is golden and a knife inserted into the center comes out clean. Let cool somewhat, then cut into squares to serve.

ONION RYE BREAD

Makes 1 loaf

Rather than make you weep, this bread will probably make you smile. It goes nicely with hearty soups—such as Lentil and Brown Rice Soup (page 26)—when they are going to comprise the main part of your meal.

1½ cups rye flour
1 cup unbleached white flour
3 tablespoons wheat germ
2 tablespoons brown sugar
1 teaspoon salt
2½ teaspoons baking powder
1 egg, beaten
1 cup buttermilk
3 tablespoons safflower oil
1 small onion, finely chopped
Caraway or poppy seeds for topping, optional

Preheat the oven to 350° F.

Combine the first 6 ingredients in a mixing bowl and stir together. In a separate bowl, combine the beaten eggs with the buttermilk and mix until smooth. Heat the oil in a small skillet. Add the onion and sauté over low heat until golden, then stir into the egg mixture.

Add the wet ingredients to the dry, a little at a time, stirring briskly until the ingredients are well blended into a sticky dough.

Oil and flour a 9-by-5-by-3-inch loaf pan and, with the aid of a cake spatula, transfer the dough into it. Sprinkle top with seeds if desired. Bake for 50 to 55 minutes, or until the top is golden and a knife inserted in the center comes out clean.

"Onions can make ev'n heirs and widows weep."

—Benjamin Franklin
Poor Richard's Almanack (1734)

ZUCCHINI BREAD

Makes 2 loaves

The grated zucchini almost disappears once this rich, cakelike bread is baked, but it leaves tiny green specks and gives the bread a special kind of moistness. This is a good way to use up those mammoth zucchini of late summer that aren't so good for cooking. If you use that type, discard the seedy pulp.

2 eggs, well beaten
⅔ cup safflower oil
1⅓ cups brown sugar
2 teaspoons vanilla extract
2 cups coarsely grated, peeled zucchini
2½ cups whole wheat pastry flour
½ cup wheat germ
3 teaspoons baking powder
1 teaspoon each salt, baking soda, and cinnamon
½ teaspoon ground cloves, optional
¾ cup chopped walnuts

Preheat the oven to 350° F.

In a mixing bowl, combine the beaten eggs with the oil, sugar, and vanilla. Stir in the grated zucchini. In another, large mixing bowl, stir together the remaining ingredients. Add the wet ingredients to the dry and mix until thoroughly combined. Pour into 2 oiled and floured 9-by-5-by-3-inch loaf pans and bake for 45 to 50 minutes, or until the top is nicely browned and a knife inserted in the center comes out clean.

TOMATO QUICK BREAD

Makes 1 loaf

This easy and unusual bread is a good companion for hearty soups.

2¼ cups whole wheat pastry flour
¼ cup unbleached white flour
1½ teaspoons baking powder
1 teaspoon baking soda
½ teaspoon salt
1 egg, beaten
¼ cup safflower oil
2 tablespoons honey
2 tablespoons finely minced fresh parsley
14-ounce can imported plum tomatoes with liquid
Poppy seeds for topping

Preheat the oven to 350° F.

Combine the first 5 ingredients in a mixing bowl. In another bowl, combine the beaten egg with the oil, honey, and parsley. Crush the tomatoes with your hands to break them into small pieces. Add them to the liquid ingredients. Pour the wet ingredients into the dry and stir until well blended. Pour into an oiled 9-by-5-by-3-inch loaf pan. Sprinkle poppy seeds over the top. Bake for 45 to 50 minutes, or until the top is nicely browned and a knife inserted in the center comes out clean.

SUN-DRIED TOMATO FOCACCIA BREAD

Makes 1 round loaf

Although this traditional Italian bread is yeasted, it does not take as long to make as other yeasted breads since it requires only one rather brief rising. The sun-dried tomatoes add surprising bursts of flavor.

1 package active dry yeast
1 tablespoon light brown sugar
4 tablespoons olive oil
¼ cup firmly packed minced, oil-cured sun-dried tomatoes
1½ cups whole wheat pastry flour
1 cup unbleached white flour
½ teaspoon salt
Garlic powder
Kosher (coarse) salt
Dried oregano or rosemary

Combine the yeast with 1 cup of warm water in a small bowl and let stand for 5 to 10 minutes, until dissolved. Stir in the brown sugar, half of the olive oil, and the sun-dried tomatoes.

In a large mixing bowl, combine the flours with the salt. Work the yeast mixture in, using your hands at the end. Turn out onto a well-floured board. Knead for 5 minutes, adding additional flour if the dough is too sticky. Shape into a round and roll out into a circle 12 inches in diameter. Cover with a tea towel and let rise in a warm place for 30 to 40 minutes. With your fingers, poke shallow holes all over the top at even intervals. Drizzle the remaining olive oil evenly over the top, then sprinkle with the garlic powder, kosher salt, and dried herb.

Bake in a preheated 400° F. oven for 20 to 25 minutes, or until the top of the bread is golden and sounds hollow when tapped. Serve warm, cut into wedges.

CLASSIC CARROT BREAD

Makes 1 loaf

2 eggs
⅓ cup safflower oil
⅔ cup light brown sugar
1 teaspoon vanilla extract
1 cup finely grated carrot
3 tablespoons apple or orange juice
1½ cups whole wheat pastry flour
1½ teaspoons baking powder
½ teaspoon salt
¼ teaspoon each ground cloves and ground allspice
⅓ cup chopped walnuts
⅓ cup raisins or currants

Preheat the oven to 350° F.

In a mixing bowl, beat the eggs together with the oil. Stir in the sugar until dissolved. Add the vanilla, carrot, and juice.

Combine all of the dry ingredients except the last 2 in another bowl. Add the wet ingredients to the dry and stir together until thoroughly mixed. Stir in the chopped nuts and raisins or currants. Pour into an oiled 9-by-5-by-3-inch loaf pan and bake for 45 to 50 minutes, or until a knife inserted into the center comes out clean.

All sorrows are less with bread.

—Spanish Proverb

CHEDDAR-OAT BANNOCKS

Makes 1 round bread

Bannocks are traditional Scottish flatbreads, similar to scones. These easy bannocks are wonderful served with hearty bean soups.

1 cup oat flour
½ cup rolled oats
½ cup whole wheat pastry flour
1 teaspoon salt
1 teaspoon baking powder
¼ cup (½ stick) margarine, softened
1 cup firmly packed grated cheddar cheese or cheddar-style soy cheese
¼ cup low-fat milk or soymilk, or more or less as needed
Poppy seeds for topping

Preheat the oven to 350° F.

Combine the first 5 ingredients in a mixing bowl. Blend the margarine into the mixture with the tines of a fork or a pastry knife until the mixture resembles a coarse meal. Stir in the cheddar cheese, then add milk as needed to form a soft dough. Turn out onto a floured board and knead briefly with floured hands. Form into a ball, then flatten. Roll into a round about ½ inch thick. Place on a lightly oiled baking sheet and sprinkle with poppy seeds. Score about halfway through with a knife to make 6 or 8 wedges. Bake for 10 to 12 minutes, until the top is nicely golden.

Shaw, as mentioned in the introduction, was a vegetarian for nearly seventy years, and really did relish good food. It was well known, however, that he had quite a sweet tooth and ate massive quantities of cakes, pastries, and honey. He managed to stay ever slender and lived to be ninety-four. In moderation, an occasional treat does not hurt.

In all the sweets that follow are included some healthy elements such as fruits, nuts, wheat germ and other whole grain substances, and dairy products.

"There is no love sincerer than the love of food."

—George Bernard Shaw
Man and Superman (1903)

BROWN RICE PUDDING

Serves 8 or more

William Vaughn, in Directions for Health *(1600), said "Rice sodden with milk and sugar qualifieth wonderfully the heat of the stomake, increaseth genital seede, and stoppeth the flux of the belly." I don't know if these claims are entirely true, but rice pudding is comforting, and children especially seem to like it.*

1½ cups raw small- or medium-grain brown rice
⅓ cup honey, or more or less to taste
1 medium sweet apple, peeled, cored, and coarsely grated
¾ cup raisins
1 cup low-fat milk or soymilk
2 teaspoons vanilla extract
1 teaspoon cinnamon
¼ teaspoon each ground nutmeg and ground cloves

Cook the rice as directed in Cooking Grains (page 214). When it is done, preheat the oven to 325° F.

Combine the cooked rice in a mixing bowl with the remaining ingredients. Mix thoroughly and pour the mixture into an oiled large shallow baking dish. Cover with a lid or foil and bake for 30 mintues. Then uncover and bake for 10 minutes longer.

APPLE CRISP

Serves 4 to 6

This version of old-fashioned apple crisp, a very easy and healthy dessert, was shared with me by a friend who assured me that it was even better served warm with vanilla ice cream.

5 medium sweet apples, peeled, cored, and thinly sliced
⅓ cup chopped walnuts or pecans
½ teaspoon cinnamon
¼ teaspoon ground cloves or ground nutmeg

Topping:
¼ cup whole wheat pastry flour
2 to 3 tablespoons brown sugar, to taste
3 tablespoons wheat germ
¼ teaspoon cinnamon
3 tablespoons margarine, softened and cut into bits

Preheat the oven to 350° F.

Combine the first 4 ingredients in a mixing bowl and mix together until the spices coat the apples fairly evenly. Oil a 9-by-9-inch baking pan and spoon the apple mixture into it.

Combine all of the topping ingredients, working everything together with the tines of a fork or a pastry blender until the mixture resembles crumbs. Sprinkle evenly over the apples and bake for 50 to 60 minutes, or until the apples are done and the topping is browned.

Serve on its own or with vanilla ice cream.

OF APPLES AND GRAVITY

The apple has been the subject of legend and proverb, in the guise of a love charm, a magical object, and a cure for every ill. But nowhere did the apple have such practical application as in the true story of Isaac Newton's formulation of the theory of gravity. In 1666, while having tea, Newton observed the falling of an apple in his garden. It was this event that led him to the concept of universal force, which is to say that although the falling of an apple from a tree seems different than the orbiting of the moon, the moon is in fact constantly falling toward the earth in much the same way. The earth's gravity pulling on the moon keeps it from flying off its orbit. Think of this the next time you have apple pie or gaze at the moon.

APRICOT BLONDIES

Makes 9 to 12 squares

¼ cup (½ stick) margarine, softened
½ cup honey
2 eggs, well beaten
⅓ cup low-fat milk or soymilk
1 teaspoon vanilla extract
1½ cups whole wheat pastry flour
1½ teaspoons baking powder
½ teaspoon cinnamon
¼ teaspoon each ground cloves and ground allspice
¾ cup finely diced apricots
½ cup chopped pecans or walnuts

Preheat the oven to 350° F.

In a mixing bowl, cream the margarine with the honey. Add the beaten eggs, milk, and vanilla and mix together until smooth. In another mixing bowl, sift together the flour, baking powder, and spices. Add the wet mixture to the dry and beat together until smoothly blended. Stir in the diced apricots and chopped nuts. Pour the mixture into an oiled 9-by-9-inch baking pan. Bake for 25 to 30 minutes, or until the top is golden and a knife inserted into the center comes out clean. Cool in the pan, then cut into 9 or 12 squares to serve.

CAROB RUM RAISIN PIE

Makes 1 pie, 6 to 8 servings

This dark pie tastes so rich, you won't believe you're eating something healthy.

Rolled-oat pie crust:
1 cup rolled oats
¼ cup whole wheat pastry flour
¼ cup (½ stick) margarine, softened
3 tablespoons honey

Filling:
½ pound soft or silken tofu, well drained
1 medium banana
⅓ cup carob powder
3 tablespoons honey or maple syrup
1 tablespoon margarine
2 tablespoons rum
½ teaspoon vanilla extract
¼ teaspoon each cinnamon and ground nutmeg
⅓ cup lightly floured raisins
¼ cup finely ground almonds for topping

Preheat the oven to 350° F.

In a mixing bowl, combine the oats with the flour. Work in the margarine with the tines of a fork or a pastry blender until the mixture resembles coarse crumbs. Stir in the honey plus enough water to hold the mixture together, about 3 tablespoons. Press the mixure into the bottom and up the sides of a 9-inch pie pan. Bake for 10 to 12 minutes, or until golden. Allow to cool before filling.

Place all of the filling ingredients except the raisins and almonds in the container of a food processor and process until smoothly pureed. Add the raisins and pulse on and off until they are chopped. Pour the filling into the cooled pie crust and sprinkle the ground almonds over the top. Chill for 1 to 2 hours before serving.

WINTER FRUIT CRISP

Serves 6

2 medium apples, peeled, cored, and thinly sliced
3 medium pears, cored and thinly sliced
1 cup chopped pitted prunes
¼ cup chopped walnuts or pecans, optional
⅓ cup carob syrup or maple syrup
¼ cup apple juice
½ teaspoon cinnamon
¼ teaspoon ground nutmeg
¼ teaspoon ground allspice

Topping:
¾ cup rolled oats
½ cup wheat germ
¼ cup whole wheat pastry flour
¼ cup (½ stick) margarine, melted
2 tablespoons light brown sugar

Preheat the oven to 350° F.

Combine the first 9 ingredients in a large mixing bowl and stir together well.

In another bowl, combine the ingredients for the topping. Spread half of the topping mixture over the bottom of a lightly oiled 9-by-9-inch baking pan. Pour in the fruit mixture, pat it smooth, and then top with the remaining topping mixture. Bake for 40 to 45 minutes, or until the fruit is tender and the crumbs are golden.

CHOCOLATE-COVERED WINTER FRUIT PIE

Serves 6 to 8

Eating this pie produces the curious sensation that one is having something very healthy yet very sinful at the same time.

1 large, sweet apple, peeled, cored, and thinly sliced
1 medium orange, sectioned and chopped
1 medium banana, sliced
1 medium pear, thinly sliced
¼ cup Amaretto or Grand Marnier
¼ cup chopped dates or black figs
1 teaspoon cinnamon
¼ teaspoon ground cloves
1 regular unbaked 9-inch pie shell
6 ounces (1 cup) semisweet chocolate chips
¾ cup rolled oats
¼ cup wheat germ
3 tablespoons margarine, melted

Preheat the oven to 350° F.

Combine the fruits in a mixing bowl with the liqueur, dried fruit, and spices. Mix well. Transfer the mixture to the pie shell and top as evenly as possible with the chocolate chips, making sure to get them into the crevices around the edges as well.

Combine the oats with the wheat germ in a small bowl. Pour the melted margarine over them and stir until evenly coated. Sprinkle the mixture evenly over the top of the pie.

Bake for 50 minutes, or until the oats are lightly browned, the fruit is done, and the chocolate chips are melted. Serve warm.

". . . It has been shown as proof-positive that carefully prepared chocolate is as healthful a food as it is pleasant; that it is nourishing and easily digested; that it does not cause the same harmful effects to feminine beauty which are blamed on coffee but is on the contrary a remedy for them; that it is above all helpful to people who must do a great deal of mental work, to those who labor in the pulpit or in the classroom, and especially to travellers . . ."

—Jean Anthelme Brillat-Savarin
The Physiology of Taste (1825)

CHOCOLATE CHIP PEANUT CAKE

Makes 9 squares

Now that chocolate has the endorsement of the famous gourmand Brillat-Savarin, let's get to it! Semisweet chocolate chips are my favorite way to indulge; here are two sinfully delicious ways to enjoy them.

¼ cup (½ stick) margarine, softened
½ cup peanut butter
⅓ cup brown sugar
1 egg, beaten
½ cup low-fat milk or soymilk
¾ cup whole wheat pastry flour
1½ teaspoons baking powder
½ teaspoon salt
⅓ cup chopped peanuts
6 ounces (1 cup) semisweet chocolate chips

Preheat the oven to 375° F.

Cream together the margarine, peanut butter, and brown sugar. Add the beaten egg and milk and stir until well blended. Stir in the flour, a little at a time, then add the remaining ingredients. Stir together until thoroughly blended. Pour into an oiled 9-by-9-inch cake pan. Bake for 25 to 30 minutes, or until the top is golden brown. Allow to cool and cut into squares to serve.

CHOCOLATE TOFU PIE

Makes 1 pie, 6 to 8 servings

This easy-to-make fudge pie is wonderfully smooth and rich-tasting.

Graham-cracker crust:
10 graham crackers
¼ cup (½ stick) margarine, cut into bits

Filling:
1 cup semisweet chocolate chips
1 pound soft or silken tofu
¼ cup low-fat milk or soymilk
⅓ cup honey
1 teaspoon vanilla extract

Preheat the oven to 350° F.

Pulverize the graham crackers in the container of a food processor until finely ground. Add the margarine to the container and process until well integrated with the graham-cracker crumbs. Press the mixture into the bottom and up the sides of a 9-inch pie pan.

Melt the chocolate chips with 2 tablespoons of water in a heavy saucepan or double boiler. Combine the tofu with the melted chocolate and the remaining ingredients in the container of a food processor and process until velvety smooth. Pour into the pie crust and bake for 30 to 35 minutes, or until the filling is firm and the crust is golden. Serve at room temperature or chilled.

OATMEAL-RAISIN COOKIES

Makes about 3 dozen

An easy recipe for this favorite cookie classic.

½ cup (1 stick) margarine, softened
1 cup light brown sugar
⅓ cup low-fat milk or soymilk
1 egg, beaten
1½ cups whole wheat pastry flour
1½ cups rolled oats
1 teaspoon baking powder
1 teaspoon cinnamon
¼ teaspoon salt
1 cup raisins
⅓ cup finely chopped walnuts, optional

Preheat the oven to 350° degrees.

In a small bowl, cream together the margarine, brown sugar, milk or soymilk, and egg until smooth.

In another bowl, combine the remaining ingredients except the raisins and walnuts. Pour the wet mixture into the dry and work together until well combined. Work in the raisins and walnuts.

Drop rounded tablespoonfuls onto cookie sheets, one at a time, and flatten slightly. Bake for 10 to 12 minutes, or until golden around the edges. Remove carefully and let cool on plates.

SESAME-DATE BROWNIES

Makes about 12 squares

Sesame seeds are reported by the Kama Sutra *to have definite aphrodisiac effects. One concoction listed results in a confection enabling a man to "enjoy innumerable women." I wouldn't make that claim for this sesame, date, and nut treat, but it does make for a high-energy snack.*

¼ cup dry, unsweetened cocoa
½ to ⅔ cup brown sugar, to taste
½ cup whole wheat pastry flour
¼ cup unbleached white flour
⅓ cup sesame seeds
1 teaspoon baking powder
½ teaspoon salt
2 eggs
¼ cup low-fat milk or soymilk
¼ cup (½ stick) margarine, melted
1½ cups pitted dates, finely chopped
¼ cup almonds or walnuts, finely chopped

Preheat oven to 350° F.

Combine the first 7 ingredients in a mixing bowl and stir together until well blended.

Beat the eggs and milk well in a separate bowl. Stir the melted margarine into the egg-milk mixture. Add the wet ingredients to the dry, a little at a time, and stir briskly until thoroughly blended.

Combine the chopped dates with the nuts.

Oil a shallow baking pan, approximately 8 by 13 inches, and pour half of the batter into it. Spread the date-nut mixture over it as evenly as possible, then top with the remaining batter. Bake for 25 to 30 minutes, or until a knife inserted into the center comes out clean. Allow to cool and cut into squares to serve.

SESAME DROPS

Makes about 3 dozen

These crisp little cookies are not too sweet, but positively addictive.

½ cup (1 stick) margarine
⅔ cup light brown sugar
1 egg, beaten
½ cup low-fat milk or soymilk
½ teaspoon vanilla extract
2 cups whole wheat pastry flour
½ teaspoon each salt and baking powder
¼ teaspoon cinnamon
½ cup unhulled sesame seeds

Preheat the oven to 375° F.

Cream together the margarine and the brown sugar. Combine with the beaten egg, milk or soymilk, and vanilla and beat until smooth. In another mixing bowl, combine the flour with the salt, baking powder, cinnamon, and sesame seeds. Work the wet mixture into the dry until thoroughly combined into a stiff batter. Drop heaping teaspoonfuls onto a cookie sheet, one at a time. Bake for 10 to 12 minutes, or until lightly golden. Cool on a rack.

"The use of Honey is so soveraigne that nothing in our cold countries comes neare it for goodnesse and perfection: insomuch that it is rightly called Flos Florum, the flower of flowers, or rather their quintessence. It makes old men young, preserving their naturall heate, if they know how to use it."

—William Vaughn
Directions for Health (1617)

HONEY SWEET-POTATO PIE

Makes 1 9-inch pie

Making this southern American classic with honey rather than sugar enhances its velvety-smooth texture. This is often mistaken for pumpkin pie, so similar is the flavor and consistency.

2 heaping cups firmly packed cooked and diced sweet potato (about 1 very large)
½ cup low-fat milk or soymilk
1 teaspoon vanilla or almond extract
⅓ cup honey, or more or less to taste
1 teaspoon each cinnamon and unsweetened cocoa powder
½ teaspoon ground nutmeg
¼ teaspoon ground ginger
1 regular unbaked 9-inch pie crust

Preheat the oven to 350° F.

Place the diced sweet potato in the container of a food processor. Add the remaining filling ingredients and process until completely smooth. Pour into the pie crust.

Bake for 45 to 50 minutes, or until the crust is golden and the pie is lightly browned on top. Allow to cool before serving.

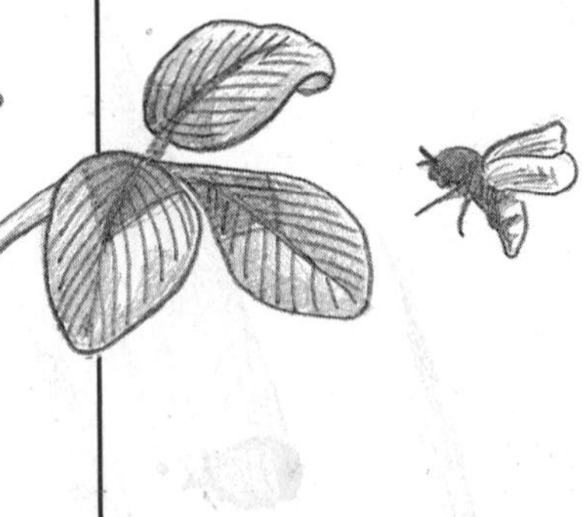

FRESH STRAWBERRY-CITRUS CUSTARD CAKE

Makes 1 9-inch round or square cake

A thin layer of baked batter serves as an anchor for a fresh citrus custard full of fresh strawberries.

Batter:
1 cup whole wheat pastry flour
1½ teaspoons baking powder
¼ teaspoon salt
1 egg, well beaten
3 tablespoons honey
3 tablespoons safflower oil
⅓ cup low-fat milk or soymilk
Juice of ½ lemon

Preheat the oven to 375° F.

Combine the first 3 ingredients in a mixing bowl. Combine the remaining ingredients in another bowl and mix together. Add the wet ingredients to the dry and stir together until well blended. Oil a 9-inch round or square baking pan and pour the batter into it. Bake for 20 to 25 minutes, or until lightly browned. Start on the custard once the batter is out of the oven.

Custard:
½ cup fresh orange juice
Juice of ½ lemon
1 teaspoon grated lemon rind
2 to 3 tablespoons honey, to taste
2 tablespoons cornstarch
1 pint ripe fresh strawberries, hulled and chopped

Combine all the ingredients except the strawberries in a heavy saucepan, dissolving the cornstarch in a little water before adding it. Whisk together and heat slowly over low heat, whisking continuously for 3 to 4 minutes or until thick. Remove from the heat. Stir in the strawberries and pour the whole mixture over the baked batter. Chill, then cut into wedges or squares and serve.

UNBAKED CHERRY-CHEESE PIE

Makes 1 9-inch pie

Any fresh berry may be substituted to top the pie, including small, halved strawberries, blueberries, or raspberries. Since the pie is unbaked, it makes an ideal summer dessert for special occasions.

Crust:
1½ cups natural bran-flake cereal
½ cup wheat germ
½ teaspoon cinnamon
1 tablespoon honey
3 tablespoons margarine, melted

Filling:
8 ounces cream cheese, softened
½ cup cottage cheese
2 tablespoons lemon juice
1 teaspoon grated lemon rind
¼ cup honey

Topping:
½ pound fresh cherries, pitted and halved
1 to 2 tablespoons cherry brandy, optional

Crush the bran flakes finely, either with a rolling pin or in a food processor. Combine them in a small bowl with the remaining crust ingredients and stir together. Transfer to a lightly oiled 9-inch round or square baking pan and pat in well.

Cut the cream cheese into several smaller pieces and combine with the remaining filling ingredients in the container of a food processor. Process until completely smooth. Pour over the crumb crust, smoothing it in evenly with the aid of a cake spatula. Arrange the cherries on top, cut side down, and drizzle with the brandy, if desired. Cover and chill for at least 2 hours before serving. Cut into wedges or squares to serve.

Walnuts were served at wedding feasts in ancient Greece and Rome, where they were regarded as favorable to the fertility of the bridal couple. Conversely, in old Rumania, a bride would place in her bodice one roasted walnut for each year she wished to remain childless.

WALNUT AND MAPLE BAKED PEARS

Serves 4 to 6

Like Apple Crisp, this easy fruit and nut dessert is wonderful served with vanilla ice cream.

5 medium firm but ripe pears, such as bosc
2 tablespoons margarine
1 cup chopped walnuts
⅓ cup maple syrup
¼ cup currants or raisins
¼ cup wheat germ
¼ cup apple juice
3 tablespoons almond liqueur
1 teaspoon vanilla or almond extract
½ teaspoon cinnamon

Preheat the oven to 350° F.

Cut the pears into quarters lengthwise (you don't have to peel them), remove the cores and stem ends, then cut each quarter in half lengthwise. Lightly oil a large shallow baking dish and arrange the pear slices in rows, alternating the thin and thick ends so that more slices can fit. Make only a single layer of pears; if you run out of room, use another baking dish.

Melt the margarine in a small saucepan over low heat. Remove from the heat and stir in all the remaining ingredients. Mix thoroughly. Spread the mixture evenly over the pears and bake 50 minutes. As suggested above, serve warm with vanilla ice cream.

ALMOND PRESERVE BARS

Makes about 3 dozen bars

In keeping with the almond tree's reputation for haste, this dessert can be made quickly. These are somewhat like cookies; each bar goes a long way.

½ cup whole wheat pastry flour
¼ cup wheat germ
¼ cup brown sugar
2 teaspoons unsweetened cocoa powder
3 tablespoons margarine, melted
1½ cups ground almonds
½ cup good quality berry preserves, such as blueberry, raspberry, or other
1 teaspoon vanilla

Preheat the oven to 350° F.

Combine the first 4 ingredients in a small bowl and stir together. Pour the melted margarine into the dry ingredients and stir together until they are coated. Set aside.

Combine the almonds with the preserves and vanilla. Stir until thoroughly mixed.

Oil a 9-by-9-inch baking pan. Line the bottom with half of the crumb mixture and pat in firmly. Pour in the almond and preserve mixture, pat in well, and sprinkle the top with the remaining crumbs. Bake for 30 to 35 minutes. Allow to cool and cut into approximately 1½-by-2-inch bars.

The Hebrew word for almond, "shakad," means to awaken early or to make haste. This name is given to the tree and its fruit due to its rapid growth, and thus, in the ancient Hebrew era, the almond tree symbolized haste, as it did in the biblical story of Aaron's rod. Its sudden blossoming was a harbinger of spring.

The Fruit of Knowledge, offered to Eve and Adam in the Garden of Eden, is commonly thought to have been an apple, but the fact is that the apple was never specifically named as such in the Bible. John Gerarde, in his Herball (1636), called the banana tree Adam's Apple Tree, and many Christians and Jews of his time considered the banana tree the Tree of Knowledge.

The fig tree, whose fruit is supposed among the first cultivated by man, was the retreat that Adam found after having eaten of the forbidden fruit. From there he plucked the fig leaf that hid his nakedness, and today, the fig leaf is still an emblem of modesty.

FRUITS OF PARADISE IN CREAM

Serves 4

The friend who introduced me to the concept of combining bananas with black figs in cream thought that the origin of this dish might be Moroccan. Although I couldn't verify this, I liked the idea and embellished it. The result is a rich spiced winter fruit melange. Black or mission figs are softer and sweeter than brown figs; you find them in imported-food shops and supermarkets.

2 large bananas, sliced
8 to 10 dried black (mission) figs, chopped
1 medium tart apple, peeled, cored, and thinly sliced
⅓ cup chopped walnuts, almonds, or pecans
½ cup light cream
½ teaspoon vanilla or almond extract
½ teaspoon cinnamon
¼ teaspoon ground cloves
¼ teaspoon ground cardamom, optional

Combine the first 4 ingredients in a serving bowl. In a small bowl, combine the cream with the remaining ingredients and stir together. Pour over the fruit mixture and mix thoroughly.

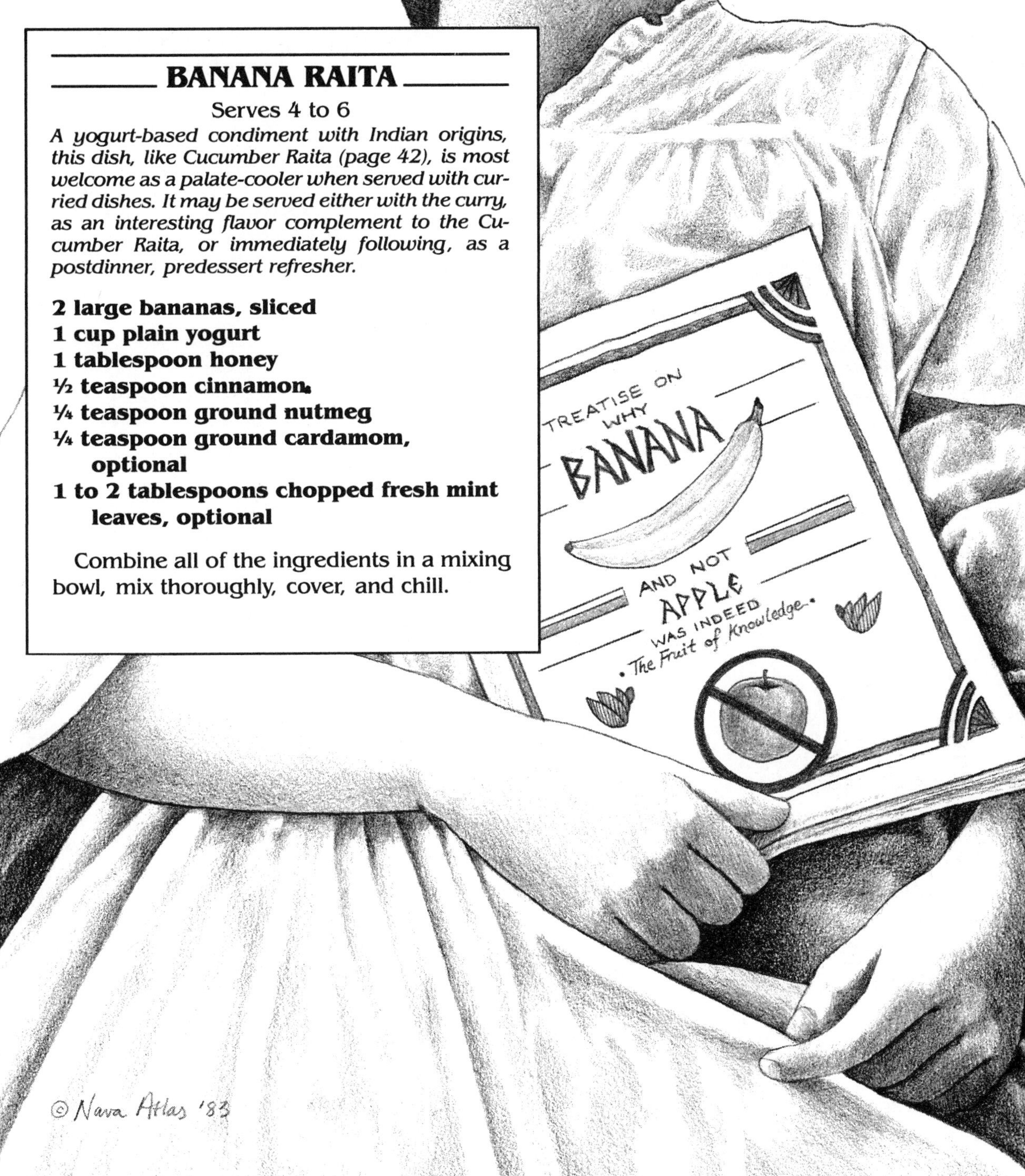
TREATISE ON
WHY
BANANA
AND NOT
APPLE
WAS INDEED
• The Fruit of Knowledge •
© Nava Atlas '83

BANANA RAITA

Serves 4 to 6

A yogurt-based condiment with Indian origins, this dish, like Cucumber Raita (page 42), is most welcome as a palate-cooler when served with curried dishes. It may be served either with the curry, as an interesting flavor complement to the Cucumber Raita, or immediately following, as a postdinner, predessert refresher.

2 large bananas, sliced
1 cup plain yogurt
1 tablespoon honey
½ teaspoon cinnamon
¼ teaspoon ground nutmeg
¼ teaspoon ground cardamom, optional
1 to 2 tablespoons chopped fresh mint leaves, optional

Combine all of the ingredients in a mixing bowl, mix thoroughly, cover, and chill.

The next time you happen upon an area with authentic colonial homes, look for a carving of a pineapple on the doorway or gatepost. The practice of carving or painting pineapples on entrances originated with the Indians of the West Indies, who cultivated the fruit and considered it a symbol of friendship and hospitality. This custom was taken back to Europe by the Spanish, who spread it to England; it was then carried back to the new American colonies. The pineapple symbol was meant to assure visitors that they would receive a warm welcome.

PINEAPPLE AND ORANGES IN YOGURT

Serves 6

This refreshing fruit salad makes for a particularly sweet finish to a Chinese-style dinner. If you like, you can serve it with almond cookies.

3 heaping cups diced pineapple, preferably fresh
2 medium oranges, sectioned and seeded
1 cup plain yogurt
½ cup chopped or slivered almonds
2 to 3 tablespoons honey, to taste
¼ cup shredded coconut, optional
½ teaspoon anise extract, optional

If fresh pineapple is unavailable and you'd like to use canned, make sure it is unsweetened. Drain it and reserve the juice for another purpose, perhaps to add to a fruit juice.

Combine all of the ingredients in a serving bowl and chill before serving.

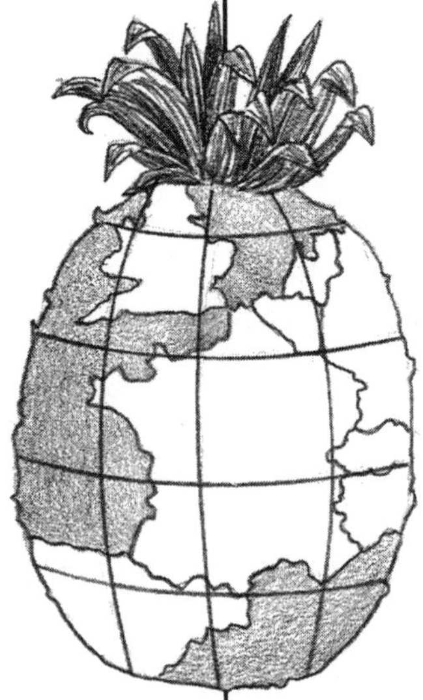

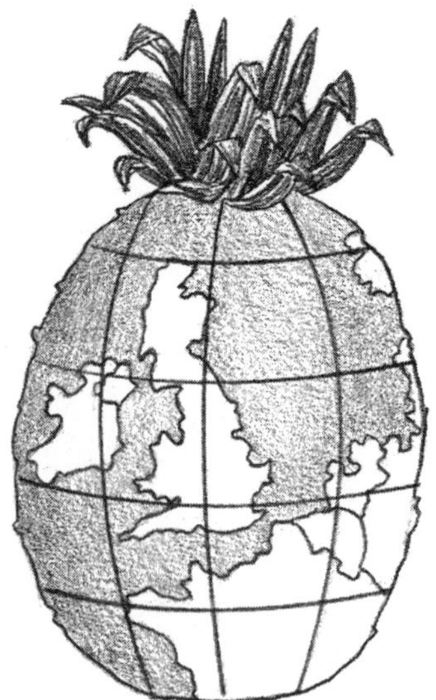

Nose, nose, jolly red nose,
And what gave thee that jolly red nose?
Nutmeg and ginger, cinnamon and cloves,
That's what gave me this jolly red nose.

—Thomas Ravencroft
Deuteromelia (1609)

SPICY SUMMER FRUIT

Serves 6

The man in this old English rhyme would have us believe that these spices (not his imbibing) caused his red nose. A light touch of the same spices enhances this ambrosial fruit salad, which definitely will have no effect on the color of your proboscis.

6 to 7 cups fresh summer fruit (choose several among strawberries, cherries, blueberries, melons, peaches, plums, nectarines, mangoes, etc.), diced
1½ cups plain yogurt
⅓ cup currants or raisins
2 tablespoons honey
½ teaspoon freshly grated ginger
1 teaspoon cinnamon
¼ teaspoon each ground nutmeg and ground cloves

Combine all of the ingredients in a large mixing bowl and mix thoroughly. Cover and chill before serving.

This is a depiction after a Chinese sculpture in wood of Shou-Lao, the God of long life. Shou-Lao holds a peach, which is in Chinese tradition the symbol of longevity and immortality. In Taoist depictions of immortality, an old man emerges from a peach. The peach is also a feminine sexual symbol in the Orient, and its blossoms are the emblem of a bride.

FRESH PEACH CRUMB CAKE

Serves 6 to 8

Lushly sweet but firm summer peaches are best for this cake.

1 cup wheat germ
¾ cup unbleached white flour
⅓ cup brown sugar
1 teaspoon cinnamon
½ teaspoon ground ginger
¼ teaspoon ground nutmeg
¼ cup (½ stick) margarine, melted
3 heaping cups thinly sliced peaches (about 4 large peaches)
½ cup finely chopped almonds

Preheat the oven to 325° F.

Combine the first 6 ingredients in a mixing bowl. Combine the margarine with the dry ingredients until they are evenly coated and resemble coarse crumbs

Oil a 9-inch round or square cake pan. Spread one third of the crumbs over the bottom. Arrange half of the peach slices in overlapping rows over the crumbs, then sprinkle half of the almonds over them. Repeat with another third of the crumbs and the remaining peaches and almonds, followed by the remaining crumbs. Cover with foil and bake for 20 minutes, then uncover and bake for 20 minutes longer. Cool before serving, then cut into wedges or squares to serve.

Better one bite of the peach of immortality than a whole basket of apricots.

—Chinese Proverb

HERBS AND SPICES

Can you make me a cambric shirt,
Parsley, sage, rosemary, and
thyme,
Without any seam or needlework?
And you shall be a true lover of
mine.

Can you wash it in yonder well,
Parsley, sage, rosemary, and
thyme,
Where never sprung water, not
rain ever fell?
And you shall be a true lover of
mine.

Can you dry it on yonder thorn,
Parsley, sage, rosemary, and
thyme,
Which never bore blossom since
Adam was born?
And you shall be a true lover of
mine...

—Old English Song

Herbs and spices once played a much more important role in everyday life than they do today, as they were valued not only for their usefulness in cookery, but for their lovely scent, their beauty as plants, and their medicinal properties. They have been cultivated and used for thousands of years, as far back as ancient India and China and classical Greece and Rome.

As objects of mystery and beauty, herbs and spices have adorned countless poetic lines, with names like elecampane, lavender, lovage, and Angelica. They were also imbued with magical powers, both good and bad. The refrain "parsley, sage, rosemary, and thyme," having been recently made familiar by the popular song, is actually hundreds of years old, and it is theorized that it was perhaps a witches' incantation, as those herbs were thought to have numerous magical and medicinal properties. Until relatively recently, herbs were the mainstays of everyday medicine, and today, with the superstition sifted out, it is known that they truly do possess wonderful curative values. The Chinese, in fact, have learned to incorporate herbal healing with modern medical technique.

ANISEEDS are the seeds of an herbaceous plant and have a distinctive, pleasant licorice taste; they are used to produce the liqueurs anisette, ouzo, and pastis. Anise is most commonly used in baking and gives an unusual twist to fruit desserts (see Pineapple and Oranges in Yogurt, page 200).

In folk belief, sprigs of anise were attached to pillows to ward off unpleasant dreams, and the seeds were eaten in hopes of restoring a youthful appearance to facial features.

BASIL, sometimes called sweet basil, has a history more controversial than that of any other herb. Basil is most delightful used fresh, either as a windowsill herb or bought in large, fragrant bunches in late summer and early autumn. If you have an opportunity to use fresh basil, substitute it in a 3 to 1 ratio to dry amounts given in the recipes. Basil has a special affinity with tomato-based dishes and pastas, but its pleasant fragrance and distinctive flavor also enhance many types of vegetables, grain dishes, salads, and soups.

This herb has many contradictory facets; its original name, basilisk, meant either "kingly" or a deadly dragon. In the Pasta chapter, basil's association with love in Italy is depicted, as well as the strange way it was sown in ancient Greece (pages 136 and 137), where it was at one time the symbol for hatred. In India, on the other hand, basil was considered a most sacred herb. Basil played an important role in the gory tales of Salome, and later in the story of Isabella and Her Pot of Basil. Strangest of all was its unfortunate association with scorpions: it was believed to be responsible for breeding scorpions both where it grew and in the brain. Paradoxically, basil was also considered an antidote to the scorpion's venom.

BAY LEAVES are the leaves of the bay laurel tree. They are used mainly for flavoring soups, stews, and pilafs.

In Greek mythology, the wood-nymph Daphne was so repelled by Apollo's pursuit of her that she prayed fervently to the gods for protection. They heard her pleas and changed her into a bay laurel tree. Apollo then declared that the laurel tree would remain forever green, and its leaves would henceforth be symbolic of bravery and accomplishment. Laurel leaves were woven into the head wreaths of worthy ancients of Greece and Rome, and thus we get the expression "to rest on one's laurels."

The bay laurel tree was once widely believed to have vast supernatural powers.

> ***"It is a tree of the Sun, and under the Celestial sign Leo, and resisteth Witchcraft potently, as also all the evils old Saturn can do the body of man... neither witch nor devil, thunder nor lightning, will hurt a man where a bay tree is."***
>
> —Nicolas Culpeper

CARAWAY SEEDS are the seeds of a biennial herb native to Europe. We know them best from their use in rye bread, but they are also good used subtly in potato and cheese dishes.

> ***"Nay, you shall see my orchard where in an arbour, we will eat a last year's pippin of mine own grafting, with a dish of carraways, and so forth..."***
>
> —William Shakespeare
> *Henry IV* (ca. 1597)

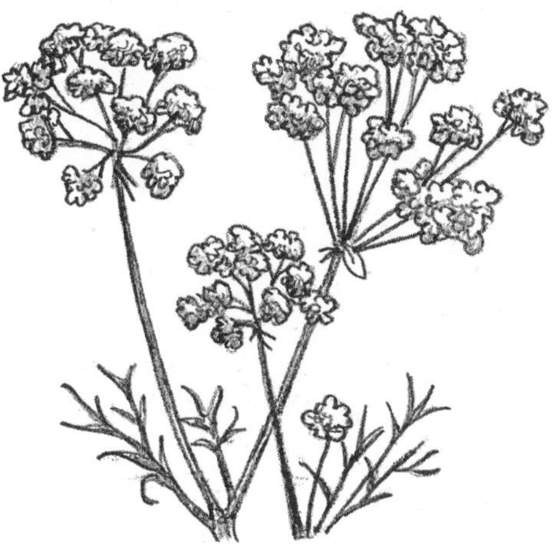

CARDAMOM refers to the whole or ground aromatic seeds of the fruit of a tall herbal plant that is grown primarily in India and Sri Lanka. The fruits are pale green pods that contain a dozen or so tiny dark seeds. Used extensively in Indian and other East Asian cookery, cardamom is not widely used in the United States. Aside from its use in curries (see Lusty Curried Peas, page 114) and chutneys, cardamom can be used in ground form for baking; it also goes nicely with bananas (see Banana Raita, page 199), apples, and sweet potatoes.

CAYENNE PEPPER comes from the ground dried fruit of the capsicum pepper, a climbing plant. It is a very hot spice, useful in curries, chutneys, chilies, cheese dishes, "hot and spicy" Chinese dishes, in fact anywhere that some fire is desired! Until you are well acquainted with its strength, use it sparingly.

> *"Powder thereof put in the nose causeth to snese and clense the brayn of flewmatyke humours as snyvell and rewme."*
>
> —Grete Herball (1529)

CHIVES, see Onion

CILANTRO, see Coriander

CINNAMON comes from the dried, aromatic inner bark of a small evergreen tree. It is one of the oldest spices known, mentioned in ancient Chinese writings and in the Bible. Cinnamon is the most widely used baking spice, and enhances any fresh or baked fruit dessert. It is also very good in curries.

> *"Cinnamon corroborateth all the powers of the body, restoreth them that bee decayed, purgeth the head, and succoureth the cough."*
>
> —William Vaughn
> *Directions for Health* (1600)

CLOVES are the dried flower buds of the evergreen clove tree, most commonly used in ground form for baking. Cloves especially enhance apple and banana desserts and may also be used in curries and chutneys.

The word "clove" comes from the Latin "clavus," meaning nail, as that is what the clove bud resembles.

CORIANDER is the seed of an herbal plant whose leaves are known as *cilantro*. The seeds are usually used ground and are a most useful spice, with a unique flavor and aromatic quality. They enhance bean and corn dishes, curries, chilies, and soups. The coriander leaves, or cilantro, are sometimes called Spanish or Chinese parsley, and are used in Spanish, Mexican, Chinese, and Indian cookery. The seeds and leaves have entirely different flavors and cannot be used interchangeably. If fresh cilantro is unavailable, use fresh Italian parsley, though there is no comparison in flavor.

In the Bible, the food of heaven, manna, was compared to coriander seed. It was mentioned as an aphrodisiac in *The Thousand and One Nights,* and was one of the plants in the Hanging Gardens of Babylon.

CUMIN comes from the seedlike fruit of a small herb native to the Mediterranean. Although the flavors of coriander and cumin are quite different from one another, they enhance each other wonderfully, and I recommend cumin for the same dishes mentioned for coriander. Its spicy yet not overly hot flavor is the basis for premixed curry and chili powders.

Cumin suffered from a bad reputation for a time in ancient Greece, where it symbolized avarice and meanness. Later, however, it was considered to have properties that would cause lovers to remain faithful (see Cumin Corn Kernel Bread, page 182), Pliny the Elder being one of those who advocated its use.

CURRY, or more specifically "curry powder," is not a spice in and of itself, but a mixture of several different spices. In true Indian cookery most of these spices are bought whole, toasted, and then ground with a mortar and pestle. A good compromise between this and using commercial curry powder is to mix a batch of good quality, preground spices and store the mixture in a tightly capped jar. A curry mix can have varying amounts of a number of spices, resulting in different types of flavors. Here is a formula that I enjoy using.

HOME-MIXED CURRY

2 teaspoons ground cumin
2 teaspoons ground coriander
2 teaspoons ground turmeric
1 teaspoon ground nutmeg
1 teaspoon salt
½ teaspoon cinnamon
¼ teaspoon cayenne pepper
¼ teaspoon freshly ground black pepper

Simply spoon each of the spices into a spice jar and shake well to mix. Compare the rich scent of this mixture with a supermarket curry powder and you won't believe the difference. Another alternative is to buy a premixed curry from a spice shop or an Indian food shop. This is what is referred to in the recipes as "good curry powder."

DILL, sometimes called dill weed, and **DILL SEED** come from a tall, feathery annual plant. Believed to have a soothing effect on both the digestive tract and the mind, dill gets its name from the Norwegian "dilla," meaning "to lull." The leaves are common in both fresh and dry form and are widely useful in soups, salads, dressings, potato and vegetable dishes, and wherever a mixture of herbs is called for. The seeds are used for pickling and are worth experimenting with for the same usages as the leaves, where they have a similar but much subtler effect than caraway seeds. Dill makes a fine windowsill herb.

The herbalist Culpeper said of dill, "Mercury hath dominion of this plant, and therefore to be sure it strengthens the brain." A seventeenth-century physician most charmingly recommended dill to stop "yeox, hicket, hisquet, or hickock," known today as hiccups. Dill was once widely used as a foil against witchcraft.

Trefoil, vervain, John's wort, dill,
Hinders witches of their will . . .

—Sir Walter Scott (1771–1832)
"The Nativity Chant"

FENNEL SEED is the ground seeds of another tall, feathery plant, different from the celerylike variety of fennel that is eaten as a vegetable. Fennel seed is aromatic and has a licorice flavor similar to but subtler than anise. It can be used for baking, for fruit desserts, and in small amounts where a mixture of herbs is called for to give an unusual twist (see Winter Potato and String Bean Stew, page 166).

Although no longer a very widely used kitchen spice, fennel seed has a full and fascinating legacy. Pliny the Elder, among others, believed that serpents ate fennel when they shed their skin, in order to renew their youth and strengthen their sight. In Italy, fennel was the symbol of flattery; the expression "dare finnocio," to flatter, literally means "to give fennel." Fennel's virtues were considered so numerous that a thirteenth-century physician said that "he who sees fennel and gathers it not, is not a man but a devil."

Above the lowly plants it towers
The fennel, with its yellow flowers,
And in an earlier age than ours,
Was gifted with the wondrous
powers,
Lost vision to restore...

—Henry Wadsworth Longfellow (1807–1882)
"The Goblet of Life"

GARLIC, see Onion

GINGER is the underground stem, or root, of a tropical plant that originated in some Pacific islands. An ancient spice, it was known to Confucius and mentioned in the Koran. Powdered ginger is acceptable for baking, but the freshly grated root is superior for giving Indian- and Chinese-style cookery an authentic character. It is also pleasant used subtly in fruit salads. Look for ginger root in Oriental groceries, produce markets, and even some supermarkets. Depending on the quantity used, ginger lends anything from a nice zest to fiery heat. Use it conservatively until you know its strength.

"Yes, by Saint Anne, the Ginger shall be hot i' thy mouth too."

—William Shakespeare
Twelfth Night (ca. 1601)

MARJORAM and **OREGANO** come from small herbaceous plants that are so closely related to one another that they share a botanical name, "origanum." Marjoram is a bit milder than oregano, although a bit more peppery, and they are widely useful for basically the same things: tomato-based dishes that are Italian-style, pastas, salads, vetetables, soups, grain dishes, chilies, and wherever a mixture of herbs is called for.

In legend and poetry, oregano takes a back seat to marjoram. Culpeper's *Herbal* says that marjoram is warming and comforting, and Gerarde in his *Herball* claims that it is "good for those who are given to overmuch sighing."

And tho' sweet marjoram will your
garden paint
With no gay colours, yet preserve the
plant,
Whose fragrance will invite your
kind regard,
When her known virtues have her
worth declared.

—Anonymous

MINT is the name for a related variety of plants with aromatic foliage. Spearmint and peppermint are the primary mints used not only for cookery but for mint teas. Mint gives a light, refreshing flavor to certain fruit desserts and raitas (the palate-cooling salads served with curries—see Cucumber Raita, page 42, and Banana Raita, page 199) and has a nice affinity with green peas. Mint is often called for in the classic Tabouleh salad (page 48).

Mint gets its name from a nymph of classical mythology who was called Mintha, or sometimes Minthes. Pluto was in love with her, so his jealous wife turned her into a mint plant.

I am that flower
That Mint
That Columbine.

—William Shakespeare
Love's Labour's Lost (ca. 1594)

MUSTARD comes from the seed of an Old World annual. It is useful wherever a subtle hotness is required, whether in soups, cheese dishes, egg dishes, grains, chilies, or curries. Prepared mustard is also made from mustard seed. I recommend the brown, Dijon-style mustard for cookery, and it doesn't have to be terribly expensive to be good.

One of the many legends about mustard relates that Alexander the Great was sent a sack of sesame seeds by Darius of Persia, to show him how vast was the Persian army. Alexander the Great then sent back to Darius a sack of mustard seed, symbolizing not only the size of his army, but its might. A tale from the Orient describes how the Buddha tells a distressed mother who seeks his help that he can bring her dead child to life only if she brings him some mustard seed from a home where no person has died. After an exhaustive search, she realizes that no family is exempt from the experience of death.

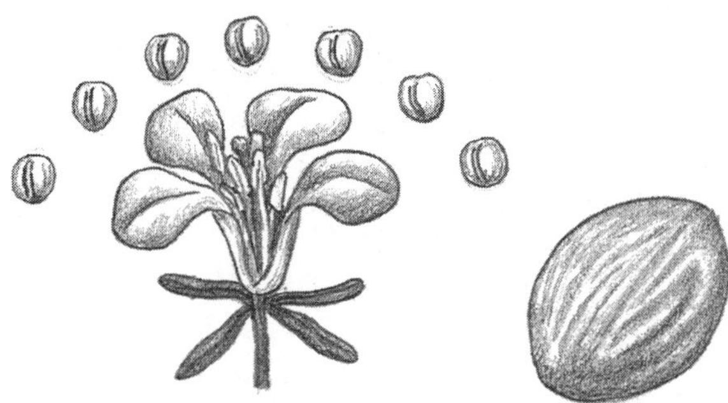

NUTMEG comes from the dried seed of the nutmeg tree, an evergreen tree that also produces mace. Nutmeg is extensively used in baking; it also enhances fruit desserts and complements the flavors of spinach, sweet potato, and squashes, including pumpkin. It may also be an element in curry.

Connecticut is known as the Nutmeg State because in the early nineteenth century unscrupulous peddlers sold wooden nutmegs to housewives.

ONION, GARLIC, SCALLION, and **CHIVES** are related herbs of the lily family. All of them, especially onion and garlic, are not only among the most ancient of cultivated plants, but also among the most widely used herbs across many cultures. Their uses are too numerous to list, and even the most basic of cooks is usually aware of their many virtues.

Both onions and garlic are highly valued in herbal medicine, believed even today to have absorptive and antiseptic qualities. If you have a cold or flu, eat lots of onion and garlic—if you can't bear them raw, make a broth of them or use them profusely in your cooking. Both onion and garlic are mentioned frequently as aphrodisiacs in numerous volumes, both ancient and modern. The onion was regarded as a symbol of the universe by the ancient Egyptians, and was the subject of vast folklore in many cultures. Garlic was considered by many a powerful charm against evil.

> *"Our apothecary's shop is our garden full of pot-herbs, and our doctor is a good clove of garlic."*
>
> —Anonymous
> *"A Deep Snow"* (1615)

PAPRIKA comes from ground dried sweet red peppers. It enhances cheese and egg dishes, potatoes, and just about all tomato-based dishes. It is also useful as a garnish to give color to the tops of casseroles and such. As widespread as its usage is in cookery, paprika has been virtually ignored by legend and lore.

PARSLEY, one of the most versatile herbs, is common in both flat and curly leaf types. It makes an excellent windowsill herb and I recommend always using it fresh, as it is always available and inexpensive, and has lots of flavor and fragrance, whereas dried parsley has very little. The uses of parsley are too extensive to list; there are few categories of cookery, aside from breads and desserts, where it would be unwelcome.

In folklore, it was believed that it was bad luck to cut parsley if one was in love. Certain parsley-lore is interchangeable with cabbage-lore, such as the old English "belief" that babies come from the parsley-bed. Like cabbage, parsley was also believed in ancient Rome to have the ability to prevent drunkenness, and was thus woven into head-wreaths or worn around the neck. Parsley is a natural breath-sweetener and has numerous nutritive values. For more praise of its virtues, see Parsley Dressing (page 67).

PEPPERCORNS are the small dried berries of an evergreen vine, and in ground form, they are what we know as black pepper. Pepper is one of the most ancient of known spices, and again, its uses are too numerous to list. Along with salt, it is the most basic of all seasonings. Any cook worth his or her "salt" knows that it is best to buy whole peppercorns and grind them in a pepper mill as needed. If you've never done this, the extra pleasant bite and fragrance will surprise you.

> *"I speak severely to my boy,*
> *I beat him when he sneezes;*
> *For he can thoroughly enjoy*
> *The pepper when he pleases."*
>
> —Lewis Carroll
> *Alice's Adventures in Wonderland* (1865)

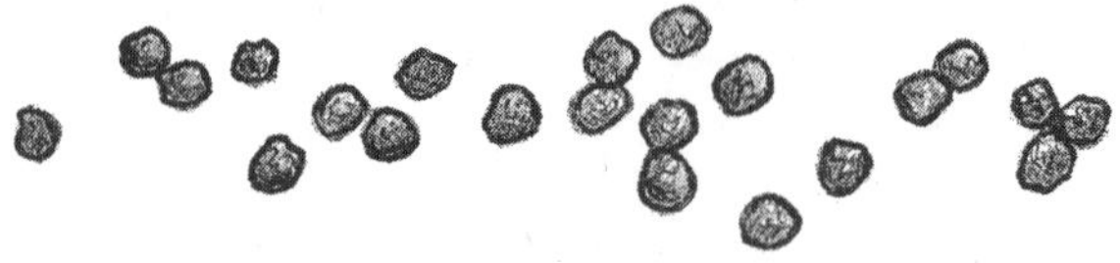

POPPY SEEDS are, predictably, the seeds of the poppy flower. They are used for certain baked goods and for garnishing breads, and lend an unusual twist to certain noodle dishes (see Bow Ties with Cabbage, page 129), cabbage dishes, and potatoes.

Poppy seeds were once used for divination by magicians: they were tossed on burning coals, and if the smoke lingered about, it was a negative omen; if the smoke ascended straight to the skies, it foretold good fortune.

ROSEMARY comes from the leaves of a small evergreen shrub and is one of the most distinctly flavored of common herbs. It is most useful in tomato-based dishes, and may also be used in small amounts wherever a mixture of herbs is called for.

Rosemary's most celebrated quality in folklore is its symbolism as the herb of remembrance, loyalty, and friendship. Students in ancient Greece wore wreaths of rosemary leaves, as it was believed to aid the memory. In some places, rosemary was called "elf-leaf," as it was believed that elves had a special affinity with it; in other places, rosemary was supposed to thrive only for the righteous, or where a woman was head of the household, thus the old proverb: "Where rosemary flourishes, the lady rules."

> ***"There's Rosemary, that's for remembrance: Pray you, love, remember."***
>
> —William Shakespeare
> *Hamlet* (ca. 1600)

SAFFRON is the dried, brightly colored stigmas of the autumn crocus. Saffron has always been valued as much for its brilliant yellow color as for its use as a spice. It is by far the most expensive of common spices, and I call for it only once in the recipes in this book (Saffron Fruited Rice, page 91). It is used mainly in Far Eastern cookery.

Saffron has a very colorful legacy. In *The Arabian Nights*, it was said to be so powerful an aphrodisiac that it would cause women to swoon. In parts of the Orient, it was used as a perfume and for painting one's body in order to resemble the Buddha. The herbalists praised its power to produce well-being.

> ***"Saffron rejoyceth the heart, comforteth the stomacke, and procureth sleepe."***
>
> —William Vaughn
> *Directions for Health* (1617)

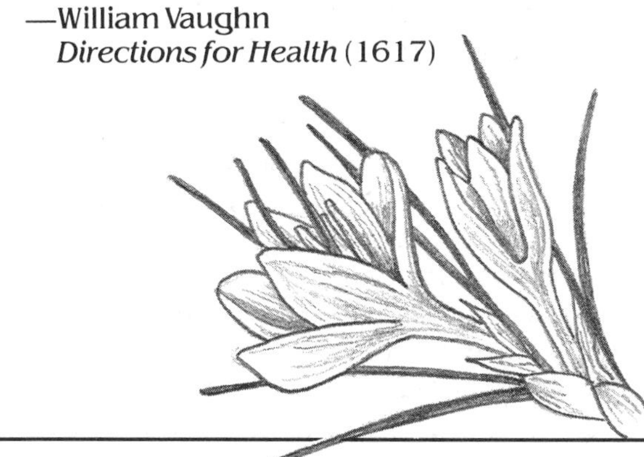

SAGE comes from the leaves of an evergreen shrub. Its strong, spicy flavor goes well with squashes, including pumpkin, certain soups, and vegetable and grain dishes. Use it subtly.

Sage's legacy is primarily medicinal; it was known as an herb of longevity, and for its ability to strengthen the brain.

SAVORY refers to two varieties of related herbs, summer and winter savory. Summer savory is more accessible and has a subtler flavor, so that is what I call for in recipes. It is extremely useful wherever a mild herb is needed or where mixed herbs are called for, such as in soups, salads, dressings, vegetable and grain dishes, etc. In addition, it has long been known to have a special affinity with beans, sometimes having been called the "bean herb."

Savory is the legendary plant of the satyrs, as is implied by its Latin name, *satureja.*

> ***"It maketh thin and doth marvellously prevail against winde: therefore it is with good success boyled and eaten with beans . . . "***
>
> —John Gerarde
> *The Herball* (1636)

SESAME SEEDS are the seeds of a tropical herbal plant. They are useful in baking and as a garnish for breads, casseroles, Oriental dishes, and salads. They are the basis for tahini (sesame paste), halvah (sesame candy), and sesame oil, which I call for in many of the Oriental-style recipes. Although it is a bit expensive, its flavor and fragrance give Chinese dishes an authentic touch.

Almost everyone has heard the command "Open Sesame!" from *The Arabian Nights* (see Crisp Sesame Vegetables, page 44), and perhaps because they are packed with vitamin E, sesame seeds are considered by some an aphrodisiac (see Sesame-Date Brownies, page 192).

TARRAGON is a perennial Old World plant and is one of the most expensive of herbs, so if I call for it in the recipes, its use is optional. Tarragon has a very distinctive, fresh, sweetish taste. It is well known for its use in tarragon vinegar, and it goes well in salads and with green vegetables.

Its name may have come from the Arabic "Tarkum," meaning dragon, perhaps because its roots resemble that fire-breathing beast.

THYME is an aromatic herb of the mint family. It is a widely useful culinary herb with a strong flavor that makes an impression even when used sparingly. It is excellent in soups, gives a nice zest to tomato-based dishes, and goes well with grains, beans, and vegetables, and most anywhere a mixture of herbs is called for.

In ancient Greece, one of the greatest compliments was to be told that one smelled of thyme; there and in other places, thyme was a symbol of courage and strength. Elves, fairies, and bees were said to have a special love of thyme.

TURMERIC comes from the underground root of a plant related to ginger. Turmeric is most useful in curries, giving them their fiery yellow color. Use it in small amounts to brighten egg and cheese dishes as well. Its scent is reminiscent of wood's, but its flavor is harder to define.

Like saffron, turmeric has long been valued for its color, and in the Far East was used as a cosmetic. In other places, it was burned in order to ward off spirits, and in India, turmeric was an element in wedding rituals and in erotic play.

APPENDIX: Cooking Notes

COOKING GRAINS

In the recipes, where a specific amount of cooked grains is needed, I give the raw amount in order to eliminate guesswork. In other cases, where cooked grains are called for to serve as a bed for vegetable or bean dishes and such and no specific amount is specified, keep in mind that grains swell to 2½ to 3 times their raw volume.

Unless a grain is cooked by simply soaking it, as is the case with couscous and bulgur,* most grains may be cooked in the following manner. Refer to the chart below for proportion of water to grain, cooking time, and yield.

1. Rinse grains thoroughly in a colander or fine sieve.
2. Bring the amount of water needed to a boil in a heavy saucepan.
3. Stir in the grain. Return the water to a boil, then lower the heat and simmer over low heat with the saucepan's lid on but slightly ajar. Cook until the water is absorbed. Do not stir, since doing so can result in a mushy texture.

*For bulgur and couscous, use the following method: simply place the rinsed grain in an ovenproof dish and pour boiling water over it in the proportion recommended below. Let soak, covered, for the time indicated, then fluff with a fork.

COOKING TIMES AND YIELDS FOR GRAINS

GRAIN	*WATER-TO-GRAIN RATIO*	*APPROX. COOKING TIME (minutes)*	*APPROX. YIELD (for 1 cup raw)*
barley			
Scotch or pot	3½ to 1	50 to 55	3 cups
pearl	3 to 1	40 to 45	3 cups
buckwheat groats	2 to 1	15 to 25	2½ cups
bulgur	2 to 1	20 to 30	2½ cups
couscous	2 to 1	15	3 cups
grits, hominy	4 to 1	25 to 30	3 cups
millet	2½ to 1	35 to 46	3½ cups
quinoa	2 to 1	15	4 cups
rice			
long or med. grain	2½ to 1	35 to 40	3 cups
short grain	2 to 1	35 to 40	3 cups
wild rice	2½ to 1	40	3 cups
wheat berries	4 to 1	50 to 55	2½ cups

COOKING BEANS AND OTHER LEGUMES

Cooked as well as raw amounts for beans are given in the recipes so that the cook can have the option of using canned beans when pressed for time. It's more practical and economical to cook beans from scratch when a large amount is needed, but the only real drawback to canned beans is their high sodium content. If using canned beans, select those that have no additives, and rinse them to eliminate the salty brine that they are packed in.

Some legumes, such as lentils and peas, need no presoaking, but most beans do. Presoaking dry beans greatly reduces their cooking time, contributes to better texture, and helps to reduce those notorious gas-causing sugars. Here are two methods that can be used. In either case, first rinse the beans and sort them carefully, removing any stones, grit, and shriveled beans.

Quick-soak method: Place the beans in a large cooking pot with water in a ratio of 3 to 4 parts water to 1 part beans. Bring to a boil, then remove from the heat and allow to stand, covered, for an hour or so.

Long-soak method: Place the beans in a large cooking pot with water in a ratio of 3 to 4 parts water to 1 part beans. Cover and refrigerate overnight (this prevents possible fermentation and spoilage, especially during warm weather).

When you are ready to cook the beans, drain off the soaking water and add fresh water in about double the volume of beans. Bring to a boil, then lower the heat and cook at a gentle simmer. Cover the pot but leave the lid slightly ajar to prevent foaming. Cook the beans until they yield easily when pressed between the thumb and forefinger, then drain. Save the flavorful stock to use in soups and sauces. Most legumes swell to 2¼ to 2½ times their dry volume.

AT-A-GLANCE COOKING CHART FOR LEGUMES

TYPE	*SOAK*	*APPROX. COOKING TIME*
adzuki beans	yes	45 minutes to 1 hour
black beans	yes	1 to 1½ hours
black-eyed peas	yes	1 to 1¼ hours
chick-peas (garbanzos)	yes	2½ to 3 hours
great northern beans	yes	1½ to 2 hours
kidney or red beans	yes	1½ to 2 hours
lentils, red or brown	no	30 to 45 minutes
mung beans	no	45 minutes to 1 hour
navy beans	yes	1 to 1½ hours
peas, split	no	45 minutes to 1 hour
pinto beans	yes	1½ to 2 hours

STEAMED VEGETABLES

When a recipe calls for vegetables to be steamed, there are two ways of going about it. One way is to use a steamer, an inexpensive gadget that serves as a basket in which the vegetables are held above simmering water. Fill a cooking pot or large saucepan with an inch or so of water and place the steamer in, followed by the vegetables. Cover tightly and simmer over low heat until the vegetables are done to the desired texture. Stir them once in a while and check on the water level in the bottom of the pot.

Alternatively, you can heat a half-inch or so of water in a cooking pot, saucepan, or skillet, add the vegetables, then cover tightly and simmer, stirring occasionally and adding just enough water, if necessary, to keep the bottom of the pot or skillet moist.

HOW TO FRY AND FLIP A SKILLET PIE OR FRITTATA

The best tool for a successful skillet pie or frittata is a good 8- to 10-inch nonstick skillet. Without that, you'll have to rely on some luck.

Heat just enough oil to coat the bottom of the skillet and allow it to get really hot. Test the heat with a drop of whatever you will be cooking; if it sizzles, pour in the remaining contents of the skillet pie. Tip the skillet or use a spatula to smooth in the batter. Turn the heat to moderately low, cover, and cook until the bottom is nicely browned and the top is fairly set.

Use a spatula to loosen the pie and then tip the skillet and slide the pie out onto a flat plate. Invert the skillet over the plate as you hold it with one hand, then quickly turn the plate upside down and skillet right side up, so the pie goes back into the skillet. Remove the plate, return the skillet to the heat, and cook the second side uncovered until it is nicely browned. Slide the cooked skillet pie back onto the plate and let cool for a few minutes. Cut into wedges to serve.

SELECTED SOURCES

Barkas, Janet. *The Vegetable Passion* (New York: Charles Scribner's Sons, 1975)

Billings, Josh [Henry Wheeler Shaw]. *His Works, Complete* (New York: G. W. Carleton & Co., 1876)

———. *Josh Billings' Farmer's Alminax* (New York: G. W. Carleton & Co., 1870–1873)

Boorde, Dr. Andrew. *A Compendyous Regyment or a Dyetary of Healthe* (London: W. Powell, 1567)

Botlan, Ibn. *Tacuinum Sanitatis—The Medieval Health Handbook,* translated by Luisa Cogliata Arano (New York: George Braziller, 1976)

Brody, Rosalie. *Emily Post Weddings* (New York: Simon & Schuster, 1963)

Butler, Samuel. *Erewhon* (New York: Penguin Books, 1970 printing of 1872 edition)

Carroll, Lewis. *Alice's Adventures in Wonderland* (London, 1865)

———. *Through the Looking-Glass* (London, 1871)

Carson, Gerald. *Cornflake Crusade* (New York: Rinehart & Co., 1957)

Chesterton, G. K. *The Collected Poems of G. K. Chesterton* (New York: Dodd, Mead & Co., 1911)

Culpeper, Nicolas. *Culpeper's Complete Herbal* (London: reprinted by Foulsham Co., undated)

Daniels, Cora Linn. *Encyclopedia of Superstitions, Folklore, and the Occult Sciences* (Detroit: Gale Research Co., 1971 reprint of 1803 edition)

Edwards, E. D. *The Dragon Book* (London: William Hodge & Co., 1938)

Ellacombe, Henry N. *The Plant-Lore and Gardencraft of Shakespeare* (London: Edward Arnold Publishers, 1896)

Evelyn, John. *Acetaraia: A Discourse of Sallets* (London, 1699)

Folkard, Richard. *Plant-Lore, Legends and Lyrics* (London: S. Lowe Marston, Serale, & Rivington, 1884)

Ford, Paul Leicester. *The Many-Sided Franklin* (New York: Books for Libraries Press, 1972 reprint of 1898 edition)

Franklin, Benjamin. *Poor Richard's Almanack* (New York: Peter Pauper Press, undated reprint of 1734 edition)

Frazer, Sir James George. *The Golden Bough* (New York: Macmillan, 1948)

Friedman, Margaret B. *Herbs for the Medieval Household* (New York: The Metropolitan Museum, 1943)

Gerarde, John. *The Herball or General Historie of Plantes* (London, 1636)

Giehl, Dudley. *Vegetarianism, A Way of Life* (New York: Barnes and Noble Books, 1979)

Hardy, Thomas. *Jude the Obscure* (New York: New American Library, 1961 reprint of 1885 edition)

Hawthorne, Nathaniel. *The Scarlet Letter* (New York: Random House, 1950 printing of 1850 edition)

Hayman, Ronald. *Kafka* (London: Oxford University Press, 1981)

Hubbard, Alice, and Babbitt, Adeline, eds. *The Golden Flute* (New York: The John Day Co., 1932)

Jones, Evan. *A Food Lover's Companion* (New York: Harper and Row, 1979)

Klaw, Spencer. "Pursuing Health in the Promised Land." *Horizon* Magazine, Spring 1976

Kronenberger, Louis. *Animal Vegetable Mineral* (New York: Viking Press, 1975)

Leach, Maria, ed. *Funk & Wagnalls Standard Dictionary of Folklore, Mythology, and Legend,* Vols. 1 and 2 (New York: Funk & Wagnalls, div. of Reader's Digest Books, 1949)

Lehner, Ernst and Johanna. *Folklore and Odysseys of Food and Medicinal Plants* (New York: Farrar, Straus & Giroux, 1962)

Leibman, Malvina W. *From Caravan to Casserole* (Miami: E. A. Seeman Publishing, 1977)

Lorwin, Madge. *Dining with William Shakespeare* (New York: Atheneum, 1976)

Mencken, H. L. *A New Dictionary of Quotations* (New York: Alfred A. Knopf, 1966)

National Pasta Association, P.O. Box 1008, Palatine, Illinois 60067

Nefzawi, Shaykh. *The Perfumed Garden,* translated by Sir Richard Burton (St. Albans, England: Granada Publishing, 1963 reprint of 1876 edition)

Northcote, Lady Rosalind. *The Book of Herb-Lore* (New York: Dover Publishing, 1971 reprint of 1812 edition)

Opie, Iona and Peter, eds. *The Oxford Dictionary of Nursery Rhymes* (New York: Oxford University Press, 1952)

Parker, Dorothy. *The Wonderful World of Yogurt* (New York: Hawthorne Books, 1972)

Paul, Anita May, and Kotlatch, David, eds. *Completely Cheese—The Cheese Lover's Companion* (New York: Jonathan David Publishers, 1975)

Penner, Lucille Recht. *The Colonial Cookbook* (New York: Hastings House, 1976)

Prezzolini, Giuseppe. *Spaghetti Dinner—A History of Spaghetti and Cooking* (New York: Abelard-Shulman, 1955)

Prochnow, Herbert V. *A Treasury of Humorous Quotations* (New York: Harper and Row, 1969)

Rhind, William. *A History of the Vegetable Kingdom* (Glasgow: Blackie & Son, 1870)

Rosegarten, Frederick Jr. *The Book of Spices* (New York: Pyramid Books, 1973)

Shelley, Percy Bysshe. *Letters of Percy Bysshe Shelley,* edited by Frederick C. Jones (Oxford: Clarendon Press, 1964)

Shurtleff, William, and Aoyagi, Akika. *The Book of Tofu* (Berkeley: Ten Speed Press, 1983)

Spence, Lewis. *An Encyclopedia of Occultism* (New Hyde Park, N.Y.: University Books, 1968)

Stevenson, Burton, ed. *The Macmillan Book of Proverbs, Maxims, and Famous Phrases* (New York: Macmillan Co., 1948)

Swift, Jonathan. *The Poems of Jonathan Swift,* edited by Harold Williams (London: Oxford University Press, 1966)

Thackeray, William Makepeace. *Vanity Fair* (New York: Dell Publishing, 1961 printing of 1848 edition)

Thoreau, Henry David. *Walden* (New York: New American Library, 1962 reprint of 1854 edition)

Trager, James. *Foodbook* (New York: Grossman Publishers, 1970)

Twain, Mark [Samuel L. Clemens]. *A Tramp Abroad* (Hartford: American Publishing Co.)

———. *Pudd'nhead Wilson* (New York: New American Library, 1964 printing of 1894 edition)

Vatsyayana. *The Kama Sutra of Vatsyayana—A New Translation* (New Hyde Park, N.Y.: University Books, 1968)

Vaughn, William. *Naturall and Artificiall Directions for Health* (London, 1600)

———. *Directions for Health, Both Naturall and Artificiall* (London, 1617)

Verrill, Hyatt. *Foods America Gave the World* (Boston: L. C. Page and Co., 1937)

Voltaire. *Voltaire, A Reader,* edited by Edmund Fuller (New York: Dell Publishing, 1959)

Winston, Stephen. *Shaw's Corner* (New York: Roy Publishers, 1952)

Yutang, Lin. *My Country and My People* (New York: John Day Co., 1938)

INDEX

Nava Atlas is the author of five books on vegetarian cookery. She is also active in the fine art field—her works on paper (including the drawings in this book) have been shown in numerous museum and gallery exhibits. Nava Atlas lives in upstate New York with her husband, Chaim Tabak, and their sons, Adam and Evan.